A BRIEFING FOR LEADERS

A
BRIEFING
FOR
LEADERS

*Communication
as the Ultimate Exercise
of Power*

ROBERT L. DILENSCHNEIDER

HarperBusiness

A Division of HarperCollins*Publishers*

HarperCollins books may be purchased for educational, business, or sales promotional use. For information, please write: Special Markets Department, HarperCollins Publishers, Inc., 10 East 53rd Street, New York, NY 10022.

FIRST EDITION

Library of Congress Cataloging-in-Publication Data

Dilenschneider, Robert L.
    A briefing for leaders: communication as the ultimate exercise of
power/ Robert L. Dilenschneider.
        p.   cm.
    Includes bibliographical references (p. 267) and index.
    ISBN 0–88730–467–2
    1. Leadership.   2. Executive ability.   3. Communication in
management.   4. Chief executive officers.   I. Title.
    HD57.7.D55   1991
    658.4'092—dc20   91–28827

92 93 94 95 96 CC/RRD 10 9 8 7 6 5 4 3 2 1

This book is for my Dad,
who was a leader of men for more than eight decades.
Without him, this volume would not have been possible.

CONTENTS

PREFACE

Most communication firms spend the lion's share of their time on communication's *output:* the speeches, letters, statements, and press releases that leaders use to communicate their viewpoints and the viewpoints of their companies. Really sophisticated firms spend more and more time on the *input* phase of communication. By input, I mean the briefing of executives on how to tackle communications problems, how to understand the landscape of communications in today's global business environment, and how to make communications fit into the broader goals of managing and leading.

Above all, it means absorbing information on the values at stake in a situation, because the courageous defense of values is the most important measure of leadership.

This switch from output to input marks a watershed in how leaders think about communications. Because a leader's communications are scrutinized today much more carefully and against far higher standards of performance than was true in the past, it has become much less easy to delegate communications work. More of it has to be done by leaders themselves, and the overarching framework has to be grasped very well by the leaders of organizations.

This shift is what first got me interested in the business of communications briefings. I realized that experienced executives—frequently those who had just moved into top slots—often wanted and needed a "crash course" in leadership communications. They weren't interested in learning about press releases or the procedure for conducting an annual meeting. What they wanted was an integrated look at communications from <u>their</u> perspective—communications as it should be seen from the helm of the ship.

One briefing in November 1988 sticks in my mind. The chairman of the executive committee of a *Fortune* 50 company called me late on a Sunday night. He and his committee had been stewing about management succession in the company. The current CEO, who had great natural talent as a communicator, was about to retire. There were several rivals for the top slot, but the one who clearly would do the company the most good was a shrewd operating executive. His chief weakness: He was a less able communicator than he would need to be, and he was not a "born leader." The exec-committee chairman would get to slot his man, but only by pledging to the committee members that something would be done fast to raise the candidate's leadership awareness and groom his skills. I had no prior business relationship with the firm, but I had a reputation for understanding communications as a problem-solving discipline. What could be done, my caller asked, to bring a highly intelligent but marginally sophisticated communicator up to spec fast?

The problem intrigued me. I said that we had the best professionals in the world and that we counseled most of the world's top CEOs. I said further that there was no such thing as instant knowledge that could make an executive a leader overnight. I conceded, however, that a truly bright manager could make a real breakthrough with the right tutoring. "How would you start?" my caller asked. Pull the best minds in the communications profession, I said, together to create a "presidential briefing," structured just like a White House briefing, and do it in four one-and-a-half-hour sessions. I said that I hoped this would form the basis for a long-term relationship. (It proved to be.)

Over the years, this "leadership briefing" has been refined many times to groom dozens of other senior executives. Generally, the briefing is tailored to the particular needs of the organization. If a company is a takeover target, more time is spent on financial issues. If it has grown overnight from a skunk-works in someone's garage to a dominant force in its industry (as has been the case for many high-tech firms), then the briefing focuses on issues of change. A core program for most briefings has emerged, and that is what this book intends to capture.

In this briefing, the reader is getting a vehicle earmarked by some of the most recent trends and perspectives in communications thinking, one that has been "road tested" in several actual situations. It's my hope that leaders and aspiring leaders for organizations of all sorts will find this briefing a useful orientation to the contemporary world of power and communications.

THE IMPORTANCE OF INTEGRITY

If I have detected one over-arching trend as a public relations counselor for nearly three decades, it is that public relations is a tool which must be used with great respect and ethical vigilance. The public relations profession is awash today with charges of the misuse of influence—falsifying government testimony, fabricating business reports, systematically misleading the press . . . the list is a long one. The charges when they are true—and some are unfortunately all too true—point to abuses which I condemn, as I am sure every responsible colleague in my profession does as well.

The fact also remains that influence strategies are indispensable to leadership—a point which the following briefing makes again and again. It is up to leaders and their advisors to make sure that influence is used ethically. The temptation and the means (especially in our age of highly sophisticated electronic communications) often exist to do the expedient, the immoral, or even the illegal for the sake of the greater goal.

My advice is simple: Don't. And make sure your people don't either. One reason I have chosen to practice through a small consultancy is that small firms may be in the best position to maintain their ethical standards. Quite simply, the small scale enables the most vigilant monitoring.

The product of a strategic communications counselor is not style. It is judgment. I am firmly convinced that the ethical dimension of judgment is best upheld when a leader works with a small, carefully coordinated group of reliable advisors. When ethics are pushed aside in communications decision-making, the resulting course will likely be dangerous and, almost always, backfires.

ACKNOWLEDGMENTS

Before I launched a new career in the fall of 1991, I spent twenty-five years with the world's largest consulting firm—Hill and Knowlton. This book would have been impossible to write without my colleagues— some of whom are now with Hill and Knowlton, while others have gone on to other careers. I've had the good fortune to work with some remarkable professionals, and I would be remiss in not singling out their contribution to my own thinking.

I especially want to thank:

Dick Hyde, Jim Lane, and Don Deaton—experts in corporate counseling and crisis management

Governmental affairs counselors Bill Timmons, Frank Mankiewicz, and George Worden

Financial relations strategist Tim Metz

Marketing and creative advisor Larry Charles

Environmental affairs experts Howard Marder and Matt Swetonic

Press relations specialist Tom Ross

Global communications counselors Claudio Belli and Arnie Tucker

Communication technology expert George Glazer

High-technology counsellor Bob Strayton

Wire-services veteran Jack Griffin

Internal communications advisor Bob Harris and

Corporate contributions counsellor Barbara Lorber.

I want to thank Karen Combs and her research staff for their help in compiling research for this book.

Jim Granger, president of the Wirthlin Group, provided valued insights on research. Dean Rotbart, editor of the newsletter *TJFR* (*The Journalist and Financial Reporting*), shared his exceptional understanding of how the motivations and agenda of the press are changing.

Among my colleagues at The Dilenschneider Group, Michelle Jordan contributed thoughtful input on marketing. Charlie Brophy, a senior advisor who spent seventeen years with Salomon Brothers, gave me some important insights on the foreign business press. Bob Stone's thoughts on media relations were, as always, incisive.

Joan Avagliano and Mary Bruno—my administrative assistants—provided tireless and indispensable support in arranging and coordinating the hundreds of details that went into the writing, checking and revising of this book, all—I might add—on their own time.

I am particularly indebted to Mark Greenberg for his help in defining the evolution of power in the discussion which appears in the introduction. At HarperCollins, I wish to thank Virginia Smith for her thoughtful editorial guidance. And, I am indebted to Jen Fleissner and Elena LePera at HarperBusiness for their meticulous fine-tuning of the final manuscript.

Finally, I want to recognize Ron Beyma, a communications counselor in Germany and the United States. Ron helped to conceptualize many of the principles in this book, and I want to thank him for his valued contribution.

INTRODUCTION

THE LOGIC OF THIS BRIEFING

Since *Power and Influence* was published in 1990, I have gotten literally hundreds of letters from serious-minded people saying that the book was a start, but not enough. Military officers and business executives, government administrators and civic leaders have all said they want to know more about the secrets of leadership and how leaders communicate. Although many detect that leadership is different today, they are not sure exactly how. Different, it undoubtedly is. But leadership is not the charismatic, mystical talent that many presume it to be. Leadership can be *learned,* and modern leadership clearly rests on the mastery of communication.

This book tackles communications and leadership in a new way. No sections are devoted to handling the press, managing crises, or playing the trump cards on special interests per se. The reader will learn a great deal about such topics as the press and special interests, but they are not the targets of the book. Focused on the mindset of the leader as a communicator, this book raises and strives to answer four questions for leaders and potential leaders:

1

1. What must I be?

2. What reality must I work in?

3. What are my tools?

4. What are worthwhile goals and how are they reached?

The reality of modern communication is actually shaping what leaders must be, and the reality demands that leaders transcend technique. This book is therefore not about media relations or crisis checklists. It is about such topics as spotting trends, managing agendas, and guiding the work of staff.

The world of communications has changed so vastly that much of communication theory, with its traditionally technical focus, is simply out of date. The time in which messages must be communicated, for example, has been remarkably compressed. A soundbite in the Truman era normally lasted 48 seconds, whereas today's network news soundbite averages 7 seconds. It's no surprise that today's leader must get messages out fast.

Compressed time is just one aspect of change. There are many others. With the press and analysts schooled in reading every signal of management behavior from the size of a picture in an annual report to the invitation list for a global teleconference, today's leader must grasp modern ritual and visual idioms and images, learning them instinctively and not getting caught up in details. In addition, electronic data bases are pulsing through modems everywhere; leaders must assume that their adversaries have access to extraordinary information and research. With satellite uplinks and fax machines poised to report a manager's every move, no leader has the luxury of creating a purely localized message for one audience in a single factory or corner of the globe. As opinion surveying and high-speed computing are developing to astonishing levels, leaders everywhere have extraordinary opportunities to evaluate their options and to pretest their initiatives.

These are just a few of the ways that the realities of modern communication are revolutionizing leadership. They are also making some of the cherished ways of thinking about communications outmoded.

- *No meaningful distinction exists today between communicating to internal and external audiences.* Employees are as likely to think of themselves as customers or shareholders as they are workers. When the latest wave of Wall Street mergers took place, raiders were cutting out their highest-priced advisers, such as investment bankers and attorneys, from key deal points. Whom can you trust at such stakes, they reasoned. Similarly, more and more outsiders have the detailed knowledge of insiders because of the profusion of data.

- *With messages plastered everywhere, from video bulletin boards to the insides of bathroom stalls, knowledge and selection of media have become specialized work.* It's pointless for modern leaders to try to understand the relative advantages of op-ed pieces versus grass-roots campaigning; of bounce-back couponing in contrast to computerized phone messaging; or of an internal videotape over a broadside on company letterhead. What leaders *must* understand is that a tremendous range of media is available, as well as tested criteria that define the methods and project the costs and results of using each. For that reason, this book has no chapter on when to issue press releases or how to write a speech. Those are techniques, not the real tools of leadership. Rather, the tools of leadership communications are to be found in analyzing trends, crafting agendas, and seeking and taking advice.

- *It no longer makes sense to talk about personal communications.* Personal as opposed to what? All leadership must be realized through people. Leaders can't afford to be any less personal on a videotape to their organizations than they can in one-on-one meetings with mentors or key advisers. Both the television eye and the collapse of hierarchies in companies and society have personalized every encounter and made it immediate. This reality has escaped many leaders.

A new concept of power is fueling these changes in leadership communications and others like them. In the second half of this century, three different concepts of power have dominated our world in nearly serial fashion. Management experts such as Harvard's John Kotter have touched on the difference between management and leadership. What remains largely unexplored, however, is the difference among administration, management, and leadership, which form three distinct eras:

- *In the fifties and sixties, there was power as administration.* Bulging staffs and tables of organization inherited from World War II regulated industry and other large organizations. Conformity and order were the watchwords. Power as administration ended when computers took over the busywork of detail; decision making became more decentralized and an emerging service industry put a new weight on interpersonal skills.

- *The seventies and eighties became the era of power as management.* Leaders ceased to be custodians of organizations that changed slowly or not at all. Instead, managers learned that they could exert power by initiating fundamental changes in their organizations.

In the business world, these changes took place in two successive phases: first *conglomerating* and then *disassembling.* Conglomerating was the amassing of assets to drive up earnings per share, chiefly through diversification. Harold Geneen was a master of this thinking, as was Harry Gray.

Disassembling—the second phase and the art form of people like Carl Icahn—was about releasing the values of companies when their break-up values exceeded the current market capitalization. The battle for control of RJR-Nabisco epitomized this phase. As the disassembling trend went forward, several things became clear: the size and complexity of large conglomerates helped conceal plush executive perquisites and rich salaries; and an increasing number of top managers were relying on outside counselors because inside staffs couldn't cope with the problems of complexity.

Smith Bagley, R. J. Reynolds's grandson, might have been talking about one manager or a specific group of managers, but his words summarized the verdict of opinion leaders everywhere as the eighties drew to a close:

> Those little bastards; those little *managers.* . . . This little guy could take the company from the shareholders to make all that money for himself. That money belongs to the shareholders. It's so *wrong.* We have to do something.[1]

In a way, disassembling was a kind of leadership reform movement, but the initial reform itself was heralded by even more egregious management excesses, such as golden parachutes and windfalls gained through leveraged buyouts.

- *As the nineties begin, we are entering the era of leadership as power.* People have had enough of management. They know that they cannot go back to an era of management as administration. Enormous changes and instability in the world will not permit it. But the public is unwilling to tolerate a continuation of that period; it has seen too many cases of self-interest and manipulation during the era of management. In part, it is this vague appetite of people for something beyond management that is fueling the interest in leadership today.

We may hunger for leaders, but it would be wrong to suggest that only they have something to teach us today. Each power era has given us role models who are important to the total repertory of executive skills. Before John Kennedy appointed Robert McNamara Secretary of Defense in 1961, McNamara succeeded in creating a new standard for administration in American business. RCA's Thornton Bradshaw epitomized the best that the era of management had to offer. Looking forward, we still lack a complete profile of the leader of the future, but GE's Jack Welch and Bob Crandall at American Airlines appear on the trend line of the future.

Although the following chart may oversimplify how power has evolved, it may help to indicate where the concept of power is headed:

THE EVOLUTION OF POWER

The 1950s and 1960s	The 1970s and 1980s	The 1990s
POWER AS *Administration*	POWER AS *Management*	POWER AS *Leadership*
Conformist	Exception-driven	Visionary
Chain of Command	Ad Hoc	Instant
Stable	Turbulent	Sustaining
Introspective	Market-driven	Positioning
Apprenticeship	Mentoring	Collegial

Leadership has become the important "value added" for being on top in the nineties. When power was administration, bosses kept nonconformity in check. When power was management, managers hunted down exceptions. If they were bad, they were ruthlessly eliminated. If they were good, they became a new performance standard. Today, the leader is focused neither on securing order nor on rooting out exceptions but on providing a vision.

Administrative power spoke through the chain of command. The era of management broke the command chain and saw the value of spontaneous dialogue. It celebrated "management by walking around." Today, managers no longer have that option. For one thing, modern communications puts them on record. Although spontaneity used to be a refreshing change, today it is a constant reality and often a trap. CEOs who openly joke that their multimillion-dollar incomes barely cover the big-city lifestyle imposed by their jobs can expect those words to ricochet around subsidiaries in Mobile or in Taiwan within hours. Unlike the spendthrift CEOs, Elizabeth Dole has given us a taste of what leaders must at times do. In a message heard by volunteers around the world, she announced that she would dedicate her first year's income as president of the Red Cross to the organization itself. Not only did Dole make a strong statement about her own commitment to the Red Cross and her belief in its mission, but the former Secretary of Labor also differentiated herself sharply from many public officials who dive from government into lucrative consulting assignments.

The three power eras differ in other ways as well:

- The goal of the administrator was to maintain stability. Managers, on the other hand, thrived on turbulence, forever trying to turn it to personal advantage. The leader's goal is to build an organization that can sustain itself and prosper in rapidly shifting circumstances.

- While the administrator was preoccupied with looking inward and keeping order, the manager was a competitive zealot driven by market forces. The leader is a positioner who knows that environmental activists or congressional oversight committees can destroy an organization as easily as can Wall Street or market forces.

- Lastly, the styles of management development differ in the various power eras. The administrator apprenticed the next generation of technocrats, whereas the manager anointed and mentored rising stars. The leader is first among equals in the essentially collegial relationship typical of today's more level and information-based organization.

Admittedly, my chart is also a generalization, aimed at depicting broad trends and tendencies. For centuries there have been spectacular leaders like Buddha, Abraham Lincoln, and Golda Meir, and for decades to come, there will be successful managers and even administrators, but for today, the needle on the meter is moving toward leadership as the cornerstone for running organizations. That fact is rewriting the rules of power and making communication the medium of power more than at any time in world history.

Leadership is a behavior that can be taught and learned. Some people, such as Indira Gandhi, Martin Luther King, Konosuke Matsushita, and Ross Perot, have a knack for leadership. But real leadership goes beyond the negative aspects of what Dr. Martin Luther King called the "drum-major instinct"—that flair for finding a parade and getting in front of it.[2] I am convinced that the core of leadership is conscious action, and it is a defining consciousness. What you say, where you appear, how you advance your messages—these factors, and others like them, create a portrait of who you are and determine how your leadership will be interpreted. The hard part is knowing what to focus on and how to invest energy. It's my hope that this book will simplify these formidable challenges.

HOW TO READ THIS BOOK

This book is structured in four parts: Part I deals with the raw materials of leadership; Part II examines the communications landscape in which leaders must work; Part III outlines the tools, or template, that leaders may use; and Part IV discusses leadership's goals. Each part contains prefatory material, which introduces the context of the four or five chapters that follow.

At the beginning of each chapter, after some introductory comments, the reader will find a series of "thinkpoints," which crystallize the content of the chapter and guide the reader through the examples and concepts that follow. The material in each of these chapters represents related, but not necessarily successive, points. As in the real world, the briefings presented here often move quickly between different slants on the same theme, paying less attention to the transitions between points and more to the collective effect of the different ideas housed under one theme.

At the end of each part, the "thinkpoints" of the chapters in that part are summarized into a brief canon of behavior for that particular aspect of leadership.

I

LEADERSHIP'S
RAW MATERIALS

One of the most remarkable managers I ever met was the president of a midwestern pharmaceuticals company back about 20 years ago. This gentleman built that company into a major force in over-the-counter drugs. He was a medical doctor, a collector of Japanese ceremonial swords, and one very tough customer. He was brought in by the family that founded the company and still owned much of the stock to build the business for the future. The president-physician (whom I will call Dr. Tim) achieved that goal by transforming a sleepy medical company into a high-powered consumer products business with brands that became some of the greatest tonics in the history of over-the-counter drugs.

Dr. Tim hired the finest marketing people in New York, people from Ted Bates, D'Arcy Communications, and BBD&O. He also insisted that the agency account teams that worked on the firm's account live in this sleepy midwestern town, at the doorstep of the company's headquarters. Dr. Tim's singlemindedness was overwhelming. His sense of mission mesmerized people, and his willingness to pay for quality lured even ardent New Yorkers away from Gotham's restaurants, theaters, and concerts. The concentration of talent that Dr. Tim built forged an outstanding marketing company in the late sixties and early seventies.

Dr. Tim was a paradox. An intensely creative man, he was one of the finest business strategists I have ever met, but he also ruled through absolute terror. In the beginning he initiated remarkable change, but as his tenure wore on, his inability to accept opposition severely capped his creativity.

As a junior account executive, I remember sitting in a marketing meeting with him and about twenty people from the company and the agency. Dr. Tim sat at the head of the conference table. Behind him was a collection of beautifully crafted Japanese swords used by samurai warriors for the *seppuku* ritual: suicidal disembowelment. I have no doubt that these swords were there to remind people about authority, loyalty, and honor.

In the meeting, two of the company's executives disagreed with an advertising approach Dr. Tim wanted to take. Their opposition was low-key and professional. Dr. Tim, whose long mane of white hair and pork-chop sideburns made him look downright imperial, had a way of peering over the top of his horn-rimmed glasses and inspiring abject terror in everyone present. After about five minutes of debate, the two middle managers still hadn't buckled. Dr. Tim stared down the table at them in an icy silence that must have lasted thirty heart-pounding seconds. Then, without raising his voice, he stated firmly, "Joe, Harry, you're finished. Pack your bags."

Joe and Harry were thunderstruck, as was everyone in the room. Many senior executives were there, but they all stayed quietly on the sidelines. Even though this was the late 1960s, no one there, including me, had the guts to face up to Dr. Tim and say, "These are two valuable executives. You can't do this." The two continued to sit there while the shock settled in. Dr. Tim got up, reached for one of the swords, took it down from the wall, pulled it out of its sheath, and said ominously: "I don't think you heard me. You're finished."

Certainly, Dr. Tim was just playacting with the sword in a macabre way, but people around the table were shocked. A few were actually quivering. I felt as if I were watching something unreal, a melodrama from "The Twilight Zone" or the "Kraft Television Theatre." As the two castoffs shuffled out, Dr. Tim called in his personal assistant and said, "Joe and Harry are leaving the company. Get their checks drawn and get them out now."

The story may seem unbelievable, but it's true, and it thoroughly illustrates my point. If the doctor was trying to win through intimidation, he clearly succeeded. There is no doubt about which advertising approach was used. But the win was shortsighted, if a win at all. It was just a show of willful power. Through incidents like this, the people of the firm grew to be scared witless of Dr. Tim. I often wonder how much further brands from this company could have gone, had Dr. Tim been more of a leader.

The use of fear and authority could once guarantee a manager influence, especially within the organization. Today, things are different. About three years ago we worked with another executive, the CEO of a major public utility in the Southwest, who prefers to remain nameless in this book. If the midwest pharmaceuticals CEO was the Ghost of Leadership Past, this second CEO, who was about the same age, was the Spirit of Leadership to Come.

This utility needed to achieve a major turnaround in performance, and the executive used an unusual method to get there. He asked all of the supervisors in the company to identify which people in the firm had unmistakable influence. "Without regard to rank and station," he asked, "which people are the will of this company?" Who, he wanted to know, were the people whose support was indispensable to implementing a decision successfully?

After thinking about the questions for a week, the supervisors came up with an interesting cast of characters. Most of these opinion leaders seemed "standard issue" if you looked at their job descriptions: a couple of engineers, a billings clerk in the receivables area, service truck drivers, a long-term secretary, and several of the supervisors themselves. One of the "indispensables" was even a janitor.

The CEO then called a meeting with the first-level supervisors and all of the opinion leaders. The group numbered about 150. He gave them his agenda and his plan: "Here's what we have to do in financial performance. . . . This is where we need to be on nuclear power. . . . As far as productivity goes, this is what we must achieve." After he presented all of the goals and challenges, he summed up: "I was going to ask the supervisors how we are going to do this, but they tell me that you are really the folks who turn the screws in the company. So it was obvious that you had to be here, too. I need your help to get the job done. What kind of incentive plan do I need to set up to get you to do it? What kind of recognition plan do I need to get you to do it?"

When the opinion leaders went back to their desks and their trucks and janitorial closets, many wondered to themselves: "What is he asking me for?" "Is my job safe?" "Is there a pink slip at the end of this?" But the CEO stuck with it and it worked. The people who turned the screws came back with amazing answers and extraordinary methods. The supervisors were aghast at what they could have learned years ago, had they only asked.

Why did this appeal work? Shock value may have been a factor but, I think, a small one. What the executive did was to reorganize the company from a communications standpoint. By finding the shortest distance from himself to the opinion leaders—the "ears" of the company—he influenced directly what the hands and minds would be doing. This performance is possibly the best single job I can recall of leading through the informal organization, and the company succeeded spectacularly. Since its turnaround, it has continued to grow with the slow, steady gait of a powerful endurance runner.

What was behind the utility CEO's success? Surely, part of it was recognizing the limits to his own personal power. People in charge everywhere, and especially CEOs, are losing the power they once had. They can no longer grab swords off the wall and behave like wanton archangels, expelling people from the company. At least, they can't do it for long. The board as well as outside groups have taken more power. Leaders are increasingly the agents of the different forces acting on them. They still have the ability to introduce enormous change, however, and can add the critical dimension to any organization's prospects of realizing its future—provided they understand the new rules for exercising leadership.

Today, in the age of leadership, bosses must use different means to exert influence. The Yale management professor Dr. Clayton Alderfer believes that there are two kinds of influence: one based on intimidation, the other based on consent. Managers who use consent must have a strong sense of empathy for their co-workers. In my opinion, influence through consent is surely the future way of running things.

Dr. Harry Levinson of the Levinson Institute, a famous center for the study of management behavior, believes that tomorrow's CEO must be willing to accept many more contributions from an organization's rank-and-file. Upper management will have to adjust to the reduced distance from the top of the pyramid to the bottom, because fewer layers exist in today's downsized corporations. Top managers will regularly get input from levels routinely ignored by managers a decade ago. This shift means that managers must sharpen their political skills, as some of that input is bound to be critical, and it won't be possible to make many of the requested changes.

Leadership can be learned, but the important things to learn are not tricks or maneuvers. Recently, I got a brochure for what looked like a silly volume called *The Black Book of Executive Politics,* written by "Z," which billed itself as an underground best-seller offering advice on "grabbing more power," "leapfrog[ging] colleagues in raises [and] promotions," and finding the "easy way to be viewed as the 'natural leader' of any group."

Black books can't buy you leadership, which requires a constant, conscious focus and hard work. More and more, leadership also means the management of information—not merely data, but the "soft," qualitative, and subjective information that deals with the motives and goals of people and organizations.

The first part of this briefing addresses the raw materials of leadership: its prerequisites. Some people are born with, or seem predisposed to use, these materials almost as a sixth sense. Others learn what leadership's raw materials are and then discover how to use them. Both leaders can be equally effective, but my experience says that the *learned leader* is generally more reliable.

In our opinion, the ingredients of leadership can be shaped into five building blocks:

1. Vision and focus

2. Practical values

3. Awareness and use of time

4. Empowerment and motivation

5. Objectivity and judgment.

The first task of this briefing is to give you a sense of those five elements.

I

A CERTAIN TRUMPET

Creating Vision and Focus

T O ME, A FITTING BEGINNING FOR A DISCUSSION OF VISION AND FOCUS is a reference to Fr. Theodore Hesburgh. Now retired, Fr. Hesburgh was the most successful president in the history of the University of Notre Dame. The *Economist* called him "God's Action Man."[1] I'm also fortunate to count him as a good friend. Father Hesburgh says this about vision: "It is the essence of leadership. Know where you want to go. That requires three things: having a clear vision, articulating it well, and getting your team enthusiastic about sharing it. Above all, any leader must be consistent. As the Bible says, no one follows an uncertain trumpet."

The following thinkpoints summarize this chapter on vision and focus in leadership. I encourage the reader to reflect on each of the thinkpoints before reading further. In my opinion, they provide a useful shorthand to understanding the seminal concepts in leadership communications.

ACQUIRING A VISION

Direction begins with vision. There are three ways for an organization to develop a vision:

THINKPOINTS
on How
a Leader Sets Direction

☐ Create a strong vision.

☐ Articulate a clear course.

☐ Bias the organization toward action.

☐ Lift the organization up.

☐ Practice communications "inside out."

☐ Earn conviction.

☐ Sustain the vision.

☐ Create unity of purpose.

☐ Leverage the strength of the culture.

☐ Support positive rituals.

☐ Harmonize vision and culture.

☐ Train people to focus.

---

1. *Impose a personal vision.* The leader can come down from the mountain, having had divine inspiration. As Henry S. Singleton, the founder of Teledyne, says, "A great company is built around a mind with an idea."[2] That mind must also be well versed in the key thoughts of the time; an informed vision entails talking with other leading thinkers. Ben Heineman of Northwest Industries was a prominently successful exponent of this kind of vision. Every year or two, Ben would travel the world and talk with the most far-sighted and ingenious bankers in the profession. Ben geared Northwest Industries to the world that the bankers foretold. His superior skills at interpreting what he learned brought Northwest Industries remarkable success. This approach to vision has two limitations, however. First, there is no reason why the organization should feel any ownership for the vision, because they played no part in its creation. Second, the leader must therefore be gifted in explaining what he or she has learned to make the vision compelling to the people in the organization.

2. *Buy a vision.* Any number of second-rate consultants will sell you a vision. There are a host of snake-oil hawkers in the business. I've known high-priced consultants who have made fortunes by cutting and pasting vision statements, carrying them from one company to the next. Consequently, the conventional mission statement of the 1980s that talks about quality, commitment to people, and a return on investment has been neutralized. It has become a factory-made, off-the-rack solution, even though it may have been arrived at in an original way. Since it's everybody's solution, it's nobody's. Like an antibiotic that has become so diluted, it registers no effect on the body and can be downright dangerous if the leader thinks it has real potency.

    There are also legitimate and effective ways to use outside talent to help create a vision. A blue-chip consultant such as Booz · Allen & Hamilton can help to generate a real vision (usually with the close partnership of the client organization). These arrangements work when the leader pays close attention to mustering the internal commitment needed to make the vision a reality.

3. *Forge a vision together with the organization's other top managers.* Generating a vision in this way probably leads to the most durable and effective results. Not long ago, Jack Malloy, who heads communications for Du Pont, told me that his CEO, Ed Woolard,

recently called together Du Pont's 25 top managers to articulate a new vision for the company. They defined the vision and then they immersed themselves in it. Woolard knew that he had succeeded when these managers not only articulated the vision but used its planks to attack or defend proposed plans and actions for the company. Collaborating to use the vision as a company resource is the key that has made Du Pont an outstandingly innovative company for so many years.

Articulating the vision does not mean saying it well. It means internalizing it and applying it. The next step is getting the 144,000 people in Du Pont's global work force to buy in to it. What I know of Du Pont's vision is fresh, but I have also sat in literally hundreds of meetings where executives have tried to articulate a vision for their firms. The same words come up again and again—and the same charts. The driving force behind these discussions is shareholder return and customer satisfaction, today keynoted by quality. Even internally developed visions, especially their articulation, run the risk of being carbon copies of other people's programs. The best visions, the most authentic ones, aren't too smooth. They have a graininess to them. Not overly polished, they take on the profile of the customers, whom they must please, and of the marketplace in which they must succeed.

Those are the three chief ways to create a vision. The worst alternative is not creating a vision at all. An organization that does not define and immerse itself in a vision, that does not articulate it and live by it, will simply lurch from one experience to another.

ENHANCING A VISION THROUGH ACTIONS

I first met Ross Perot, the steely entrepreneur who founded the computer firm EDS and went on to sell it to General Motors and recently declared himself to be a U.S. Presidential candidate, at a formal dinner at the Chicago Club. When I came up to him in the reception line, Perot—whose concern for American POWs in Vietnam was already widely known—bellowed, "Where's your American flag, boy?" I said, "Excuse me?" "Come now, you're not hard of hearing, young man, your American flag?" With that, one of his John Wayne–like aides stepped forward and pinned a lacquered American flag medal on my lapel. Perot is a bold man, whose clarity of purpose is infectious.

What you find in Perot the person, you see in Perot's organizational style. Because he knows where he's going, he moves from ideas to action nearly automatically. Perot's EDS was a success because of the organization's do-now bias—exactly what was lacking at General Motors, as Perot learned when General Motors acquired the company. As Perot put it in one of his speeches: "When people at EDS spotted a snake, they killed it. When people at General Motors saw a snake, they formed a committee on snakes, hired a consultant on snakes, but never got rid of the snakes."

LIFTING THE ORGANIZATION ABOVE THE IMMEDIATE TRANSACTION

Vision is being able to think beyond the immediate transaction. Bernard Arnault, the Chairman of LVMH (Louis Vuitton Moet Hennessy), has created the world's most renowned and successful luxury-goods firm because he resolutely steers the firm to become a realizable "ideal company"—the epitome of French quality. With LVMH's diverse goods and businesses—champagne, cognac, haute couture (houses like Dior and Lacroix), leather, and luggage—he asks how every deal and every new product will help realize that vision. LVMH's recent strategic acquisitions give the company a powerful share of the world champagne market.

As a *Wall Street Journal* article put it, "A luxury-product company has to balance quality, originality and cachet—the aura of exclusivity—with mass production and marketing."[3] Arnault knows that each part of his business cannot operate in the same way. Because a critical mass is integral to distribution, size is vital to the wine and spirits business, as it is to perfume brands such as Dior and Givenchy. In beverages and perfumes, therefore, LVMH has built leverage from enormous size. But for Louis Vuitton and the couture trade, the distribution is highly selective. Not only is volume unnecessary, it undermines the exclusivity of the product.

Doing 70 percent of its volume outside France, LVMH is sensitive to public affairs trends. When the U.S. trade representative tried to impose a tariff on cognac that would have effectively tripled the importer's cost in the United States, the French cognac industry, led by firms like Hennessy, launched a tightly focused counteroffensive. It raised the voices of American opinion leaders—the people who drink the cognac—and eventually succeeded in rescinding the proposal.

In listening to Arnault, you can hear his mind switch gears like a precisely timed Ferrari or Porsche as he talks about the differing factors influencing each line of business. When he speaks of a brand strategy, he'll frame it in a plan stretching over 10 or even 15 years. And he will always return to how the brand links to the umbrella vision of French luxury goods.

KNOWING COMMUNICATIONS "INSIDE OUT"

Even a strongly cast action-oriented vision, one which lifts thinking beyond the next transaction, must be conveyed expertly. No leader can communicate a vision well unless the leader's organization knows communication inside out.

What does being an *inside-out* communicator mean? As I am using the term, it does not refer to knowing the details and techniques of communicating. It means understanding communications from a management standpoint. Too many managers, I find, jump to worrying about how a message will be perceived without ensuring first that it will be received. Managers who think communications inside out are constantly asking themselves such questions as:

1. What signals am I getting (or not getting) that people in the organization grasp our direction?

2. What business issues should we be addressing in our next meetings and letters?

3. How is our behavior—what we are actually doing about an issue—consistent or inconsistent with our declared vision and values?

Not worrying about the print calendar for the house organ, not fretting over the editing of the videotape, but focusing on the content issues of keeping a vision on course highlight what I mean by managing communications inside out. A manager needs to know what kind of stimuli to put into place to make strategic communications understood. Many organizations are insensitive, in a way illiterate, about making messages register. G. D. Searle, the pharmaceutical company and the creator of NutraSweet, was once like that.

In 1977, soon after leaving the post of Secretary of Defense, Donald Rumsfeld became CEO of Searle and brought in Bill Greener to head communications. (Rumsfeld had made his concern for quick, effective communications legendary as Defense Secretary, when he decided to test the "hot line" to President Ford and ended up being put on hold by an operator for 10 minutes. Needless to say, the systems were changed.) Searle was a tired, sleepy business, but it had enormous potential and tremendous strength in research. Rumsfeld had a vision for Searle. Greener's job was to open the ears of Searle so that the articulation of that vision could be heard. In status meetings, Greener and his associates, Billy Vaughan and Dick McGraw, would listen to what Rumsfeld wanted to achieve and would then draw up action plans for various parts of the Searle vision. These wonderfully insightful documents, usually seven or eight pages, each addressed some change in Searle's communication that would be needed if Rumsfeld's vision were to be realized.

Bit by bit, 10 or 12 position papers later, Greener was literally writing the book about communications at Searle. After a few months, the time was ripe to open the ears of G. D. Searle's management everywhere, and Rumsfeld allowed Greener to do it by staging a revolution in the writing of the company's annual report. Historically, the Searle report had been a cursory exercise. But its very blandness carried other messages:

1. The company didn't know how to communicate.

2. The company didn't expect its employees to communicate about their sectors of the firm.

3. The company didn't understand its businesses very well.

With the CEO's endorsement, Greener spearheaded the writing of a comprehensive annual report that set the power of Searle ringing in people's ears both inside and outside the company. Although the report itself was important, the writing of the report was far more momentous. The writing process sensitized everybody to the new power and priority of communications. To have one's story told corporately was now seen as a badge of honor. The annual report overhaul created an "event" that changed the whole culture of the company.

Searle's managers were asked to explain the results of their respective divisions and to characterize the contribution of their individual units to the total G. D. Searle business. No longer accountable just for results, they were now also accountable for explaining results in a corporate context. Going through this process created a burning desire to understand the context. This communications tactic whetted the appetite for—you guessed it—Rumsfeld's vision. Writing the report was actually a two-way communication that unleashed the desire for guidance and made the Searle team say, "We need a vision."

At the same time, a new standard for communicating had been put in place. There were no cowboys out there telling private stories. There were no leakers. Rather than using the annual report just to satisfy the SEC objective of disclosure, Greener gave Searle "disclosure plus"— disclosure that meant more on the inside than on the outside.

Greener himself is a communications visionary. Coming out of his shop since those days have been Tod Hullin, who now manages public relations for Time Warner; Dick McGraw, who stopped at Eastern to help out Frank Borman and now heads communications for COM-SAT; and Mark Brand, a highly respected independent consultant. Greener became a widely acknowledged expert in leadership communications. His expertise also no doubt helped make possible Searle's marriage with Monsanto. While the Searle team still enjoys plenty of sovereignty today, there was no way Searle could break out of the middle of the pack without the major capital infusion a major player like Monsanto could provide. The combination was just another step in realizing the vision.

SUSTAINING THE VISION

Creating and communicating a vision are tough, but sustaining a vision is the toughest problem. After vision making, everyone is happy, basking in the emotional exhaustion because of the accord achieved. None of this has any importance to the lasting value of a vision. The risk, in fact, is that you think the job has been accomplished.

What will motivate people to strive constantly to fulfill the vision? Will the vision survive the tests that are put before it?

Vision will not survive in an organization fixated on control. In a *Harvard Business Review* interview, General Electric CEO Jack Welch talks about a leader's responsibility for motivating people, especially staff. His comments target the positive bias a vision must have:

> Leaders have to find a better fit between their organization's needs
> and their people's capabilities. Staff people, whom I prefer to call

individual contributors, can be tremendous sources of value in an organization. But each staff person has to ask, "How do I add value? How do I help make people on the line more competitive?" In the past, many staff functions were driven by control rather than adding value. Staffs with that focus have to be eliminated. They sap emotional energy in the organization. . . . [M]iddle managers . . . have to see their roles as a combination of teacher, cheerleader, and liberator, not controller.[4]

In the article, Welch is seen as leading a "transformation of attitudes" at GE aimed at releasing what he calls "emotional energy." He says, for example, that people should challenge their bosses with such questions as, "Why do you require me to do these wasteful things?" And he sees that a demanding part of leadership work is intense communication. "Real communication," says Welch, "takes countless hours of eyeball to eyeball, back and forth. It means more listening than talking." This is high-powered vision at work.

As well as energy, a vision needs endurance—staying power. The critical moment in the life of any vision is the testing of its values. The most successful visions are articulated with a clear eye toward how they will be tested. What will be done to prove or disprove the vision's validity? Will the vision and its articulation in mission and strategy statements stand up when we are interacting with employees or responding to pressure groups in real life? You have to be prepared to defend an undertaking and to repel all assaults on the vision.

Johnson & Johnson's creed has long stood as one of the finest articulations of a business vision. With only a few fine-tunings of the original words over decades, it remains the essentially same document. When consumer safety was at peril some years ago as a result of criminal tampering with Tylenol capsules, Johnson & Johnson withdrew the product and redesigned it at considerable expense. The creed demanded it. That response is an excellent example of withstanding the test, but it is a negative example. To my mind, the real strength of the Johnson & Johnson creed is how it sustains positive action. Andrall Pearson, who was PepsiCo's president for fifteen years, is an admirer of Johnson & Johnson and has written this about Johnson & Johnson and its network of 100 companies:

This highly decentralized organization is skilled at marketing and product innovation and [is] supported by a corporate credo that glues everything together into a very humane yet competitive company.

Managers throughout J&J know exactly what they're trying to do and how they are to do it.[5]

In comparison, Perrier is an example of a firm with a vision that didn't work. When faced with a product contamination problem, it did pull the product from the shelves, but I don't believe its customers sensed the thoughtful attitude that pervades a company like Johnson & Johnson. Perrier jumped from issue to issue. It tried to paper over its problems with advertising. When its vision was tested by a crisis, this outstanding brand of the past two decades incurred heavy losses.

EARNING CONVICTION

Visions can be well founded, superbly articulated, and doggedly supported by their leadership—and they can still fail if the organization doesn't have conviction. Even though the selected course of action may be difficult to follow, everyone must believe that it is right. It's the leader's job to build conviction. Everyone at Hertz knows that CEO Frank Olsen is right when he wants Hertz to be number one in every respect. That objective demands extraordinary effort and achievement to hold on to that franchise in the highly competitive car rental industry, but the Hertz people know the goal is worth the struggle. Everyone knows that when Dick Mahoney wants a 20-percent return on equity for Monsanto, he's right. Its employees understand that their future growth can be funded only with that kind of performance.

Both managers have patiently and continually schooled their organizations on the realities of their markets and their businesses. They have mapped out what will happen if their people lose a grip on the goals. And they have recognized how important it is to sell rightness emotionally, not just intellectually.

PROVIDING UNITY OF DIRECTION

A remarkably powerful and desirable aspect of communicating a vision is that it periodically provides an organization with a feeling of unity in its sense of direction. I say *periodic* because unity of purpose happens only for brief periods of time, even in the best organizations. It's self interest that drives moment-by-moment behavior in almost all organizations, unless you're talking about a band of saints. Even most religious organizations require their faithful to congregate and demonstrate unity of purpose only once a week. For the typical company, unity of purpose might be expressed at a quarterly meeting or an annual outing. Usually, it doesn't last long after the upbeat theme music in the meeting hall dies away.

While the organization is rallied to express its united purpose only periodically, leaders have to remind an organization constantly of the need for unity. To do so, the leader must continually be alert to the negative things on people's minds and must express the organization's vision against those negatives. Leaders must perpetually take the temperature of people around them. Reagan did it with polls. When he found that drugs were a divisive force undermining unity of purpose in American society, he declared war on drugs, just as if it were a menace such as Noriega or Hitler or Saddam. That the war on drugs was not particularly successful may say more about the methods used to wage it than about its rightness as a cause.

While American leaders use polls to gauge attitudes, the Japanese are more inclined to amass scores of subjective analyses. They lean more on collecting intelligence than on polls. No matter what the method, the sampling for threats to a unified sense of direction must be constant.

LINKING VISION TO CULTURE

In addition to the persistent sampling for new or changing views and attitudes, the leader must also understand the deeply ingrained cultural traits that have evolved in the organization. Vision and culture—the values and the unique characteristics of an organization—go hand in hand. In a young organization with a short history, the leader must use the vision to shape the culture. In a long-established organization, a vision must often accommodate the culture of the organization. Changing culture quickly—the way that Rumsfeld and Greener did it at Searle—requires a master stroke of planning and execution. The idea that a corporate culture can be overhauled overnight is a fallacy that's making a bunch of huckster consultants wealthy. Don't fall victim to it!

LEVERAGING A STRONG HERITAGE

Corporate cultures truly do exist in many companies. Strong, colorful founders underpin the most vibrant organizational cultures. At Weyerhauser, they still spin yarns about George Weyerhauser, Sr., trekking through the logging camps and pausing to jawbone with the lumberjacks while he propped one boot up on a tree stump. His son George, Jr., is a model professional manager, and you are far more likely to think of him in a well-tailored suit than in a plaid flannel shirt and a leather logger's jacket. He doesn't, and can't, manage today's vastly bigger business in the same way that his father did, but George, Jr. understands the importance of preserving the imagery surrounding his father, too. Weyerhauser knows how to use its legacy to leverage its vision: An enduring and thoughtful reference to the past and its values and achievements is striking in the company's communications.

IBM has a great culture, as do 3M and Ford. But even a mediocre culture is difficult to change. Don't be deluded; it takes generations and generations to put a corporate culture in place. And it usually takes years to alter its character.

I have seen some top managers seize a momentous event, such as a takeover or an LBO, and presume that they can redefine a culture with one radical jerk of the carpet. The image doctors are out there proclaiming that you can incubate a corporate culture as though it were a hot-house tomato plant. Presto! A new culture in twelve to eighteen months. It just doesn't work that way. Although it can be remolded with great ingenuity, most cultures are shaped by lore, not by quick fixes nor executive orders.

UNDERSTANDING RITUALIZED BEHAVIOR

Culture is evident in the little things as well as in the big ones. At Marathon Oil, the headquarters staff in Findlay, Ohio, would religiously stop business for a coffee break at ten every morning. Marathon would hire the best bakers in the region to create the toothsome platters of cupcakes, sweet rolls, and cookies that were the high point of this ritual. Pity the unaware manager who tried to schedule a staff meeting that coincided with the Marathon coffee break.

Marathon was a well-disciplined business and had a very conscientious work force, *but those factors had nothing to do with the ritual.* I'm sure that if Marathon were still around today and OPEC had been dissolved this morning or the world's largest oil reserves were discovered in Findlay, the Marathon people would still punctually be off to their ten o'clock break. Smart Marathon executives understood that there was no percentage in trying to work against the grain of this institution in running their business.

Managers who want to shake up the organization had better choose their shots carefully. When you tread on culture, you tread on quicksand. Slandering a founding father or mother or nixing the traditional company picnic as an expense move may cost you dearly.

MATCHING CULTURE TO VISION

Culture and vision are tied together. Sometimes culture constrains vision. Sometimes a faulty vision can demoralize a workforce and undermine a healthy culture, as when Allegis Corporation (once the parent to United Airlines) tried to become *the* travel company, with positions in air travel, travel reservations, car rental, and hotels. The plan didn't work. On June 9, 1987, reported *Business Week,* "the board ousted Chief Executive Richard J. Ferris, repudiated his travel supermarket strategy . . . and announced that a major stake in Allegis' flagship United Airlines might be sold to its employees." The article quotes one Allegis executive as saying that the "reason for [Ferris's] resigning was simple: The strategy was his vision and it wasn't accepted."[6] Internal pressure against the Allegis concept was strong and came from forces as diverse as nonmanagement directors and airline unions.

When culture and vision are well matched, magic can happen. No example in American industry demonstrates this better than Wal-Mart. Conceived in 1962 by the late Sam Walton and headquartered in Bentonville, Arkansas, Wal-Mart is now the country's largest retailer. It breezed past K-Mart at the end of 1990, and its monthly sales surpassed Sears' in the first months of 1991.

Although Wal-Mart appears to have an easy-going, down-home quality, underneath is a culture that is so well anchored in a vision that it should be in every leader's textbook. There are many facets of the Wal-Mart culture that deserve study: from the total involvement that Wal-Mart's associates (as the company's employees are called) demonstrate daily, to the latitude that in-store department managers have to merchandise and promote a certain portion of their inventory, thereby exerting considerable control over the destiny of their business, to the slogan, "What's important is you," which creates a mindset for how both customers and employees are treated.

Three other aspects of the Wal-Mart culture that I find particularly striking are the concept of customer as guest, the total commitment to communication, and the belief in fun as an important part of the workplace. Let me shed more light on each of these points.

When you walk into any one of the 1578 Wal-Mart stores, 176 Sam's Clubs, or 4 Wal-Mart Hypermarket U.S.A.s, you will be welcomed by an official "people greeter." These hosts and hostesses are well qualified to answer a shopper's questions, but their primary function is to let customers know that Wal-Mart wants to treat them as guests in their store. Obviously, their effort makes a strong, positive impression on customers, but it also creates a standard for the Wal-Mart associates in the stores. They, in turn, help realize the expectation of the customer-as-guest, set by the greeter at the front door. The Wal-Mart greeter is a simple, but powerful means of helping to fulfill the vision each day of customer satisfaction.

I especially relish communications, as Wal-Mart manages it. Wal-Mart's top managers, including its headquarters executives, spend much of their time in the field during the week. But everyone homes in on Bentonville on Friday, for Friday is what is known as "Meeting Day"—the day set aside for staff and interdepartmental meetings.

The crescendo of Wal-Mart's week is actually reached the next day when the "Saturday Morning Meeting" is held. Convening at 7 or 7:30 A.M., the Saturday Morning Meeting is attended by several hundred managers. Merchandising, marketing, and operating issues dominate the discussion. Lasting generally about two hours, the meeting is both a give-and-take session and a direction-setting session: It provides all the participants with the opportunity to speak and to adjust the course of the business—even if only a degree or two—thereby positioning the company to pursue the hottest opportunities for of the following week.

Through conference calls to field managers throughout the United States, the results of the Saturday Morning Meeting can be, and generally are, communicated nationwide within minutes of the meeting's conclusion. A pillar of the Wal-Mart's culture, the Saturday Morning Meeting gives the Wal-Mart calendar a regular rhythm. It helps calibrate and adjust the vision on a constant cycle while it provides the organization with an open forum to air issues and the follow-up mechanisms to communicate direction with great clarity and urgency.

The third facet of the Wal-Mart culture that I find remarkable is that Wal-Mart people have fun on their jobs. If you ask the company's veterans which part of the Wal-Mart lore best sums up the company's character, they will probably say it was in 1984, when Sam Walton wiggled down Wall Street in a grass skirt, dancing the hula and making good on a bet and a pledge to his associates at Wal-Mart if they exceeded their earnings target. Sam Walton, when he died, purportedly the richest man in America, believed in enjoying his work and in fulfilling his promises. He was also the architect of one of the most successful cultures in modern business.

Not every business is like Wal-Mart. Occasionally, culture and vision work in a perfect harmony, even though they produce a feisty, rough-and-tumble organization. Such is the case with Iowa Beef Processors, a company that wants to be the low-cost producer of beef, first in the United States and then in the world. They attack their competition at every point from the chain of processes, beginning with slaughtering the steer.

Iowa Beef plays tough. Instead of setting up one battle-plan, it takes on some competitors at the meat case in the grocery store and tackles others in the stockyard. CEO Bob Peterson has told me, "I don't care if it gets down to me, my secretary and a desk; this company will make it." He says that he wants his people to experience first-hand the rain, the grime, and the mud that go along with this business.

Iowa Beef is the company that invented boxed beef—the packing system essential to keeping meat prices down for consumers. Although its processing plants are still not a sight for the fainthearted, Iowa Beef's facilities set the industry standards for cleanliness and efficiency; and the firm is guided by the most sophisticated computing system in the industry.

A clenched-jaw company loaded with hardball players, Iowa Beef conveys a tension that grips you when you walk into the company's four-story headquarters in Dakota City. But in their business, it works. The company attracts the positive, confrontational people who can make such a style successful within the framework of a company that has the highest standards of integrity.

ACHIEVING VISION THROUGH FOCUS

Iowa Beef also has focus. There is no gap between the firm's vision and the actions that each player must perform to realize the vision. Focus can be achieved in many different ways, but no vision can be realized unless it is acted upon in a persistent, sustained way. It is the unique ability to concentrate one's energy and attention totally on the task at hand. Any organization that can focus its people with that kind of intensity is unbeatable. It may sound simple, but cultivating the ability to focus is the most powerful attitudinal advantage a leader can bring to an organization.

Wendy's is an organization with great sensitivity to people, yet it also has a relentless commitment to focus. In my opinion, this has made Wendy's the real ground-gainer in the quick-service food industry. Dave Thomas and Jim Near, the top executives at Wendy's, have almost an obsession with focus, which is giving them a powerful marketplace edge:

1. Their customer is more sharply defined.

2. Their workforce is better trained to specialize.

3. Their menu is tighter.

4. Their advertising is more sharply centered on the product.

5. Their packaging is more carefully designed to avoid the anger of environmentalists.

That dedication of energy and attentiveness to product and service comes from leadership. Wendy's has it—the ability to translate vision into task. Without a focus that sharply evokes and clearly defines the important issues of the business, all the other important aspects of the vision will falter and be for nought.

2

SMASHING
THE CRYSTAL
*Making a Commitment
to Practical Values*

NOT LONG AGO, I HEADED UP A STAFF PRESENTATION BEFORE A major potential client in the Southwest. This client had been wooed for years, but in the last two months the preparations reached a high point. Environmental and marketing problems were slapping this firm right and left. This battering made them increasingly receptive to bringing in skilled outside counsel—a step they should have considered years ago. Now, it looked as though they were finally ready.

A month before the presentation, the firm invited me to address their international marketing conference on the trends that the leader in their industry—and they are—could expect to face in the next decade. It was a good day. An audience of 500 cheered me off the podium. But I knew that I hadn't really given a speech. My appearance merely previewed our thinking on communications to the middle managers to pave the way for the company's announcement that it had retained us. When the applause meter pinned on the high side, the senior managers could feel comfortable that we were *their* kind of people.

The whole mating dance culminated in a final presentation made in the boardroom eight days later. We approached the prospective client

THINKPOINTS
on How
a Leader Upholds Values

☐ Smash flawed crystal.

☐ Focus on practical values.

☐ Measure the values' performance.

☐ Make national values internationally competitive.

☐ Create an agenda of values.

☐ Humanize personal values.

☐ Stress values leading to quality.

☐ Respect the resurgence of traditional values.

---

with slides, charts, and handouts—all the vital material needed to close the deal, but the delivery of the presentation itself was done in the best professional, low-key style. About midway through our pitch, the president of the company, an angular, athletic man known for his arrogance, started thumping the eraser of his pencil on the long oak table. Then the senior managers unleashed a cascade of questions and challenges at our staff. The challenge was fine—the tougher the better. But their comments were framed with the epithets "handler" and "flack" and barbs such as "All you people are good for is putting a shine on things"—insults like that, and much worse.

At first, I tried not to notice. After the second disparaging remark, I was disappointed, figuring that we had lost the business—$1.6 million a year, not a small account—and that this man was having a bad day and using us as a whipping post. When the third and fourth comments came along, I got furious. After the fifth show of rudeness, I slowly stood up and said that there was no point in continuing this presentation, was there? "No, no, Bob, sit down," the president countered, slowly rolling his words out in a reedy, malevolent voice. "You've *got* the business. I just want to make sure your people understand how things work around here."

"You may have given us the business," I said flatly, "but we're not taking it. If you treated your own people the way you just talked to us, you would be blown out of the water in two days. If you put flexing power ahead of treating people decently, this is not business we want." With that solid rejoinder, we walked out and took a long elevator ride down to the lobby. Two of our staff members asked me if I hadn't been a little hotheaded, but it was obvious they were proud that we had walked.

Our exit was a statement about values: the topic of this chapter. In my view, a leader without strong, practical values has few prospects of realizing a meaningful vision. When Steuben makes a bad glass bowl, the company destroys it if there's the slightest flaw. Sometimes, you have to smash the crystal, despite its apparent worth. Upholding a standard is what values are all about.

Not long ago, a story about the Village Cheese Shop in Southampton, Long Island, appeared in *New York* magazine and was retold in the *Financial Times*. It is the version excerpted here:

The mood [in the United States] has turned.

[Recently, a] fur-coated corporate raider . . . walked into the crowded Village Cheese Shop in Southampton, a Long Island seaside town much frequented by investment bankers in the 1980s.

Standing at the end of a long [line of customers], he lost patience and shouted: "I'll give $10 to anyone who'll give me his place in the line." Mistaking the contemptuous stares of other customers for a challenge, he upped his bid to $20.

Finally, a distinguished man turned around and said quietly: "Sir, this may come as a surprise, but there are people in this store with less time and more money than you."[1]

Chalk one up for the good guys. I think of that story as a parable for what is happening in American industry. The traders and junk-bond barons who dazzled us in the eighties are headed south.

The real industrial leadership of this country is waking up to the true problems of running American business. To me, this awakening means they now realize that they must take a stand for values, just as the gentleman in the line at the cheese shop did.

EMBODYING A CODE OF VALUES

Some people may think that leaders have a direct relationship with their followers, but that notion would pin everything on the charisma and motivational efforts of the leader. Few leaders can withstand that burden. In fact, the relationship is triangular. Although leaders relate to followers, both leader and followers have to relate to a commonly held set of values. The antiquated, arbitrary leaders of the past often tried to be either the law or the values of a company. The tobacco baron R. J. Reynolds said once, "I have written the book. All you need to do is follow it."[2] Or, worse yet, old-style leaders tried to be above the law.

Today's leaders must embody and uphold values that the organization considers worthwhile. A code of positive values, shared by both leader and followers, keeps an organization on course in the absence of minute-by-minute direction from the leader. The need to sustain that code explains why organizational values must be actionable, practical, and easily communicated.

When I go to conferences on business values and ethics, I still hear many abstract discussions, preoccupied with remote "what-ifs." Instead, leaders should invest their energy in defining the values that will get the job done responsibly and morally in the vast majority of cases. Leaders have a responsibility to their employees and their organizations to think and act in exemplary ways.

FOCUSING ON CORE VALUES

There are many fine values, such as courtesy, confidence, ingenuity, thrift, and so on. The trouble is that the list of values grows easily and can cause many employees to lose their focus. They fail to prioritize. A "short list" of values is far more useful in putting the workplace back on track.

Moreover, when the core values exceed four or five points, it becomes difficult to communicate and reinforce them. The following are five candidates for the practical values having foremost importance:

1. Integrity

2. Accountability

3. Diligence

4. Perseverance

5. Discipline

I know companies—strong organizations—centered on these values. They are invariably successful. Almost always, these core values generate other values in employees.

But what if all our organizations started with the same short list? Wouldn't that give American industry, or the industry of any culture, an important leg up?

INTEGRITY

Integrity is no simple matter. It is particularly easy for business people to lie. Recently, I compiled a list of 46 reasons that executives lie. They include

> If I didn't lie about my loyalty to the firm, they would never have promoted me.

If the union knew our real profit prospects, they would beat us black-and-blue at the bargaining table.

If I hadn't lied, I would have exposed our firm to an unfair lawsuit.

There seem to be some compelling reasons to lie in certain situations. Although I've heard a few plausible defenses of lying, I'm not sure it is ever justified. Once a company starts to condone lying as a matter of course, it is headed for serious trouble. In such businesses, lying becomes a game. And success goes to those who play it best.

In an article titled "Where Lying Was Business as Usual," *Business Week* reviewed a recent book on the Wedtech Scandal, a Washington scandal of the late eighties in which a few government officials fed fat contracts to a dubious supplier. The reviewer Harris Collingwood concludes his piece, saying: "In the end, what's remarkable about the Wedtech gangsters isn't that they were crude and thuggish. It's that among the sharp-elbowed hordes pushing through Washington's corridors of power, they didn't even stand out."[3]

ACCOUNTABILITY

The value of accountability is the willingness to take responsibility for one's own actions.

Bob Waterman has written a penetrating little book, *Adhocracy: The Power to Change.*[4] It narrates an engaging story about accountability in an energy-cogenerating firm called AES. The people in the Beaver Valley, Pennsylvania, AES plant learned what many workers and managers know across the country: They learned who is responsible for the way things run. The answer, of course, is that *they* are. "They," however, is not any one of them, but rather a nameless, faceless force hiding in the organization. These powerful secret terrorists, these mega-gremlins—"they"—are always there to gum up the works. *They* send the wrong material handling orders. *They* misprocess the medical claims. *They* forget to clean and maintain the machinery.

A courageous top manager in this firm, Bob Hemphill—who is a leader, no doubt about it—decided to declare war on "they." He sent out coffee mugs emblazoned with "Who is they anyway?" He put up posters that read: "Send *they* a letter."

With a healthy sense of humor, AES eliminated the rationalization *"They* make us do it." It was no longer an acceptable excuse. In a particularly clever step, the workers created a system of organization called the honeycomb structure and organized themselves into families: the turbine family, the coal-pile family, and the scrubber family. Workers were also encouraged to move from family to family to expand their range of skills. In this way, AES was able to make the breakthrough on accountability, as each "family" also provided a framework of values that, in turn, became a basis for improving accountability.

DILIGENCE

There are scores of individuals who equate diligence with drudgery. Too often, managers demand diligence about the wrong things: filling out forms is one glaring example.

According to Arno Penzias, the head of research at Bell Labs, the mother of one of his teachers at Columbia used to ask her son persistently when he was just a young schoolchild: "Did you ask any good questions today, Isaac?"[5] The question was not what did you learn in school today, but what good questions did you ask. The mother's priority must have had an impact on Penzias, because he eventually helped institutionalize the practice of asking useful questions at AT&T Bell Labs. Asking tough questions has become a hallmark of AT&T research culture and has helped to establish Bell Laboratories as one of the great creative institutions in America. The best firms are diligent about uncommon things—for example, asking creative questions.

I'm afraid that we lose the value of diligence as a positive force early in life. Too often, schools turn diligence into drudgery. Peter Drucker has pointed out that our educational system is obsessed with people's weaknesses.[6] Rather than making their powerful writing skills even stronger, children weak in geography waste time on remedial geography with few results. "How do we make our strengths stronger?" is a positive, productive question that we should ask ourselves each day.

Diligence that nurtures strength makes a difference. Indeed, a diligent commitment to improving their already powerful position is what makes the Japanese a formidable competitor in the electronic and automotive industries. Similarly, the Japanese philosophy of perpetual quality improvement is a restless, but positive diligence.

PERSEVERANCE

The developers of the ulcer drug at G. D. Searle knew they had something when they invented aspartame. It took years to learn, however, that aspartame was not an ulcer drug but the heart of the revolutionary sugar substitute NutraSweet.

Perseverance presupposes confidence, and few companies can match Xerox for its sense of confidence and determination. Xerox, which pioneered the photocopying business, lost important ground to the Japanese on price. Now, Xerox is reviving its copying business by focusing on the value added by advanced technologies and color copying. Focused leadership over time implies productive, useful perseverance.

In the eighties, "cutting your losses" quickly was fashionable thinking. In the future, companies won't be able to exit and enter businesses as quickly as in the last decade. The initial costs of entry, especially for marketing, will be prohibitive. Once the massive investment has been made, it becomes increasingly awkward to justify abandoning the business. The vice chairman of the holding company that includes Revlon recently said in the *Wall Street Journal:* "[W]e aren't going to spend $30 million to launch a deodorant."[7] The minimum stakes can be staggering, and the entry costs for other kinds of products are, in fact, much higher.

Employees must be prepared for prolonged competitive horizons. The battles of entrenched foes, such as Pepsi and Coke, will be more the norm than the exception. Just think: The Cola Wars between Pepsi and Coke have already lasted longer than the Cold War between the United States and the Soviet Union.

DISCIPLINE

How little we know about discipline in modern business! Because of our passion to make things simple, we err and also try to make them easy. As the great battlefield strategist von Clausewitz pointed out, the simple and the easy are not synonymous.

Al Neuharth launched *Today,* the prototype for *USA Today,* in Florida back in 1966. Two weeks before the first issue, Neuharth reported that his employees "produced complete prototypes of the paper every day—printed them, put them on trucks, dropped them at delivery points to pinpoint timing, then picked them up and burned them at the local dump to keep them out of the hands of the competition."[8] In my view, *USA Today* is assured great commercial success in journalism. In no small measure, it stems from the remarkable discipline that went into building the paper.

Discipline does not always imply following orders. Sometimes, it points in the opposite direction. *Business Month* named MCI one of the five best-managed companies in 1990. The late Bill McGowan, MCI's former Chairman and CEO, did "his best to ban . . . standard procedures and practices." He would get up in front of his people and say: "I know that somewhere, someone out there is trying to write up a manual on procedures. Well, one of these days I'm going to find out who you are, and when I do, I'm going to fire you."[9] For McGowan, I think, discipline meant that individuals are required to think on their feet. They have to solve problems sensibly from the earliest days of their careers.

Obviously, there are many ways to sort and define the five cornerstone values: integrity, accountability, diligence, perseverance, and, discipline. It's hard to contain the focus to these attributes before other supporting values come into play. Diligence presumes a sense of urgency, for example, because you can't be just busy; you must be busy in the context of time. Perseverance also requires judgment because no one would ever persist in a patently wrongheaded course. Although they may presume other values, the five cornerstone values are a credible starting point, and, I think, can be considered a priority list of the key workplace values.

In my view, management now has no choice but to teach values. Business leaders in the United States have shunned talking about values, because they seem to suggest a religious or moral outlook. This implication is not necessarily the case. Further, it's not possible to sustain industrial competitiveness without attention to them. Ask a Japanese CEO to define his primary job, and he's likely to tell you that his role is to "harmonize" values. It is to help employees to adjust to the ever-shifting structure of priorities and demands. Values are what motivate and sustain behavior over the long run, and this perseverance is something the Japanese understand particularly well.

MEASUREMENT OF VALUES

If we're going to get serious about values, we had better prepare to do more than just preach; we must do. Most important, we must measure what we do.

Not surprisingly, measurement has also been central to America's industrial resurgence in the 1980s. We've measured defect rates, productivity, and the time needed for nearly every job. Now I propose that leaders measure values. Managing values in the modern organization requires leaders to assess the values' performance, communicate the results, and focus employees on the communication.

A SEVEN-POINT PROGRAM
FOR MANAGING VALUES

1. *Gather reliable data on the values that you have, need, and want.* Undertake exhaustive studies, not esoteric reports. Forget the boardroom. Start at the factory floor. Talk with your sales manager out in the real world—in the coffee shops at Holiday Inns in Nebraska and Oklahoma. Get the purchasing agent to tell you about how sealed bids really work. It's easy to stencil your standards formed on the best of the Business Roundtable; it's tough to address the hard realities facing a business in operation.

2. *Formulate a plan centered on values.* Ask probing questions: What kind of values do we need? Where does the marketplace support our values? Where are we in conflict? Everything won't come clear in an instant. The best values statements I've seen in business are constantly debated.

3. *Convert the values plan into a communications agenda.* Look for the ways to publicize the key values through routine communications. I know two CEOs who praise rank-and-file employees who typify positive values at the company's annual meeting. Waste Management built a terrific commercial around one of their finest garbage truck drivers, a model of reliability, courtesy, and humanity. His example gave garbage truck drivers a better reputation than that of many politicians.

4. *Find the values lessons in unexpected, critical events.* I've made a career of turning away new business because it doesn't meet high standards. It is an event publicized throughout the organization. The bigger the account rejected, the more it's celebrated.

5. *Set up measurement systems to monitor how well the values perform.* This is an opportunity for company-wide participation. How will we measure productive diligence, diligence that strengthens our strong points? Are we going to track "forms completed on time" or "hours invested in training"? Shall we pay bonuses for "serving customers in a disciplined way" or for "having no worse quality than our leading competitors"? Every measurement standard sets a tone.

6. *Teach management how to "harmonize" decisions based on values.* That often means explaining the logic of an organization's decision making, especially key decisions. Let people know what can be compromised and when—and what can't ever be compromised. Sometimes supposedly cherished values *will* be compromised. There comes a point where customer loyalty ends. There is also a point when the bottom line can't absorb more discipline. The best companies generally agree on where to draw the line of limits.

7. *Make values a continuous concern.* It can't be a one-year program. You know the routine: "This year we're doing values; last year, it was quality; and next year, it will probably be globalization." Values cannot be a hot-button item. They must abide.

These points may sound hopelessly corny. But the way world competition is shaping up is forcing us to choose between being cynical, sophisticated, and self-destructive or corny, ethical, and competitive.

VALUES AND GLOBAL BUSINESS

We Americans are not very realistic when we talk about values in global business. We become purists and let esoteric cultural problems overwhelm our focus. If bribery is a common practice in certain countries or if prices are artificially supported in others, we allow these practices to disturb us, rather than mastering certain core values for ourselves and making those values powerful competitive advantages.

Almost never do we talk about the weaknesses in our own values, and rarely are we critical of our weakness in sustaining the values in which we believe. Are we too independent? Are the problems too complex? The reasons for our behavior are debatable. I know only that our most successful international competitors aren't timid about teaching values. The companies in those countries set crystal clear expectations for values.

At every international business conference I attend, I am constantly embarrassed at the lack of preparation U.S. participants evidence. We have forgotten how to do our homework. But the Japanese are ever-ready with a second or even a third position paper as a debate unfolds. They think that far ahead in the chess game.

Last October, I tracked the countries that responded fastest to my faxes. The Japanese won, of course—not a single unanswered fax, not a single one answered in longer than 24 hours.

Yet the Japanese themselves are looking over their shoulders at the Koreans these days. *Business Week* reports that "signs in the elevators at the Daewoo group's headquarter advise employees that 'the hand of the diligent shall rule.' Koreans work an average of 2700 hours a year, 40 percent more than Americans do and 25 percent more than the Japanese work. The Korean saying *minjok chajon,* which means 'We can do it by ourselves,' amounts to a national slogan."[10] That sounds a lot closer to the Puritan work ethic and Yankee can-doism than anything you are likely to see in the standard-issue U.S. factory these days.

THE VALUES AGENDA

In my opinion, every leader needs an agenda of attitudes on values, one that challenges commonplace notions about accepted values. Each organization has its own false assumptions with which to deal. Looking at the assumptions that leaders wrongly make, we can perceive four challenges to past practices, which, I believe, should be instilled in the consciousness of our leaders. Perhaps, they can be a starting point for creating specific agendas for values.

1. *We will not automate ourselves out of our values weaknesses.* Even the engineering of our factories rests to a great extent on our ability to master values. Richard Schonberger, a management consultant

on manufacturing in Seattle, has pointed out the hazards of automating factories for the sake of automation. Just putting in robots
won't help us keep pace with the Japanese. "[U]ndue haste in
adopting advanced technologies" can simply lead to "automating
bad practices," he maintains.[11]

Before automating, you have to simplify the work. You must
consider new ways of arranging the flow of work—moving subas-
semblies between different work groups rather than down a single
assembly line. You need workers who are flexible, alert, and cooper-
ative. But this kind of clarity and coordination in the workplace
requires values, such as cooperation.

Peter Drucker, who predicts that the greatest changes in our
society will be in education, sees an important transformation
needed in our elementary schools. All of us will have to function
as colleagues in a less hierarchical society. Drucker contends that
"in the elementary schools, greater attention needs to be paid to
teaching 'management of the self,' the responsibility everyone has
for constructively participating in group endeavors."[12]

2. *Our accounting principles must reinforce positive values.* Right
now we stimulate more wrong moves than right ones. Some of our
roadblocks to values are indeed subtle, but no less powerful for
their subtlety. The accounting laws are one such barrier.

Another obstacle is evident in the accounting principles that
drive decision making in our factories. The accounting principles
applicable to costs and investments in American factories have
actually hindered the new industrial values that managers want to
instill.

Some businesses, such as the Allen-Bradley division of Rockwell,
are tearing up their accounting rule book when making decisions
about factory design. The British newsweekly the *Economist* goes
on to explain:

Yesterday's sort of management accounting used to encourage
presses in the car industry to churn out body panels for four-door
models, even while salesmen screamed for two-door models. . . .
Japanese accounting systems [are different from those used in the
West. They] are used to motivate employees into producing products
at a "target cost" and to reduce that cost over the lifetime of the
product.[13]

Some may say accounting rules are just financial principles. I disagree. Positive accounting rules embody a series of fundamental cultural disciplines, ranging from individual worker accountability to the pursuit of a continually improving standard of excellence. In the same *Economist* article, the experts call the emerging accounting principle "activity-based costing." I call its moral counterpart "reality-centered work values."

3. *We must be open to the reality of other value systems.* And we must see this both ways: from the standpoint of economies less successful than ours as well as those economies more successful than ours.

Should we actually worry about less developed countries, too? For very sound reasons, the answer must be yes: It's impossible to contain an increasing list of issues within national boundaries. As one example, the transnational environment is really heating up as a values' theme. Everyone is concerned about the ozone layer, global warming, and South American rain forests. These are genuine concerns, and the United States has made impressive progress on the environmental front in the last two decades. I can remember that day in June 1969, when Cleveland's Cuyahoga River was so polluted by oil slicks that it actually caught fire.

In some respects, it's healthy that American activists are leading the international initiative on the environment. In other ways, American visibility has drawbacks. It is yet another example of our widely disdained "moralism" versus our morality. I talk regularly with business leaders in Southeast Asia and South America who are livid about the American attitude. They say: "Sure, it was great for Americans to pillage their landscape and resources for more than a century. It was fine for U.S. firms in the fifties and sixties to move offshore and build pollutant-belching factories. Now the United States is a service and information economy, however, and they want to change the rules.

"Today, we [in South America or Southeast Asia] are just entering our manufacturing era, and Americans want us to spend on the environment as if we were a developed economy." These opinion leaders in less developed countries want to know whether this is part of an economic conspiracy. They ask: "Isn't this just a convenient way for the United States to slow our growth and keep us as a permanent underclass of less developed nations?"

I don't think those opinions represent our agenda, conscious or otherwise. I do think some U.S. views on the global environment, such as our whining about the lack of a level playing field in global trade, show astonishing naïveté about the goals and values of other cultures.

On the other side, some American companies are earning respect from our toughest competitors. Not too long ago, *Business Week* had an excellent cover story on Motorola titled "The Rival Japan Respects."[14] Under Robert Galvin, and now under CEO George Fisher, Motorola has managed to stay afloat in cellular phones, automotive electronics, and microprocessors. Motorola knows how to mix it up in the world of international business. Galvin himself taught Sony's redoubtable Akio Morita, the article describes, how to windsurf in 1986 in Barrington, Illinois.

The electronics businesses in which Motorola is excelling have been seriously challenged by foreign competitors, especially the Japanese. While the U.S. chip industry gets thumbs-down reviews in many Japanese companies, Canon—the Japanese camera giant—is using a Motorola microprocessor "as the heart of its hot-selling EOS 35mm camera."

It was more than excellent technology. It was also common values drawing Canon to Motorola, says *Business Week*. The Canon people felt Motorola had the same *netsui*, or passion for doing business, as Canon management has. I am sure that Motorola has also studied the values of the global electronics industry, and the Japanese in particular. The company knows that it must fit into that framework to be a viable resource in the business. Similarly, it's no surprise that the former CEO of Philips in Holland, Wisse Dekker, spent years living and working in Japan.

On the one hand, you have Philips, with a consumer electronics business continuing to show good growth, and Motorola, doing a terrific job in semiconductors, studying the Japanese and other international values and adapting to them. On the other hand, you have a bunch of CEOs primarily in the United States bad-mouthing Akio Morita. They are outraged because Morita, co-author of *The Japan That Can Say No!* (the Japanese edition's title), wrote that America had better fix its quality problem.

I ask you: Which firms will win as global competitors? Those that study and adapt to differing values systems? Or those that do not? Those that stop bellyaching and demand a tough system of domestic values that make sense for America? Or those who want the World Court in the Hague to send in a carpenter with a level and measure how flat the playing field is?

Indeed, there are various healthy systems of values. That is not to say they are all easily made compatible. The controversy between Japan and the United States is an excellent case in point. We should focus less on how our value systems differ and more on how to strengthen our own values. In the end, if we don't manage values in our own companies and in our own culture more vigorously, I am certain of this: Our opportunities to shape values on a world stage are diminishing. But if we advance values aggressively through communications, the American spirit will rise again and make its mark in the world we're about to face.

4. *We must come to grips with our overlitigated way of life.* A stronger commitment to positive values would diminish our tortuous investment in litigation. The pervasiveness of litigation has diminished our capacity to take risks. It has sapped the determination of many leaders to stand up and be accountable. Excessive litigation, in lieu of genuine values, has been an unintentional but massive disruption to achieving the vision of so many organizations.

If we could make progress on just these four challenges, think of the added latitude and energy our leaders would have to take the initiative and to lead!

There are three other ways in which leaders must reflect on values:

1. How leaders should project their values in the context of their own humanity

2. How values are fundamentally related to the pursuit of quality

3. How a resurgence of traditional values is redefining our concept of power.

HUMANIZING THE VALUES OF LEADERS

Many leaders are perceived by the public to have weak values. Television helps create a bad impression for leaders among the public at large, and both news and entertainment shows put business management in an especially bad light. In entertainment programs on television, the company executives make phenomenal sums of money. Many of them seem to make it illegally. Why shouldn't employees transfer the fantasy they see on television to their own company? After all, they know more about the boardrooms of Ewing Oil and "Falcon Crest" and the skill-fully edited world of "60 Minutes" than they know about the upper management in the company where they work.

Businesses have failed to use their clout to change the ethical fabric of television. A Mobil op-ed piece pointed out that before a child reaches adulthood, he or she will see businesspeople commit 10,000 murders on TV dramas. Real-life business leaders always complain to me that there is too much violence, sex, and dishonesty on television. Unfortunately, they communicate a different message in the way they use their advertising dollars to present programming.

Are these matters of values? Businesspeople must assume that the average citizen has sizable and automatic doubts about the integrity of business. If managers want their messages on ethics heard, they will have to convince their audiences that managers live with the same realities as those of everyone else. On the day after his appointment to the Presidency, Gerald Ford was photographed in his bathrobe eating toast at the breakfast table with his family. Some years ago, a news team videotaped Lee Iacocca eating a family-style dinner with his daughters in their suburban kitchen. The Bush family dog has succeeded the Reagan family dog as a center of attention on Sunday afternoon under the whirring blades of the presidential helicopter.

In speeches and informal meetings, intelligent executives will under-stand the importance of "humanizing" their lives—that is, conveying what their lives are like. I often advise executives to remind their own employees of the everyday "realities" of executives' lives, which are far more "normal" than many persons think they are. If leaders don't build an awareness of this ordinariness, they make it easy for people to believe that managers live in lavish corruption. Sometimes a casual comment in a speech will help: Turning down a child's request for more allow-ance or a new bike suggests that managers have budgets, too. Using illustrations from the daycare center or the subway ride to work can also help bring the world of that manager down to earth for the people around him or her.

QUALITY AS A PRODUCT OF VALUES

In addition to humanizing their values, leaders must also understand the connection between values and goals such as quality, or else they will limit their ability to make material improvements in realizing these goals. People keep getting things backward. Quality is not a value. Quality is the output, the product of a series of values—chiefly the practical values I cited earlier.

William Wiggenhorn is corporate vice president for training and education at Motorola and president of Motorola University. In an article he wrote in 1990, he emphasizes the importance of quality:

> At Motorola, we require three things of our manufacturing employees. They must have communication and computation skills at the seventh grade level, soon going up to eighth and ninth. They must be able to do basic problem-solving—not only as individuals but also as members of a team. And they must accept our definition of work and the workweek: the time it takes to ship perfect product to the customer who's ordered it. That can mean a workweek of 50 or even 60 hours, but we need people willing to work against quality and output instead of a time clock.[15]

What a superb convergence of values and skills! It's the foundation for achieving consistent quality over time: unembellished virtue without glamour or banners. But it should allow Motorola to achieve the venerable standard of Six Sigma by 1992—Six Sigma: 99.99966 percent defect-free production. Motorola is a leader because it conveys the same message outside the company that it sends to its employees. Motorola demanded that 3000 suppliers compete for the Malcolm Baldrige National Quality Award.[16] About two hundred companies said no. They're no longer Motorola suppliers. Everybody goes down the same chute, which is a sensible beginning point to create standardized values leading to quality.

More and more leadership companies are improving quality and their overall performance by making values more practical. What CEO Robert Haas of Levi Strauss has to say about this realization makes sense to me:

> In the past . . . we always talked about the "hard stuff" and the "soft stuff." The soft stuff was the company's commitment to our work force. And the hard stuff was what really mattered: getting pants out the door. What we've learned is that the soft stuff and hard stuff are becoming increasingly intertwined. A company's values—what it stands for, what its people believe in—are crucial to its competitive

success. Indeed, values drive the business . . . Values are where the hard stuff and the soft stuff come together.[17]

NO TEFLON, EVEN FOR THE FORMIDABLE

My last point on values is that the resurgence in traditional values is transforming the kind of power that leaders should aspire to possess. Recently I saw a cartoon by Leigh Rubin. In it, an empty platter rests atop a kitchen counter, and two bloated dogs are sitting on the floor beneath it, surrounded by a pile of turkey bones. One dog philosophizes to the other: "What it really comes down to is a question of values. . . . Is a delicious, succulent turkey, baked to perfection, worth a few whacks on the nose with a newspaper?"

The world of business in the 1980s, especially the world of Wall Street, fed on that kind of Power Snack, big helpings of booty accompanied by a relatively light slap on the wrist for punishment. But as the fur-coated investment banker in the cheese shop line discovered, that world is changing. What I call a "reining in" is taking place for visible figures of every stripe. Leaders and leaders-to-be would do well to pay attention to it. It is making aggressive, highly independent leadership behavior more and more risky to pursue.

The heightened awareness of values put the high-flying criminals such as Ivan Boesky and Michael Milken on the sidelines. That same awareness censured and sidelined executives such as F. Ross Johnson in the RJR Nabisco takeover for their monumental bad taste. It is also reining in what other big-league executives—who are neither criminal nor clumsy—can get away with. Nearly every day I get calls from CEOs who find that their aggressive business behavior is making them a target for attacks from the press, from special interests, and from competitors. In the main, these executives have very high standards of integrity. While they make considerable efforts to stay informed about what is happening in their own organizations, some things are bound to escape their notice, while others may deliberately be shielded from them. Because these are aggressive executives who don't shrink from a fight, they have made enemies. As a result, everything done by their organization is being held up to the microscope. An investment banker working on their behalf may engage in insider trading. An overseas office head in South America may mount a program of disinformation against a business rival. A family member may unwittingly commit a conflict of interest. Suddenly, the executive and the business are in trouble, because there is no Teflon coating for leaders anymore.

Much of my week is spent visiting executive suites on cases such as these—suites with dazzling art, endless hallways of mahogany or oak paneling, and lobbies with exotic floral arrangements and elegant furniture. When I talk with these executives, I will often glance out their office windows. The view is usually a knockout. It's easy to feel you could run the world from such a place. Manhattan has literally thousands of offices that give you this perspective on the world, that whet the appetite for power. The forces surrounding leaders today, however, demand that they exercise their leadership with more care.

When you visit Reinhard Mohn, the former head of Bertelsmann's supervisory board and now head of the Bertelsmann Foundation, (Bertelsmann is the global publishing empire, which owns Bantam, Doubleday, and RCA Records in the United States), you go to the fringes of a little German town called Gütersloh. You need to travel by car, because only local trains stop in Gütersloh, and there's no airport. You visit a company that started out publishing biblical tracts—one that has remained true to its founding values while it pulses ahead in expanding an information empire of far-reaching power. Communication quietly hums in and out of Gütersloh over fax and phone lines while power is effectively decentralized to its operating divisions throughout the world. And Reinhard Mohn, one of the world's wealthiest individuals, is a modest, low-key personality, even though he had the foresight to build an aggressive growth strategy and to bring gifted talents such as Mark Woessner into the firm.

From the heart of Bertelsmann, at the top of a three-story, block-shaped building in the town of Gütersloh, you don't see much of anything, except a stolid German landscape built on conventional, somewhat boring values. I wonder, though, as I compare that landscape with the dramatic panorama one sees from the pinnacles of Manhattan or Chicago, which vantage point, which values—the audacious and the dramatic or the traditional and the sober—will be center stage for leaders in the years to come? I think I know.

3

THE
POWER CLOCK
Managing Time Effectively

ECENTLY, THE CEO OF A MAJOR SECURITIES FIRM ON THE WEST
Coast confided in me that he didn't know what to do with his
time. Several months earlier he had named Carl, a strong lieutenant,
to the post of president and chief operating officer to prepare him to
take over as CEO in the next 18 months. To give the new president
free range to build his own relationships, the CEO had effectively
locked himself in his office, wary of having meetings with anyone in the
organization lest he seem meddlesome to the evolving order. In truth,
the CEO was longing to have his regular lunch and dinner conferences
with the other officers of the firm.

"Go ahead and dip down into the organization," I told him. "Hold
the luncheon and dinner meetings. You will be doing Carl a service.
He's overweight and doesn't need the calories." We talked about ways
that the CEO could use the contacts to reinforce Carl and not undercut him. So far, it looks like the partnership is working. I hope it does.
In my opinion, a CEO's time is a terrifically expensive asset. Even
though a management transition has not been completed, the top
manager is still obligated to make that time productive and not be
inhibited by fears of being meddlesome. Most fears of this sort—and

THINKPOINTS

on How

Leaders use Time Wisely

☐ Balance your commitments.

☐ Steadily move your agenda forward on multiple levels.

☐ Practice issue-driven time management.

☐ Stick to the timetable in dealing with peers.

☐ Sustain a leadership rhythm.

☐ Keep your limited tenure in perspective.

☐ Prepare for your exit from the day of your appointment.

---

leaders often succumb to such anxieties—are simply phantoms, which can be overcome by simple planning and setting objectives.

This CEO's problem was symptomatic of many I see in the category of time management for leaders. You would think that executives get better at managing time the higher up the ladder they climb. Indeed, most improve their time-management skills as high-level executive *subordinates*. But when they get to the top, a new set of skills and criteria must be used to handle time. When leaders wind up their power clocks, they face entirely new challenges involving time:

1. How many of their present activities are important to their new role as leaders? Which of these activities are simply the things they enjoyed doing, or excelled at doing, when they were top-level subordinates?

2. How do they measure their effectiveness as time managers, since the time frame for measuring results and effectiveness is generally much longer for leaders?

3. How much time should be devoted to the often ceremonial functions of civic affairs, philanthropy, and trade associations?

Setting the power clock to run effectively in the leadership time zone has stymied scores of executives. This chapter is intended to give you some tips on managing leadership time for better results.

Leaders should expect of themselves and their people a balanced use of time in everything they do, especially in community affairs. Howard M. "Pete" Love, who retired as chairman of National Intergroup in 1990, was criticized by a shareholder group, Walker Street Associates, for being an "absentee manager."[1] Some felt that he spent too much time away from the business. In a *Business Week* article titled "National Intergroup: How Pete Love Went Wrong," reporter Gregory L. Miles notes, "[C]ritics say Love relished the trappings of his office far too much. Described as an 'absentee manager' by former colleagues, Love spent a good deal of time on outside boards and civic organizations."[2]

Shareholders, financial analysts and others are starting to project the time distribution of an executive's calendar from what *Who's Who* will tell them about board and civic involvements. A leader can be compromised if it looks as though the right focus on running the organization is missing.

MANAGEMENT ON MULTIPLE LEVELS

A leader's best insurance policy against wasting time on the wrong things is having a clear plan to invest time productively. All of us remember the geologic time scales from high-school science books showing the various strata of rock in the earth's crust. Leadership time—the time a leader is empowered to do the job—is layered like the earth's surface. But rather than individual layers being added on top of each other with the passage of time, all the layers are present at once. Managing leadership time successfully requires leaders to make progress on realizing the multiple levels of their agendas simultaneously.

Weak leaders look at their tenure as a one-dimensional experience to be weathered until they reach the safe haven of retirement. Leaders who savor their roles enjoy the complexity of advancing on several fronts simultaneously, but they also have the focus to know that there are five key layers that demand constant, conscious attention:

THE LAYERED-TIME SCALE OF LEADERSHIP

1. *What must I achieve?* While I am leader, what goals must the organization realize? How do I wish to leave it positioned? How do I break the negative molds that inhibit the organization's future? As the former CEO of RCA Thornton Bradshaw once pointed out, the average CEO may have several years' tenure but only six months to initiate dramatic change before being neutralized by subordinates who find the CEO's changes painful.

2. *What is my economic context?* How do I structure the timetable, the sequence for goals to intercept or avoid the economic trend line? How can I meet the needs for short-term profit performance and still support the necessary investment in research and development for the future?

3. *What is my succession plan?* Whom am I grooming or testing for succession? What are the milestones for measuring the progress of contenders? How do the key goals to be achieved mesh with the advancement of contenders?

4. *What obstacles are foreseeable?* Which of the biggest nonproductive time-eaters, such as litigation or building a new headquarters,

are most likely to intrude, and how do I minimize their interference with the agenda?

5. *Where is the trend line of managing headed?* Am I mindful of what is happening generally in the world of managing? Am I evolving a leadership approach that has, for example, more global awareness and is more effective in dealing with information workers, or will I leave the helm an anachronism and my organization dated and floundering?

In the periodic communications of all great organizations—IBM, Ford, the Red Cross, and others—you will see attention to these themes presented as proof that leadership has an abiding focus on getting the right things done. With the average tenure of today's CEO about five years, down from the ten-year term of two decades ago, the multidimensional management of time has become a foremost leadership skill.

TYRANNY OF THE EXECUTIVE CALENDAR

The desire to control time should not result in leaders' becoming slaves to their own calendars, a pitfall that surfaces all too often. Executives who rigidly schedule themselves six to nine months in advance are really missing opportunities. A leader has to maintain some flexibility in the calendar to take advantage of the changes and chances that will come along.

I tried for weeks, in fact months, to reach an executive who used to head a major media corporation in Los Angeles, but I couldn't get an appointment with him. It was unfortunate for him, because I had been empowered to offer him a board position with a blue-chip Fortune 100 company. He was always scheduled so far in advance, jetting here and there, and I could only say so much over the phone to his staff. When I finally reached him, he said to me, "Gee, it's been a long time that we've been trying to get together." I said, "Yeah, I'm embarrassed to tell you why, because the board position I had been asked to offer you has gone to someone else."

Leaders today demonstrate their importance more through their flexibility than through their inaccessibility. The effective leader will constantly be flexing the calendar, zeroing in on problem areas as well as opportunities. Issues have to drive a leader's calendar, but enough time must be put aside to study innovative ideas and to consider fresh ways of doing things. Above all, leaders must recognize that their personal use of time will become a symbol and a standard for the management of time within the organization.

NO BEATING THE CLOCK

For years I handled the publicity for Gatorade. One day I was scheduled to meet with Hank Stram, then coach of the Kansas City Chiefs, in Miami to ask him to be a paid spokesperson for Gatorade. I was flying in from Dallas for the meeting, and fate had it that the guy in the next seat to me was none other than Hank Stram. Since we couldn't sit there in silence, we ended up running out of things to talk about. It's almost impossible to sit silently on a flight, especially if you're an American and if you have a deep desire to influence the person next to you.

Midway in the flight, I screwed up my courage and decided to pitch Stram on the Gatorade proposition. I explained that the reason I was on my way to Miami was to meet with him and some of the Gatorade people and ask him if he would be willing to endorse the brand. After my improvised sales talk, Stram turned to me and simply said no. Can you imagine the stony silence afterward? I'm sure Stram thought that I had fixed my seat reservation through travel agents and spies to contrive this midair sales call. When dealing with other leaders, it's important that events follow a certain order and form. In these cases, stick to the timetable. Otherwise, you could end up seizing defeat from the jaws of victory.

FIELDING LINE DRIVES

Another dimension of leadership time is rhythm. Leaders really do create a rhythm, a recognizable pace within the organization. Back in my days in Chicago, the staff at the Chicago Symphony told me that when the Music Director Sir Georg Solti was in town to conduct his series of concerts, he would ignite a perceptible tempo change in the entire organization, creating a rhythmic pace of heightened enthusiasm. On a more modest scale, I have tried to do the same thing in the businesses I have run, as do most leaders who help their organizations by creating some sort of rhythm. They also propel themselves through the day better if they create and sustain that rhythm.

The biggest challenge is not letting unforeseen events break your rhythm. For example, a senior government official from an Eastern European country recently visited me. After exchanging some niceties, the man looked at me with urgency and begged me to help him defect. I, in turn, felt as though I had been hit by a line drive in the gut, feeling sorry for him on the one hand and being committed to my organization on the other. As it happened, my management team was expecting my undivided attention at a review of strategic plans over the next three hours.

This event might seem like a bizarre, dated espionage tale from the seventies, but it is still true in the spring of 1991 that people are being killed every day in Eastern Europe for political reasons. Organizations such as the Shining Path and the Grey Wolves continue to spread terror throughout southern Europe and the Balkans. Communications firms land in the middle of such intrigues because of the involvement as go-betweens in many political missions.

I visualized myself spending the afternoon walled up in my office with this poor soul until he could be turned over to a safe haven with the FBI. I smiled and tried to say reassuringly, "Look, you don't have to defect any more. Your country has been liberated. It's had free elections. People are buying copies of the *Wall Street Journal* and *Penthouse* at your airports." Then my guest convincingly explained that much of this was show, and the secret police was still very much alive and would gun him down if he tried to defect. Finally, it dawned on me to turn him over to a Washington think tank, which could do far more for him than I could. The truth is that once my mind was back in stride, I was genuinely able to help the person and could also get back to leading my own organization effectively.

KEEPING TIME IN PERSPECTIVE

Time is unusually difficult to keep in perspective. It's as easy to be distracted and side-tracked by a "line drive" of the moment as it is to neglect the long-term time line of the organization. Recently, I reread Paul Kennedy's awesome tome, *The Rise and Fall of the Great Powers*. I was struck by a passage about the United States in the context of world history. Since the United States has been a world leader for so long, we tend to think that our country has been a leader in world affairs since its inception. In fact, it was "not until 1892 [that is, less than a hundred years ago] that the European Great Powers upgraded the rank of their diplomatic representatives to Washington from minister to ambassador—the mark of a first-division nation."[3]

Just as my preconception about U.S. history had been wrong, many leaders have a faulty perspective about time and leadership. They think they have been, and will continue to be, around forever. That's the underlying truth in the old joke about DeGaulle not wanting to spend too much money on a tomb, because he needed it for only three days or in the "Saturday Night Live" newscasts that perennially mentioned General Francisco Franco as "still dead."

LEADERS WHO WILL NOT LEAVE

All leaders of organizations, including founders, are guests in their own homes. They better know when to leave if their organizations are to have a successful life ten or twenty years into the future. In the last quarter of 1990, two of the most determined leaders who would not let go passed away. Both were founders—Armand Hammer of Occidental Petroleum and William Paley of CBS.

Hammer—confidant of Lenin and every Soviet leader since, medical doctor, and founder of Occidental—died at the age of 92, the day before he was to celebrate his bar mitzvah and 79 years after the age most Jewish males participate in that ceremony of passage. Hammer was the epitome of individualism and ran Occidental in an unabashedly personal way, holding annual meetings on his birthday and spending company assets on charities so lavishly that shareholder groups started to sue the company to restrain him. There is no doubt that Hammer was a genius, but some experts believe his willfulness helped to erode Occidental's earnings toward the end of his life.

Like Hammer, William Paley could not let go. Several fine executives in succession were first placed as Paley's successor and then replaced by Paley himself. Until his death at age 89, Paley remained chairman of CBS, having forged a partnership with Lawrence Tisch as president and CEO. But what about CBS? In the seventies and eighties, it sold off valuable assets, such as the New York Yankees to an investment group, and then CBS Records to Sony. Its position in the television ratings plummeted. There is no doubt that modern broadcasting would be inconceivable without Paley's contributions. Had Paley kept his eye on the clock and stuck to his original transition plans, however, CBS would probably be a much healthier organization today.

In all fairness, both Hammer and Paley *tried* to formulate succession plans, and brought in some remarkable talent to attempt to transfer their power, but they didn't have the same resolve to manage succession through to a conclusion that they evidenced in all the other aspects of running their businesses.

THE ELEGANT EXIT

At the Metropolitan Club in Manhattan, there is a mezzanine foyer that leads to the balustrade of the main staircase. Marbled in Florentine elegance and artfully perched, there is perhaps no more effective setting—at least none of which I know—for making an entrance. Leading society figures have emerged there countless times to host parties during the holiday season. While the beautiful people of this world are always in pursuit of a stunning entrance, nothing becomes a leader more than an effective exit. The way a leadership job is left speaks volumes to me.

When Walter Wriston left Citicorp, he walked out the door and never looked back. He was ready for other things. Because he had so painstakingly prepared the succession that led to John Reed's selection, Wriston felt no need to tamper. But he also accomplished three other assertive things, which guaranteed the success of the transition:

1. *He handed over contacts and relationships to his successor and the management team.* It isn't the milestones you surpass in performance or the job description you leave on the desk that ensures the successful passing of power. It's how you create and fine-tune the relationships to power—government and community leaders, industry peers, leading thinkers—that speaks of your sincerity and commitment to help your successor be a success. These are not turnkey legacies. From the day you are the leader, you need to think about how the connections that support leadership will be turned over to the person coming next.

2. *He took his hat and coat.* So did Ted Hesburgh when he left the presidency of Notre Dame. He traveled for a year and wrote a

book. Most important, he got off the screen and allowed his successor Father Molloy to develop a unique profile for leadership to carry the university forward to its next phase as an institution.

3. *He wrote his own epitaph.* Wriston wrote one book and maybe more are in the works. That's one way of summing up. He, and the financial community, had a keen grasp of his own contribution. Too many leaders agonize over what they have achieved. They unsettle everyone around them by speculating endlessly about the significance of their contribution. Have done with it.

THE COST OF ABRUPT SUCCESSIONS

J. Franklin Smith, the head of marketing for the Pennsylvania Electric Company, became the CEO of this utility. Unfortunately, his predecessor never prepared him for the job. Smith, an extremely able executive, ultimately proved a fine leader. Fortunately, he inherited a good staff assistant named Mary O'Donovan and a top-notch communicator named Sandy Pollan. For several years, these professionals were taxed heavily and unnecessarily to help compensate for Smith's lack of preparation. Executives will rationalize that a tough, broad-gauged executive will be able to handle an abrupt change. Sure they can, but what about the implications of wasted time for the rest of the organization as it tries to compensate for the lack of preparation?

When William Bennett resigned as drug czar in the Bush administration in November 1990, A. M. Rosenthal wrote a thoughtful piece in the *New York Times,* praising the work Bennett had done but saying some felt that Bennett may have left his job too soon.[4] Most of all, he left it unexpectedly, and that suddenness threw an understaffed and "talented" team off beat. For whatever bona fide reasons that a gifted leader such as Bennett had for leaving the post, the abruptness of his move made the transition much harder for his successor Bob Martinez and the drug-war team.

Al Neuharth did an outstanding job of passing the baton to John Curley as the new CEO of Gannett. Over time he prepared the organization for the transition and an executive who had, and needed to have, a completely different agenda. As part of his orderly exit,

Neuharth also quit the Gannett Board. When he explained his decision to Peter Ueberroth, the former baseball commissioner praised Neuharth for his wisdom, saying:

> A former CEO can't win by staying on the board. If you disagree with your successor on issues, it sounds like sour grapes. If you always agree, it sounds condescending. If you stay mute, what are you doing there?[5]

I must add that CEOs who overstay their welcome in corporations are not always "too old" to do the job. Age and ability are very personal attributes. Peter Grace, for example, has been the longest tenured CEO of any major corporation in the United States and has a vitality and clarity of strategic vision surpassing those of managers half his age.

SECOND COMINGS

Two years ago, I witnessed a speech given by Richard Nixon at the Harvard Club in New York. Before he began, Nixon walked down the rows of people, about 150, and shook the hand of everyone in the audience. This was not the Richard Nixon most remembered: the President who gave the fewest news conferences of any modern Commander-in-Chief; the President who, because of his imperial pretenses, some said, wanted to put White House Guards in uniforms rivaling the Beefeaters or the Swiss Guard; the President who was tumbled by Watergate—in short, the least accessible President since World War II. Contrary to every expectation, Nixon was warm and gracious to each individual as he skillfully moved down the lines, making small talk and greeting each person with a warm smile and a firm handshake.

His remarks were remarkably effective. Nixon stood in front of a microphone, unaided by a script, and talked for about an hour. This man in his late seventies drew the most cogent picture of world affairs I have ever heard. His powers of concentration were astonishing, and his sheer knowledge overwhelmed a hostile audience. Before the event, there was enormous anticipation of what a Nixon, with Watergate behind him, would be like. After it was over, he again shook the hand of every member of the audience, and people are talking about the impression he left to this day.

The same turnaround is now being experienced by Jimmy Carter. His activist work in support of the poor and human rights caused the *Economist* to write recently of Carter's "second coming" and to note that "scarcely a month goes by without someone, somewhere saying that he is the best ex-president the country has."[6]

Sometimes, leaders do get a second chance to influence how they are remembered, but image comebacks require enormous effort. Life is short, and a leader would do well to get it right the first time.

CHAPTER

4

RALLYING A
GREAT FOLLOWING
*Winning Support Through
Motivation and Empowerment*

ABOUT FIFTEEN YEARS AGO, I WAS ASKED TO COACH A PLANT manager named Jim, who worked for a national lumber company. It was Jim's responsibility to announce to his workforce that the plant was going to shut down. Two days before the event, I went up to the tiny logging town that was home base to the plant and met with him.

Jim was scared to death about what he had to do, but he kept nodding his head when we talked and saying he understood the mill had to close. There was just no way to make it profitable and keep it open. Over and over again, we rehearsed the brief statement he would make to open the meeting. Then we spent half a day trying to anticipate questions the workers might pose to him. I kept stressing to him that the way the workers and the community would perceive his company depended on his ability to explain the company's decision honestly and clearly and to emphasize the generous severance benefits and job retraining program the firm was offering the workers. After many hours, Jim appeared to have both the command of the information and the confidence to pull it off.

The meeting was scheduled for 4 o'clock in the afternoon. There

THINKPOINTS
on How
Leaders Motivate and Empower

☐ Instead of controlling behavior, empower and motivate people.

☐ Empower and motivate through trust.

☐ Establish trustworthiness before events test it.

☐ Uphold the dignity of people in everyday business.

☐ Whenever given the chance, be a model follower yourself.

☐ Tailor your messages to key niches within the organization.

☐ Empower women and other groups through special agendas.

☐ Encourage decentralized divisions to share ideas.

☐ Cultivate the effective flow of lateral communication.

☐ Give pointed, not reckless praise.

---

were 300 men in that plant, most of whom looked like Paul Bunyan's ox Babe. The loggers stomped inside the huge milling room. Late afternoon sunlight streamed into the mill through air clouded with sawdust. I stood at the back with my fingers crossed. Jim looked at his audience and said, "My friends . . ." His voice cracked perceptibly. He paused and then continued, now pointing at me: "My friends, Mr. Dilenschneider has come here from New York today, and he has something to tell you. . . ." With that, 300 burly hulks—some with no teeth, many with tattered shirts, and at least five with "Mother" tattooed on their arms—flipped around in their steel folding chairs and stared at me and my three-piece suit with looks of pure malice. As I figured it, there was no way out. I took off my jacket, rolled up my sleeves, strode to the front of the room, and told them the plant was closing. It was a lonely moment, but nothing happened after my statement and during the question-and-answer session that followed. There were groans, of course, and some curses, but no one tried to saw me in half or break my arm.

The secret to great leading is rallying a great following. What prevented Jim from leading at the decisive moment was the greatest single flaw undermining leadership: fear. Often employees are afraid of, and are intimidated by, their bosses. But even more often, management is afraid of their workers and will not share information and plans with employees. They are intimidated by worker demands and concerns. In a word, they don't trust the very people on whom they must primarily rely to be successful leaders.

The backbone of effective empowerment and motivation is trust. If you have genuine trust within an organization, you cannot contain it. Trust transcends the borders of the organization and extends to its surrounding environment. Regulators, the press, community leaders, and customers will feel that trust as well. Transacting business under an umbrella of trust is the best atmosphere in which to run a company. Trust is also a tremendous asset if a crisis or a problem should arise.

This chapter looks at trust and other aspects of empowerment and motivation critical to leaders' achieving their agendas within their own organizations.

THE FALLACY OF CONTROL

Too often, management gives employee communications a low priority because management thinks it is "in control." Managers assume that workers are more or less a captive audience. It's a power thing. As a result, much less time is spent deciding how to involve employees in the organization's strategic plan than, for example, in creating the launch for a new product. As good employees are becoming harder to find and are exercising more mobility between firms than ever before, which communication is more important? If the leader takes the long view, can there be much doubt about the answer to that question?

The audience within the organization is the toughest audience to fool—much harder than Wall Street or special interests. And an internal audience can't be force fed. Some consultants compare the relationship between leader and employee to that of parent and child. A dangerous analogy. If anything, it's a relationship between parent and a child who has grown up, respectful but collegial. Smart leaders know that they can't "control" their following and don't even try to manipulate them. They address the issues that concern their followers before they attend to their own. It's essential to understand that the grapevine is always more important than any official channel and that "reserved-for-management" parking places in the employee lot shout louder than any management claim about equality. To create the right environment, leaders must ask, "What do I need to do to empower and motivate the persons in my organization in a sustained way?"

TRUST AS RISK TAKING

My experience tells me that an atmosphere of trust is the most important aspect of motivating top managers. Building trust at the senior level—and increasingly at every level—requires sharing confidential information and involving people in decision making. But I must also admit that their involvement isn't always successful.

I'll never forget when Fred Ackman, the CEO of Superior Oil, tried to coalesce his top management team of seven people during a take-over. Fred had been in the oil and gas business for more than 30 years and was one of the finest technical managers I've ever known. On the day of this particular management meeting in the late seventies, an article had appeared in the *Wall Street Journal,* causing the stock price of Superior to shoot upward several points. Right after the story broke, Superior had to put out a press release confirming the accuracy of this material information.

Sitting in the company's boardroom with me and those seven top managers, Ackman asked: "How could this have gotten into the paper? Nobody outside of this room knew about it. All of you kept your commitment not to share this information with anyone, didn't you?" Everyone there nodded their assent. Ackman didn't know what to do next, but he was sure he had to get to the bottom of this. I suggested we make a call. He and I then went to a corner of this walnut-paneled boardroom and sat down by a small coffee table where there were two chairs and a telephone. I called the reporter at the *Wall Street Journal* who wrote the story and said, "We're outraged that this is in the paper. Nobody had this information. Fred Ackman, myself, and the seven executive committee members who knew this information are all sitting here with us, and each denies having revealed the story." Then, the reporter asked me: "Who are the seven other people in the room?" I named them. "I won't tell you *which* one, but one of those people gave me the information," he said gravely. Having worked with this reporter over the years, I believed what he was saying.

What did Ackman do wrong? Nothing in particular, no mistake that managers at his level don't make every day. Trusting his colleagues with key information at a critical time was not the error. It was in failing to verify their trustworthiness in advance, before the need to take a risk arose. Being more attuned to technology than to people, Ackman had not spent enough time appraising the human values of Superior's key players. Ackman never discovered who leaked the information, but after that day he was never able to manage with the same enthusiasm and confidence again. Moreover, even if Ackman had been expert in assessing the trustworthiness of his colleagues, the incident could still have happened. The goal, however, is to improve your odds.

Trust is not blind faith, especially not at top levels. Leaders, I believe, are accountable for assessing the integrity of their key subordinates. The best way to accomplish that is by direct experience over time or through third-party endorsements whose opinions are reliable.

Sometimes, you have to bring a new, unknown person into a group where trust is critical. What then? Is there a way to predict how someone will handle confidential information? One CEO whom I know, who is very successful at controlling this problem, has an effective, if slightly crafty, solution. It's an integrity test. The CEO will tell a person whom he is testing a confidence. This confidence is a fabrication. The subject will be the only person to get that tidbit and usually it's a juicy one. If the story gets back to the CEO from another source, he calls the subject in for a conference. He tells the person that "something-that-wasn't-so" was leaked and that the individual was the only one who knew it and must therefore be the one who leaked it. The employee almost never makes that mistake again, for to do so would be to run a serious risk of being fired.

To some extent, trustworthiness is an accountability that a follower owes to a leader. On a larger scale, it is an accountability that every member of an organization must honor. Clear violations against trust deserve, therefore, swift, certain punishment.

LEADERS' SLEEP AND *NEMAWASHI*

If trust were a defined expectation and were more openly managed in U.S. business, I suspect that our business world would have less stress and tension. A recent study showed Japanese CEOs average an hour and a quarter more sleep than their U.S. counterparts. Experts believe it is partly attributable to *nemawashi*—a strongly developed sense of mutual trust in the Japanese approach to managing businesses and solving problems.[1] The most destructive erosion of trust has occurred, I believe, in the relationships that U.S. business leaders have with our country's workforce.

Bitter labor problems can sour every part of a company's communication. Just as firms want investors to hold a company's stock and to consider the company a good investment, leaders want employees to have a positive attitude toward the organization. But the firms, usually by simple neglect, will then sour the very attitude they want so much to foster.

Remember, an employee, talking informally over the backyard fence or at the neighborhood grocery store, is always the most credible spokesperson for a company, especially in a crisis. The Action News camera interviewing a disgruntled employee will register more impressions than anything the "official" company spokesperson says. Above all, an unhappy workforce will not realize the vision of an organization. It will punch time cards and will put forth only minimal effort in the most uncaring way possible. If employees acted with trust and with confidence, how much more could be achieved!

Most labor problems, I have found, stem from a neglectful breach of trust, usually by management. Some time ago, Iowa Beef was having problems with its union. The company asked me to find out why. I started my probe the way I normally do for any internal problem: I scanned the supervisors' work reports. In this stack of greasy, blood-stained documents, I found a clue. The report suggested that an employee pitting eyes out of cattle heads severely cut his hand with an awl, nearly severing his thumb. The wound was cleaned and wrapped, and the employee was sent back to line. I went into the office of Bob Peterson, the CEO, and said: "If you think you're having problems, this is the reason. The worker walked back out there [after the accident] because he needed the job. He wasn't treated right. Not only that, everyone saw he was pushed back to the line." Iowa Beef is one of the best-managed businesses I know. The solution, which consisted of reprimanding and retraining a couple of supervisors, took less than a week to implement.

To sustain trust, leaders must be continuously visible in their leadership. The management expert Harry Levinson predicts that an organization will soon become demoralized if it senses that the leaders are not actively leading. With that demoralization, productive employee relations and mutual trust are bound to collapse. To keep the organization on track, a leader should constantly be implementing knowledge and demonstrating effectiveness. Above all, the leader must certify that the basic values of the organization, especially the dignity of its workers, are being upheld.

LEADERS AS FOLLOWERS

Leaders can be excellent role models for the support they want inside an organization by the way they behave in their outside roles. A couple of years ago, Frank Cary, the former CEO of IBM, headed a blue-ribbon, volunteer commission charged with helping New York City find ways to trim its budget.

Booz · Allen & Hamilton, Morgan Stanley, American Express, Arthur Andersen, the top law firms—the best New York City business had to offer—sent their highest level people to chip in. CEOs and presidents of international stature went to all the meetings, supported Cary fully, offered informed opinion, and brought extraordinary work from their staffs and their years of knowledge to the sessions. Persons normally leading the charge were now working as enthusiastic spear carriers.

For me it was a heady experience, sitting as a peer with some of the finest leaders around. Participation of this sort also sends a strong, positive signal back into the organizations of these executives. It tells a leader's own staff and employees that the leader understands the art of following, too, when the situation demands it.

TALKING TO THE INFORMATION WORKER

To motivate and empower one's organization most effectively, leaders should approach the various key audiences within it as if they were separate marketing niches—niches needing distinctly tailored marketing messages. To empower information workers—focusing on just one important work group of the future—leaders must truly understand the motivations of the information employee. Most firms remain remarkably ignorant of using niche communications to reach different in-house segments, especially information workers. Leaders are no longer talking to Patton's army. With the increasing importance of "information work" in most organizations, speaking effectively to the "information niche" of employees is pivotal.

The late Hedley Donovan, former editor-in-chief of *Time*, penned a singular article for *Fortune* in 1989 called "Managing Your Intellectuals."[2] It's a primer for leaders as we enter the age of information-based organizations. As I interpreted it, here is the gist of what Donovan had to say:

- Downward loyalty to one's employees is as important as the upward loyalty that employees show their bosses, especially for naturally skeptical intellectuals.

- Since they often complain, intellectuals need to be reminded that they like what they are doing because they were, after all, smart enough to pick the job they have.

- Just as a salesperson generates sales, an information worker generates ideas. The leader's job is to "keep those ideas coming."

- Intelligent criticism is vital. That criticism can take three reliable forms: (1) "You can do better work than this." (2) Your peers are being measured against the same standards as you are. (3) You are being held to the same standards against which I measure my own performance in managing information.

Information workers are just one niche. Older workers are another. Today's blue-collar and "new"-collar workers are third and fourth niches. It's possible for a leader to reach these niches in a meaningful way that will motivate and empower each one to work more productively without communicating in a discriminatory or condescending manner, on the one hand, or conveying mixed messages that detract from the organization's single clear vision, on the other.

If a leader wants peak performance from an organization, communication specific to key work groups is crucial. When any major internal program is going to be introduced, I urge leaders to define exactly which internal groups are essential to the initiative's success. Has the program a special appeal to each particular group? What reward will it look for if the program is well accepted? How and when can the group's successful contribution be publicly celebrated?

Let's say that a major systems overhaul has been entrusted to two data-processing facilities staffed largely by workers in their late twenties and thirties, many of whom are raising young families. Perhaps a special family get-together or an outing at a theme park is the ideal way to build group comradery for this niche: an opportunity in which the president, wearing a sport shirt, chatting over hot dogs and pop corn, can acknowledge the group's contribution. The possibilities for such targeting among the different niches are endless.

EMPOWERING WOMEN

Even talking about empowering women is a sensitive matter. In one respect, women are critical to the workforce and have been so long accepted as equal in every respect by perceptive leaders that it sounds patronizing to make special comments on empowering and motivating women as a separate group. Nonetheless, many organizations, including large and otherwise sophisticated ones, still blunder terribly in the way in which they communicate with their women employees.

Most leaders have gotten the picture right, whereas some of their organizations often exhibit vestigial behavior. This section is included in the hope that some of the tools I propose can help both women and men leaders ensure that their organizations excel in empowering women across the board. In my opinion, the central issue is motivating managers at all levels, and of both sexes, to fulfill their responsibility, that is, to enable women to attain the career goals they want to achieve.

Again and again, the most advanced organizations on women's issues are those having strong cadres of women in all functional areas and especially in middle-management. Some companies actually damage themselves and their credibility by placing a woman in a senior but token position, while completely overlooking or bypassing advancement opportunities for the mainstream. When I look back at the last two presidential elections, women, I believe, made considerably more progress in 1988 than they did in 1984. In the last election, women had powerful roles in managing campaigns and shaping agendas. That fact had more impact than Geraldine Ferraro's appearance on the ticket in 1984, partly because before 1988 the groundwork for women exercising power in politics had been poorly prepared.

In my own experience, I have witnessed the power of solid groundwork. In 1978, Hill and Knowlton moved me to Chicago to acquire and merge a then-associate firm, Gardner Jones & Company, into the business. The strategy was to turn that beachhead into the dominant force in an important market. It worked; but it wouldn't have, if I hadn't hired people such as Joan Krga, Kate Connelly, Debbie Gordon, and Mary Moster. Since then, all have advanced to solid positions, such as general manager or managing director in major metropolitan centers. Eventually, Mary Moster became the corporate communications vice president at Navistar International. Debbie Gordon established her own firm, which is well regarded. Kate Connelly today heads the Chicago office of The Dilenschneider Group.

Recently, a Chicago civic group invited me to speak. I was asked to outline what leaders could do to advance women in their organizations. Here's what I suggested:

A LEADERSHIP AGENDA
TO ADVANCE WOMEN

1. Create a truly nondifferentiated culture. That means no sex-differentiated language, no "girls" getting the coffee and no other vestiges of antiquated times.

2. Lobby for a female presence at critical meetings, not when a "woman's viewpoint" seems suitable.

3. Determine whether your organization has a disproportionate number of women in staff or advisory jobs with little real power versus

line operations, or actually running the business. (This imbalance is often a symptom of an organization's trying to window-dress its way out of real equality. The argument over women's qualifications has long been settled; the problem for leaders is making sure that women are enabled to rise to those positions that they deserve.)

4. Tie advancement of women to competitive advantage for the organization and for America when commenting on management practices and issuing leadership messages. (There are plenty of statistics to support it.)

5. Assign excellent mentors to highly qualified women, but even more, make sure that women are encouraged to *be* mentors early in their careers. Implement this practice systematically.

6. When qualified women leave your organization, study their case histories rigorously and hunt for any fundamental problems your firm may have in retaining highly qualified women managers. Get the word out that you have learned something from the loss.

7. Pay bonuses for career development and promotion and extract penalties for the failure to develop and promote female executives.

THE HAZARDS OF DECENTRALIZATION

The empowerment of women is one sensitive aspect of the internal agenda for leaders. Another difficult topic is the motivational problems resulting from a decentralized organization, which minimizes centralized control. Although these organizations are voguish today, and for some good reasons, they can also cause problems when motivating the organization toward achieving its broader unified goals—goals crucial to everyone's self interest.

Put simply, decentralization drowns out the company song. It also often cripples the leader's capacity to motivate and empower by destroying the leader's reach. Decentralization has been a sister principle to many expense-reduction programs but has also inadvertently crippled the communications power of many leaders. The breakdown may happen in this way: Controllers will argue that the line executives in the field are in the best position to estimate in dollars how much communications support will increase the bottom line. The bean-counters contend that the employees in the trenches can best make that assessment, and they should propose the needed communications budget in their profit and loss statement.

If corporate communications staffs have been ravaged at headquarters, how willing is the average, bottom-line driven manager to maintain any communications personnel? Not willing at all. The upshot is sure to be a further weakening of morale and motivation and may well lead to some dangerous departures from the company vision as the company's overall sense of direction loses visibility and influence.

We spend a fair amount of time today—and earn a tidy sum of money—bailing out companies who are in jams with their employees and the press because they "economized" on hiring staff or on having a clear corporate message. At the very least, decentralized companies should maintain strong central control of communications in specific policy areas. Leaders can fight back and motivate even the most strongly decentralized organizations toward important goals, provided the right techniques are used. I learned a tactic to rally loyalty in a decentralized corporation from a very smart man by the name of Louis Austin, the retired chairman of the construction giant Brown & Root, who was then CEO of Texas Utilities. That firm included Dallas Power and Light, Texas Electric Service Company in Fort Worth, and Texas Power and Light—three highly independent companies.

Whenever Louis sent down an order, the divisions nodded and then turned away to do their own thing. Louis was one of the first CEOs of a modern holding company to recognize that he had power only with Wall Street. He had no real power with the companies for which he was ultimately accountable. When he gave up operating power to the divisions, these units didn't give a damn about corporate destiny. They were competing with each other for such scarce resources as expansion capital. This rivalry was okay for running the day-to-day business but became a problem in other respects.

Louis saw the need to ally these companies in some key areas, such as lobbying government. If each division lobbied in its own way, as they were doing, the separate businesses of Texas Utilities were just small, squeaky voices in the Texas capital of Austin. If these subsidiaries worked together, they could be a powerful force. Louis looked for a way to get the divisions to recognize their common interests. He knew that dictating cooperation wouldn't work, and he had an idea about how to solve the problem for which he asked our help.

As a neutral facilitator, my colleagues and I set up a series of meetings. In each of those meetings, we assembled a different group of management representatives from each of the divisions. We showed them data on issues facing utilities and asked them what they thought should be done. Each of the groups independently arrived at a strong consensus that all of the Texas Utilities' firms confronted the same problems. They demanded unified campaigns on nuclear power, the use of coal, and rate hikes. They built a strong fraternal network. Some of the group members wondered why "those guys at corporate" didn't have the horse sense to put together a program such as this before, a program linking their common interests. But you and I know that "those guys at corporate can never get anything right."

Louis Austin shrewdly created a will to unify on external issues that compensated for decentralization and made Texas Utilities a powerful, single voice. It was a voice that achieved an expansive legislative agenda in Texas and influenced national policy in such areas as rates and transmission lines. And to add the final touch of skillful understatement, Louis himself always rejected being the leading industry figure at the Edison Electric Institute—the industry's trade association. Whenever talk of industry initiatives came up, "I wonder what those bureaucrats are up to now," Louis would muse aloud. Yet behind the scenes, Louis and his companies were clearly setting the national agenda in the utilities industry.

LATERAL COMMUNICATION'S NEW PRIMACY

Decentralization is just one phenomenon affecting how leaders motivate organizations. The leaner organization with fewer management levels is another. It is re-routing communication, thereby altering the ways that organizations can influence the morale of their employees.

In factories of the future, for example, Peter Drucker observes that much "information will flow sideways and across department lines, not upstairs. The factory of 1999 will be an information network."[3] This structure will have a decided effect on how leaders attempt to empower and motivate their organizations. As information logjams and poor coordination increase, ensuring that parts of the organization share information effectively may become the maximum contribution that a leader can make to an organization's morale. Just because more information is flowing across the organization doesn't relieve any pressure on the leader to guide communications and make it successful. Unless leaders ensure that lateral communications flow smoothly, the information-driven business, more and more today's norm, will quickly crash.

RECKLESS PRAISE

A final aspect of motivation and empowerment deserving comment is a mistake spreading among leaders: dishing out heaping servings of unwarranted praise. Who would have ever thought this would become a problem? But it is a serious one. Many companies thoughtlessly encourage squandering praise. And cost containment has fueled the problem. How many times have you heard the expressions: "Praise is cheap"; "give more praise and fewer salary increases"; and "praise the manager instead of adding to headcount"?

Cheap praise is the squeezed penny of modern business; it can also get a company into serious problems. Praise is important, but its foundation has to be honest feedback, and it will never be an effective long-term substitute for proper working conditions and wages. The praise cult has transformed many managers from being straight-shooters into being politicians.

A wonderful article in the *Harvard Business Review* by J. S. Ninomiya, called "Wagon Masters and Lesser Managers," identified a rogue's gallery of the key types of bad managers who rove the modern company.[4] One of these prototypes is called "The Politician." Politicians are long on praise and short on candor. "A colleague of mine," Ninomiya writes, "received 37 notes of commendation in one year, though the boss who sent them rated his overall performance average. . . . The Politician's relentless insincerity wears subordinates down." Along with worrying about the dollar's eroded value, we ought to worry about how nearly worthless the phrase "nice job" has become.

John Hill, Hill and Knowlton's founder, was a master in handing out "pointed praise." When I was at Hill and Knowlton in the late sixties, I remember preparing at a feverish pace a 200-page report for a client. I was nonetheless proud that I had created a quality document so quickly. The next morning it came back from Hill's review. On the cover were scrawled three words: "Great report! Typo." I found the error. To this day, I believe that there was only one. It took me longer to find it than it did to write the report. Hill was a stickler for detail, but he was right. In our business, a casual punctuation error on a news release can drastically change the meaning and endanger a client.

Ever since that experience with John Hill, I have been a staunch advocate of administering pointed praise instead of handing out insincere platitudes. Leaders must set the standard for how praise is rendered in an organization, and they should manage it as carefully as they manage cash. Through a regimen of carefully administered succinct and justifiable praise, leaders can lift their organizations to new levels of performance and keep strong internal standards vital.

5

THE BIG I AM
Maintaining Objectivity

A T THE AGE OF TEN, I PLAYED IN A LITTLE-LEAGUE BASEBALL game, which I'll never forget. There was one out in the ninth inning, and I was on first base after hitting a single. The next batter hit a fly to right, which I thought was going over the outfielder's head. I started running around the bases. The right fielder caught the ball and made a double out by tagging me at second base. Our team lost. A teammate of mine, Mike McCort, raced away from the bench, screaming that I had lost the game. I felt awful about it. My older brother came over with a smile on his face and said, "Cheer up. You know, you were behind by sixteen runs."

My brother's advice always comes to mind when I see people overestimate their own importance, either on their own or through the instigation of others. During my early years at Hill and Knowlton, a time when it was still a relatively small firm, another experience further tempered how I saw the contribution of people at the top. Dick Darrow had become CEO of the firm and, under his leadership, we expanded our operations in Europe and entered Australia. It was a tragedy that Darrow, a victim of a harsh, crippling illness, passed away while he was heading the company.

THINKPOINTS

on How

Leaders Preserve Objectivity

☐ Keep a clear perspective on your contribution.

☐ Act primarily for the organization.

☐ Study how adversaries view your role.

☐ Accept recognition on behalf of the organization.

☐ Shun charisma in favor of steady vision.

☐ Maintain a suitable profile for the organization.

☐ Learn the agenda of the press in serving the public.

As is still the case today with many businesses, the company held a life insurance policy on Darrow with itself as the beneficiary. When he died, the company used the million dollars it collected to make investments and expand the business dramatically, on a scale that would have been impossible, quite frankly, if he had still been alive. That may have been a heartless observation, but some of my colleagues made it, and they were right in a way. As a CEO myself, I have recalled Darrow's contribution from time to time. It helps me put the limited importance of a single person at the top in perspective and to steady my own sense of objectivity.

In this chapter, my focus is on the most common challenges to a leader's objectivity and how best to overcome them.

Leaders must fight an ongoing war, trying to keep perspective on how good and how important they are. When things are rotten, the people in the spotlight reap an undue share of the blame. When things go well, some persons with high visibility try to collect more credit than they deserve.

In addition to teaching me the art of pointed praise, John Hill taught me another great lesson: how much damage the "Big I Am" can do. Look at any letter or memo, listen to any speech or interview where a supposed leader constantly says, "I did this" or "I caused that," and you are likely to bristle at the show of self-importance. Focused on acting for themselves rather than acting for their organizations, leaders disenfranchise their followers and alienate all the other audiences around them. Leaders who constantly find it easier to say "I" than to say "we" have some thinking to do.

Genuine leadership is selfless, even in business, and perhaps most especially in business, because the opportunities for greed and self-interest are so numerous. Influence belongs to those who have a vision, demonstrate a concern for the development of others, and have the ability to help people adjust to change. The Yale management psychologist Dr. Clayton Alderfer says that genuine leaders "come across as rich and complicated individuals who are comfortable with their own richness. They don't usually radiate an 'I'm-the-greatest' tone. The most influential have a mix of confidence and humility. What they do radiate is a sense of vision about themselves and their organizations. They also evidence a constant interest in the development of younger managers. They are teachers, mentors in the general sense of the word. Lastly, they cause people to look at themselves in a different way." This last skill makes the leader an indispensable mirror for the organization and the people within it and is crucial in the management of change and growth.

POWER DELUSIONS CREATE VULNERABILITY

Too many leaders in organizations think they *are* the organization. In fact, they are dispensable. Throughout the last decade, it was common for analysts, investment bankers, and lawyers to view leaders in companies as naïve souls who did not grasp their place in the world. A high-level manager who lacks perspective can be manipulated by someone who has the money or the black book of the law on his side. CEO after CEO has been led like a lamb to the slaughter in precisely this way.

The corporate leader is supposed to be a renaissance man or woman, capable of everything. Most are not. The outside directors, who have enormous fiduciary responsibility to safeguard, are on to that fact. Those directors always want reassurance that the business is being superbly managed. Some CEOs have resolved the problem by going on an outside shopping spree, in which they hire the best advisers to shape or endorse company direction. If there is a problem in manufacturing, Booz · Allen & Hamilton is contracted. If it's a personnel problem, a Proudfoot or a Kwasha Lipton is hired.

Nowhere is this truer than in financial matters. If a takeover attack is mounted, an enormous cast of prestigious attorneys, bankers, and strategists is assembled. Many CEOs have become aristocratic shoppers. No doubt these advisers give superb advice and help the companies measurably. But Wall Street knows what quality counselors cost, and it sees how they ease the weight from management's shoulders. The Street, in its own circle, is scornful of those corporate managers who contend they carry such heavy responsibility while they rely excessively on outside support, often just to "paper" the file behind many decisions.

Any CEO who believes that the description I've just sketched is true will be both bitter and suspicious. In fact, that's how many CEOs behave on Wall Street. They think that security analysts are arrogant and that investment bankers are cannibals. The CEO's contempt bubbles up easily. When I see CEOs react that way, I immediately counsel them to rein in their emotions. The financial people may be brutal, but leaders can demonstrate leadership and professionalism only by being detached about their own importance and unflinching at the barbs of cynics.

DEAD OR ALIVE

When Armand Hammer was 88, he slipped in his bathtub. That accident set off a wave of panic buying of Occidental Petroleum as analysts figured that, with Hammer potentially out of the way, Occidental might be a buyout candidate. Hammer recovered, but the incident was enough to include Occidental on a list of what the *Economist* newsweekly calls "death-watch companies."[1]

When John Dorrance, majority shareholder and former chairman of Campbell's Soup, passed away, the *Wall Street Journal* quoted a family friend who said: "As far as the children are concerned . . . Wall Street is dancing on their father's grave."[2] The arbitrageurs had struggled to put the company in play for years. Until John passed away, they couldn't budge the family interests, which owned 58 percent of the stock.[3] When he died, the remaining family members were believed to lack John's commitment to holding on to the company. The stock shot up five points. When David Johnson took the helm of Campbell's, his remarkable leadership stabilized the situation. By presenting a vision beyond the viewpoint of one individual, he was able to persuade the major shareholders not to sell their stock. Campbell's today is back on a steady and successful course.

They used to say: "The king is dead; long live the king!" Now they say the same thing about the principal shareholder. I recently saw a cartoon with two statues in front of a company headquarters. One had a plaque inscribed, "To Our Beloved Founder and Chairman." The other plaque in front of the bigger statue said: "But this guy offered us $40 a share." It instantly made me think of Occidental.

With the enormous responsibility most leaders must shoulder, it's often hard to keep one's self-importance in check, but objectivity demands it. Any leader having trouble controlling personal importance should think about previous great leaders who Wall Street said were worth more dead than alive.

THE PRICE OF MODESTY

Some business leaders I know play a part that is the exact opposite of "The Big I Am." They project "I Am the Big Nothing." They won't play the role of visible leader on behalf of the organization. They shun publicity and demand that attention be showered on the divisional managers who run the subsidiaries.

Excessive modesty and restraint can damage the leader and betray the organization as badly as an unbridled ego can. Misperceptions on either end of the spectrum not only handicap the leader, but can also bring on his or her eventual ouster. In three cases I know of personally, undue showcasing of subordinates led to the recruitment of a president's successor. They were picked off by a competitor, whose head was turned by the outpouring of favorable press given to the division head. In two more glaring cases, too bright a spotlight on an organization's subsidiaries triggered the actual breakup of the companies, because all the attention was riveted on the value of the company's component parts.

OUT IN THE OPEN

Leaders' ample compensation packages often become a battleground of opinions, which impair their own objectivity and cloud the perspective of others. If the law requires that the compensation be disclosed, being completely candid about the package usually defuses most of the controversy for the press and others and allows the leader to attend to other issues. In the most recent wave of acquisitions and buyouts, those companies that were forthright about the financial benefits to management generally fared best. Candor gets the issue off the screen.

LOST OBJECTIVITY AND
THE LOSS OF SUPPORT

Leaders must be able to look at their salaries, their personas, and their roles with objectivity. They must also be vigilant about *appearing* objective to the public, which watches and evaluates leaders. Jim Granger, president of the Wirthlin Group, the strategist behind the

Reagan presidential campaign victories, once pointed out to me how a leader's perceived loss of objectivity can put an end to his or her leadership. In 1980, the United States presidential campaign was a dead heat until incumbent Jimmy Carter made a major mistake and asserted that Reagan's election would divide North from South, Christian from Jew, and rural from urban. Reagan countered, more in sadness than in anger, that Carter was reaching a point of hysteria that was hard to understand. Carter lost credibility and was tagged as a dirty campaigner, whereas Reagan was seen as more "presidential" than the president. The encounter marked an important turning point in the campaign.

THE CHARISMA TRAP

Those management gurus who say that charisma is the essence of leadership are talking bunk. Peter Drucker, a management expert who understands the hazards of charisma, once wrote: "Effective leadership doesn't depend on charisma. . . . Indeed, charisma becomes the undoing of leaders, it makes them inflexible, convinced of their own infallibility, unable to change."[4]

Harry Levinson, head of the Levinson Institute on management, finds that influential managers are often not spectacular personalities. He points to Bristol-Meyers' CEO Dick Gelb as a manager who has enormous influence and a low-key personality. Gelb has acquired his influence on Wall Street and within his company through years of credible communication and steady, consistent performance. Dick Mahoney, the CEO of Monsanto, is another case in point. A great marketer and a highly influential CEO, Dick is also a low-key fellow. When he headed Columbia Gas, Barney Clark, a true intellectual and an uncharismatic leader, was followed and loved by the organization. Even though he preferred to stay in his office, Barney was wired into every part of the company, and his employees knew he was wired. That intentness helped give employees an absolute conviction that Barney was right. The success of leaders such as these is the best proof I know that leadership is usually a learned skill, as I said earlier, not a dose of God-given chemistry.

David A. Nadler and Michael L. Tushman have written a brilliant paper for the *California Management Review* called "Beyond the

Charismatic Leader," in which they pinpoint the limitations of charismatic leadership.[5] These include

- Setting unrealistic expectations

- Creating an organizational dependency, where everyone freezes "and waits for the leader to provide direction"

- Disenfranchising "the next levels of management . . . [who] lose their ability to lead because no direction, vision, exhortation, reward, or punishment is meaningful unless it comes directly from the leader"

- Impeding "management's ability to deal with various issues" owing to the "range" of the leader's skills and other characteristics

- Perpetuating "the need for continuing magic."

Charisma-based leadership can turn an organization into a pack of charisma junkies, constantly hungering for a fix of dash and magnetism instead of focusing on the clear and steady vision that is the core of leadership.

HIGH OR LOW PROFILE?

Leaders keep asking the wrong question. Donald Trump and the late Robert Maxwell were two of the highest profile executives of the eighties. Both sought the limelight, and the images of both have paid a heavy price as a performance of their respective business enterprises suffered problems. At the same time, other big-company CEOs, such as Exxon's Lawrence Rawl, who faced the Valdez crisis, are lambasted for having too low a profile. Who's right? How much of a profile should a major company leader have? Doesn't a global economy demand that a leader have a "bigger" profile?

Answering these questions intelligently has little to do with a leader's preference for a high or low profile. It concerns phrasing the profile question the right way, that is: What kind of profile is demanded by an organization's situation, condition, or goals at a particular point in time?

No leader can, or should, decide that he or she *in principle* will have a high or a low profile. The valid comparison is between the "right" and the "wrong" profile, not the high and the low profile. Every organization will encounter situations in which the leader must be visible and other situations in which the leader stays in the wings. Leaders dedicated to courting continuous high-profile visibility for themselves or to shunning visibility are generally asking for serious trouble. In learning to spot either syndrome in their own behavior, managers keep a step ahead.

High-profile leaders lean on these rationalizations:

1. *"I'm a natural with the press."* No one is a "natural" with the press any more. Dealing with the press is no longer a personality game, if it ever was one. Media are increasingly analytical and investigative. This includes the once more benign European business press.

2. *"The CEO should be there to comment on all matters big and small."* In the last two years, I have been called for three cases in which the CEO was a spokesperson too early in a crisis. Minor incidents were actually escalated into national issues because the CEO's "voice" determined at what level the debate would be conducted, and that level was absurdly high.

3. *"Stirring up controversy keeps our competitive profile sharp."* I can count on one hand the number of firms benefitting from their leaders' raising constant controversy. Remember those companies that churned out an endless flow of op-ed pieces and advertorials in the early eighties? It's not surprising; they're not doing them any more.

Low-profile managers, on the other hand, are trapped by these deceptions:

1. *"The limelight belongs on my people, not on me."* I've already spelled out the gruesome consequences of this position carried to its extreme.

2. *"The crisis will pass if we keep our heads low and wait it out."* This "bunker" attitude turned Watergate into a political watershed and Three Mile Island into a communications debacle. It also nearly destroyed Johns-Manville several years ago. (Fortunately, under its present CEO, Tom Stephens, Manville has

become one of the most forthright and accessible companies in industry today.)

3.   *"Our actions speak for themselves."* Nothing speaks for itself in a society where individuals are bombarded by 18,000 discrete messages a day.

The worst fate is reserved for those who think that they can turn profile off and on like a light switch. Barricading the press for months on end and then suddenly inviting them to hype a triumph or currying favor in advance of an impending disaster is a setup nearly every seasoned reporter will smell.

The best management profiles are seen at firms like Merck, Shell, PepsiCo, and Sumitomo. Management has a steady, low-key presence, but it is immediately present to help the firm reap positive acknowledgment for successes as it would be there to assist should serious problems arise.

There are four "reality checks" that I recommend to leaders to gauge whether their profile is being managed properly:

1.   *Are my board memberships, civic involvements, and trade association roles roughly equivalent to those held by counterparts in my key competitors?* Managers in companies with serious performance problems may have a bona-fide excuse for cutting back these involvements. Others rarely do. These memberships establish important networks, often valuable in crises, which no leader should be without.

2.   *Are major strategic and marketing breakthroughs celebrated in the press to enable the company to derive the recognition it deserves?* In 1990 German Chancellor Helmut Kohl managed the process of German unification with consummate skill, always ready to accept recognition at key triumphant moments—recognition accelerating the momentum of his party and his policies.

3.   *Have I fostered relationships with analysts, vendors, and industry observers to secure the necessary support when the organization's profile periodically rises?* Woolworth and Philip Morris are just two companies who do an uncommon job of maintaining excellent analyst relations. The investment has come back as staunch endorsements when these companies have been the center of public attention.

4. *Has an organization chart for defining spokespersons been prepared?* That chart should answer questions such as the following: What kind of issues and opportunities is the company likely to face? Who will be involved in choosing the issues and in tackling them at what levels? How will we monitor a situation to see whether its complexion changes and needs a different response?

Maintaining a continuous high profile is only justified when leaders are identified with issues that transcend themselves and their companies. Ford's former CEO Don Petersen has been a remarkable ambassador for quality in manufacturing. Cummins Engine's Henry Schacht is the pacesetter for linking true industrial competitiveness with long-term performance.

If there is a "broader profile" that goes along with being part of the global economy, it is taking a stand on the big issues. Smart leaders in the 1990s are now searching the issue landscape and staking out turf that can help thrust them to a higher plain, while they hold the "right" profile, not a "high" profile in everything else they do.

STRATEGIC LIMBS

If you speculate too publicly about your organization's strategic possibilities, you can signal a loss of objectivity and catapult yourself into an undesirable high profile. In 1985, Charles W. Parry, then CEO of Alcoa, walked out on such a limb. An article in *Business Week* reported that Parry "was so serious about developing new business ventures that he forecast in 1985 that Alcoa would get as much as 50 percent of its revenues from nonaluminum business by 1995. The company's $6 billion aluminum business accounted for 90 percent of sales and was expected to continue growing. Thus, Parry would have to create a $7 to $9 billion business from scratch in a decade. . . . Both inside and outside Alcoa, the proclamation caused confusion. . . . [The directors] began thinking about a replacement for Parry, and they decided they needed someone from outside."[6] Some leaders will attempt to set direction by setting a longer-range objective. More and more, that speculation is likely to encounter an immediate, abrupt, and objective *"How?"* from all the people affected by, or interested in, the organization's destiny. Leaders have much less license to speculate about the future than they once enjoyed.

THE PRESS: ULTIMATE ARBITER OF
OBJECTIVITY

The press's powerful role in defining the "objective" truth makes the press the most difficult outside institution to relate to among leaders. The press is feared because it determines the agenda of the interest groups who make up the public. It is maligned by many leaders because it is not "objective," thereby conveying distorted images of organizations and people. In fact, the press is usually objective, given its motives and goals.

Many leaders' failure to understand the charter of the press and its reporting is the beginning of their misunderstanding and hostility. Take, for example, the charge that reporters miss the point in the stories they do. Look first at how reporters are rewarded or penalized, as one writer points out:

> It doesn't matter if the story is slanted or meretricious, if it misinterprets or misses the point of the week's news. That is the responsibility of the editors. What matters—and what seems to attract most of the hostile letters to the editors—is whether a championship poodle stands 36 or 40 inches high, whether the eyes of Prince Juan Carlos of Spain are blue or brown, whether the population of some city in Kansas is 15,000 or 18,000.[7]

Many leaders confuse the reporter with the ultimate audience of an interview. The reporter is a vehicle to a target. Back in the Wilt Chamberlain years when the University of Kansas team were the lords of college basketball, reporters from the New York newspapers would besiege the team's coach after every game of the tournaments in Madison Square Garden in New York. The first interview would unfailingly go to the wire service reporter from the UPI. "Why? Why?" exasperated reporters from the Gotham papers would ask. The coach explained why, and it went something like this: "Because the wire service operator writes for 1600 American newspapers. He writes for the people of Salinas, Humboldt and Topeka. He writes for Kansas." That coach was a leader who understood the reporter as medium.

Moreover, many leaders confuse their comfort level with a reporter as a person for a license to speak candidly. In September 1990, Air Force chief of staff General Michael J. Dugan lost his job after an interview he gave to Rick Atkinson of the *Washington Post.* The resulting article portrayed Dugan as spelling out U.S. military strategy for a possible attack on Iraq during the Gulf crisis of that year.

In the story-after-the-story, Atkinson commented that Dugan outlined "his vision of how the war would unfold, how 'the cutting edge would be in downtown Baghdad,' how Saddam would be personally targeted, how the Israelis had advised hitting Saddam's family, personal guard and mistress. . . . A few of Dugan's comments seemed improbable and naive. . . . And, we wondered, frankly, why the Air Force chief of staff was telling us all this."[8] It's easy to paint a portrait of reporters as craftily tricking vulnerable people into spilling their guts. More often, reporters simply take advantage of prominent people who let their hair down and lose sight of their objectivity.

A leader's objectivity will constantly be challenged by manipulative advisers, by earnest fans, by cunning reporters, and by would-be supporters from unexpected places. During the height of the Civil War, Abraham Lincoln received an offer from the King of Siam, a devoted admirer of Lincoln, to send over a troop of elephants to aid the battle against the Confederacy. True to his vision and to common sense, Lincoln declined.

THE CANON
OF RAW MATERIALS
Conclusion to Part I

L EADERSHIP IS FOUNDED ON THE SKILLED USE OF FIVE RAW MATERIALS: vision, values, time, empowerment/motivation, and objectivity.

VISION

The essence of leadership is not born talent but the ability to impart a strong vision to an organization. That vision must be articulated as a clear course that biases the organization toward productive action while it gives people a sense of purpose above the everyday.

True leaders practice communications "inside-out," making communications work effectively rather than worrying about how they look. They communicate to earn conviction in the vision and to sustain that vision. Periodically, the leader will celebrate the organization's unified sense of purpose and will leverage the strength of the organization's culture. The leader harmonizes the vision and the culture and trains people to focus on both the vision and the task at hand.

VALUES

The leader is the custodian of the organization's values. Destroying inferior work and voiding transactions that fail to meet the standards of the vision, leaders create an agenda for values and measure how well the organization's values are upheld. The leader fine-tunes the organization's values to keep them healthy and competitive.

Leaders project their own humanity into the organization and diminish their own aloofness. They emphasize practical values, especially those supportive of quality, and endorse values of proven strength.

TIME

Time is the leader's scarcest resource. The leader masters time through balancing commitments and by keeping a constant eye on the limited time available to get the job done. Great leaders start to prepare for their departure the day they start their job.

Leaders understand that their agenda must be conducted on multiple levels. They avoid inflexibility by managing their time based on the priority of the issues confronting them, but they also respect set timetables in dealing with peers and outside organizations. The leader creates a rhythm, a pace of accomplishment within the organization.

SUPPORT THROUGH MOTIVATION AND EMPOWERMENT

The leader unleashes the power of the employees within an organization: their capacity to work and advance the organization's goals. Leaders empower and motivate through trust. They also establish the trustworthiness of people, especially the organization's key players, before events test it.

Effective leaders uphold the dignity of individuals and their contributions in the daily business. When leaders serve as followers outside of their own organization, they do so in an exemplary way. When speaking inside the organization, leaders sharpen their messages by addressing key niches. Leaders empower women and other groups through special agendas and cultivate the flow of lateral information within the organization. Leaders set the organization's style of praise, making it pointed, not reckless.

OBJECTIVITY

Leaders keep a clear perspective on their own contributions. When they act, they recognize that their action is interpreted as a statement for the organization they serve. Leaders study how adversaries view them, internalizing the information and suppressing the emotions animosity can trigger.

Leaders accept recognition on behalf of the organization as part of their ceremonial role, but they shun charisma in favor of a steady vision. Rather than engineering a high profile or a low profile, a leader maintains the "right" profile for the needs of the organization at any point in time. Leaders learn the agendas of important outside institutions, such as the press, to give themselves and their organizations the optimal chances of being fairly regarded by outsiders.

II

THE

COMMUNICATION

LANDSCAPE

A story I've been told concerns the Dutch subsidiary of a multinational company in the business of buying up scrap metal and scrap-metal dust from different companies using electric arc furnaces. This scrap and dust is a by-product of making other kinds of metal. In 1989, the firm ran aground of environmentalists in an incident outside São Paulo.

In 1989 the firm consolidated two separate dust and scrap shipments from Denmark and Italy in Rotterdam. Properly seen, the dust and scrap were raw material for a next stage of industrial production. Some environmentalists saw it differently. They viewed it as solid waste, which was being transported over international borders.

Greenpeace discovered that this material had been shipped to Rotterdam. The environmental activist organization learned this because it now has a sophisticated computer system that tracks international shipments of what they call hazardous wastes or toxic wastes, using, some believe, definitions arbitrarily. The system was first put into place to keep the First World or Second World from shipping its wastes to the Third World. Greenpeace believes that if a country makes waste, it should dispose of it on its own turf. As a general principle that belief makes sense, if the waste is really waste.

In this case, the loaded ocean barge was destined for a firm in Santos, a port outside of São Paulo. Basic elements would then be extracted from the dust to make fertilizers used in Brazilian agriculture and produced at a very low cost. Saving Brazilian farmers the expense of buying new basic elements and making agriculture more efficient have tremendous value to a country in which there has already been great concern about protecting the rain forests.

These arguments made economic sense to everyone except Greenpeace. In my opinion, Greenpeace regarded it as an attempt by a multinational company to inflict the wastes of the First World onto the Third World. In less than 12 hours, environmental special interests mobilized and sent in at least three strategists to Brazil, 11 days in advance of the ship's arrival.

As I heard the chronicle, environmentalists in Brazil told the dock-workers in Santos that a ship was coming filled with toxic garbage and warned them that if they went anywhere near the ship, they would become deathly ill. And they were advised not to unload it. The matter caught the eye of the Brazilian government agency CETESB, which is in charge of environmental matters.

Environmentalists repeated their claims to CETESB that unloading the ship in the port would expose people to a serious health risk. They moved to block unloading the cargo at another Brazilian port. These accusations were being made and the authorities were responding to the scare despite the fact that no one seems to have asked what was in the cargo. No one pointed out that although this kind of cargo is shipped to Brazil all the time, there are no records of anyone getting sick from it. When the ship arrived, the dockworkers refused to unload it. The ship's immobility was costing the Dutch firm thousands of dollars a day.

While the ship was offshore, none of the dockworkers had contact with it. The newspapers had written articles, however, referring to the cargo as "toxic waste." Then 82 dockworkers in Santos showed up for sick call and medical exams, becoming ill—toward the end of the week, incidentally—with dizziness, nausea, and scales on their hands. The next day 47 more workers came in for exams. These people may have had legitimate complaints, but they had never even been near the ship, which was then out of port in anchorage.

The environmentalists' next tactic was to plant even grimmer doubts about the chemicals involved. We know that cadmium, lead, zinc, iron, chrome, and copper are present in this cargo, they said, but who's to say there aren't radioactive chemicals in it, too? The activists launched rubber motorboats and equipped their crews with Geiger counters. Then they called a little press conference and solemnly said to the media that they were going out to take readings because they suspected that this ship could be radioactive. After they rode around the ship, they never reported what they had learned when they came back. Their foray was enough, however, to jolt the Brazilian press with the fear that the ship might even be spreading radioactive contamination. Thereafter, the story continued to deteriorate for several reasons; the trend lines in this situation spelled trouble.

Trend line is the term I use to mean the growing or waning course of public opinion. One trend line, as so often happens, layers atop another. When that occurs, an earthquake or an avalanche can result. In fact, this shipment of metal dust was sitting atop a San Andreas fault of public opinion. Brazil was being attacked by every ecologist and environmentalist in the world. The situation was ready-made for the opposition. The government, harassed on a spate of environmental fronts, said in effect: "This is an easy one. We're going to look like good guys. You can't unload that ship." And unloaded it never was. Fortunately, the dockworkers at Santos went on strike for a 62-percent pay increase, which gave the metals recycler the option to withdraw gracefully. But that was not the end of the story.

The firm tried to bring the cargo back to Europe. The Brazilian hysteria had ignited, however, wild speculation in the European press. Public opinion said that Europe didn't want that cargo either. Things were getting desperate. On the high seas, the crew even tried to paint over the name of the ship for fear that it would never dock again. Finally, the ship was allowed to unload its cargo in Rotterdam, but only after huge and needless expense to the firm involved.

This tale has all four ingredients that make up the modern communication landscape in which any leader is today an actor:

1. There is no longer a single audience either participating in a problem from within or observing it from outside. No longer is it environmentalists against industry. Just as often, it's Brazilian environmentalists against Belgian environmentalists. Today the audience is always fragmented, always plural. It continually watches events with the perspective of multiple agendas.

2. Situations are overwhelmed by an enormous clutter of information and messages. In this case, everyone was screaming: environmentalists, Brazilian dockworkers, the press on two continents, govern-

ments, and a host of others. An organization's messages must rise above that clutter, thereby enabling the organization to act successfully. In this case, that did not happen.

3. Events move with remarkable speed. During this crisis, faxes were flying in every direction 24 hours a day through command posts in New York and Amsterdam. Wire services and electronic media were monitored continually to track each unfolding step in the rival agendas. The institution of 24-hour financial markets over an electronic network has made information instant, and instantly important.

4. More and more events pass over national boundaries. Indeed, as McKinsey consultant Kenichi Ohmae contends, we have entered the era of the "borderless world."

A communications counselor's role in the episode of the "Flying Dutchman" would definitely be one of damage control. But the adventure is rich in lessons for leaders today:

- *In any conflict, bear in mind the information resources of potential adversaries.* Information is increasingly becoming the decisive force in winning wars of influence. Once you know where the information advantage is, the rest is simply a matter of logistics.

- *Avoid the world's "fault lines of issues".* A geological map of the world will tell you to stay away from Japan or San Francisco if you are afraid of earthquakes. Good intelligence will tell you where the fault lines of issues are, because they can be equally potent in disrupting business—negatively and positively. Like the earth's tectonic plates, these too are forever shifting. Last year it was a campaign on nationalist grounds against English language publications in Malaysia. This year it could be an insatiable hunger for English-language everything in Hungary as it seeks to align itself with the high-tech world of modern business. That need could represent a huge opportunity. Because of our aggressive media and the American appetite for debate, the United States has a perpetual menu of volatile issues. To cite just one, I would suggest that unless a firm has a brilliant solution to the controversial "mommy-track" issue in the career advancement of women, this is not the time to take a high-profile stand on how to combine pursuing a career with raising a family.

• *Look for the flip side of every trend line.* The other side of global garbage is global growth. The environmentalists knew how to thump the drumbeat of global garbage, but over time, people in all countries will welcome the intelligent transporting of waste products. Leaders need to articulate the flip side of messages and have the persistence and dedication to help draw those viewpoints into the public consciousness, and hopefully displace uninformed opinions.

For a leader, the communication landscape should be as vital as the factory floor where products are made and as vital as the conference room where ideas are debated. When leaders think about communicating, they must put their heads in that landscape and consider any messages in the landscape's four realities:

1. Its fragmented array of many audiences

2. Its clutter of messages

3. Its speed of movement

4. Its transnational scope.

CHAPTER

6

BUSTING UP THE
GENERAL CONTEXT
Searching for Pluralism

ABOUT A WEEK AFTER MARGARET THATCHER RESIGNED AS PRIME minister of Great Britain in November 1990, and only through coincidence, I ran into her and her grandson in Hamley's, London's foremost toy purveyor. Never having met her, I still felt obliged to congratulate Mrs. Thatcher on the many contributions her 11 years in office had made to restoring pride and direction to the United Kingdom. She was polite and appreciative but obviously preoccupied with keeping an eye on her six-year-old grandson, who was rambling through the hobbyhorse display.

As I turned and made my way down the crowded department-store aisle, I heard the Iron Lady's voice resonate over the din. "Young man," she called out, stopping me in my tracks, "the sign clearly says that there will be no riding of the hobby horses. You shall not ride the hobby horses!" Relieved that the remark wasn't aimed at me, I must say her directive was delivered with the same zeal and decisiveness as if she were dressing down a Westminster backbencher, or even a cabinet minister, for writing a sloppy brief or failing to have a bill reported out of Parliament. I'm sure she got the young gentleman's attention.

THINKPOINTS

on How
a Leader Deals with Diversity

☐ Differentiate between the consent and consensus issues.

☐ Prepare for and monitor the consent issues.

☐ Reserve consensus for key, strategic goals.

☐ Establish an overriding community of interests.

☐ Recognize individuals are a composite of different subgroups.

☐ Tailor communications for both input and output.

☐ Constantly find ways to unify the diversity.

Of all the leaders of modern history, none was more capable of getting her nation's collective attention, of assembling a coalition of fragmented social and philosophical viewpoints than Margaret Thatcher. But after 11 years, her power was dismembered by this same diversity of forces that had empowered her—as if the Lilliputians had banded together, not to tie down this Gulliver-like giant called Thatcher, but to draw and quarter her, to tear her apart—and they succeeded.

On November 23, the day after the Thatcher resignation, the London papers talked of nothing else than the End of the Era. "Last days of Maggie: the agonised calculations, and the men in grey suits," read the banner in the *Daily Mail.* [1] "Cabinet revolt ends Thatcher's 11-year reign" was the splash in the *Daily Telegraph.* [2] Analysis of what had happened and why was everywhere. Colin Brown, writing in the *Independent,* chronicled the events leading to Thatcher's demise as beginning October 18.[3] A day later the *Economist* took the longer view and said the disintegration began in October 1989 and was propelled by three converging, hostile forces: inflation, Britain's future as a part of Europe, and "a steady disintegration of trust at the heart of Mrs. Thatcher's cabinet."[4]

In truth, a series of events cascaded from those three central themes. The March 1990 riots over the poll tax were a symptom of rising unhappiness with the economic decline, which had cost Thatcher her supporters among the middle- and lower-middle classes. The balking over Britain's participation in European economic union caused the business community, Thatcher's strongest supporters in the past decade, increasing concern that the United Kingdom would be cut out of the rapidly developing framework of the new Europe. Social idealists, who had winced over Nicholas Ridley's anti-German comments in the *Spectator* during the preceding summer, saw England as isolated from the spirit of pan-Europeanism. Problems in the cabinet mirrored the problems of support in the populace. It's crucial to note that what happened to Thatcher was not the forging of a dump-Thatcher coalition, but it was the collective pressure of *individual* opposing factions, causing the polls to turn against Thatcher and encouraging her party to withdraw its support and unseat her.

The sharpest lesson of the Thatcher resignation is, for me, the finale itself. On Wednesday, November 21 at about 3 PM, Margaret Thatcher stood in front of Number 10, Downing Street and declared: "I fight on. I fight to win." Less than 24 hours later, she quit. The abrupt change of course is a by-product of today's fragmented world. Margaret Thatcher's departure is a result of what I call the dawning Age of Consent.

This chapter describes the new structure for the decision making surrounding today's leader—especially the growing importance of consent in steering issues and the tremendous diversity of viewpoints forging a common direction.

AGE OF CONSENT

After many months of heated protests, Star-Kist, the leading canner of tuna and a division of H. J. Heinz, announced in April of 1990 that it would only buy and use "dolphin-safe" tuna.[5] Immediately, all the other major tuna producers followed Star-Kist's suit. Just days after the Iraqi military machine rolled into Kuwait, an unprecedented international coalition imposed sanctions and barriers against Iraq. When Perrier mineral water was found to contain minute traces of benzene,[6] the market authority of a brand built on years of painstaking work evaporated overnight.

These three cases have at least one factor in common: They were all reactions to the power of "consent," a force of rapidly emerging importance in the world of leaders. Not coincidentally, consent is gaining significance just as another influence tool, consensus, is losing it. The touted management skill of the eighties, consensus is proving too slow an approach to many business and political situations, particularly crises. While consensus still plays a vital role in crafting strategy and building commitment to long-term direction, organizations and leaders are being bombarded by more and more issues that cannot be addressed by consensus.

Consent moves directly from issue to action: Major tuna packers didn't fall in love with Flipper overnight, but the polls and the boycotts told tuna packers—in my view—that it was cheaper to make even a costly change in fishing practices than to ignore the animal rights advocates. When that point of diminishing returns was reached, policy shifted 180 degrees.

The *San Francisco Chronicle* published a fascinating account of the dolphin-tuna controversy.[7] It reported that Heinz had proposed a middle-ground proposal on the dolphin issue to the environmentalists, who were increasingly considered the public voice on dolphins, as late as

April 3. The environmentalists nixed the proposal. It was not until April 11 that Heinz offered a revised position, just a day before a scheduled major press conference and only four days in advance of National Dolphin Day, April 14. Heinz's new position was totally fresh and close to what the activists wanted. The ensuing negotiations with environmentalists, one gathers from the *Chronicle* report, took place within 29 hours. These negotiations dealt with points as fine as controlling Heinz's canning practices in Samoa and guarantees that only dolphin-safe tuna would be used in their frozen Weight Watchers brand of entrees. The environmentalists agreed to the Heinz proposal. A dispute that had dragged on within this industry since the 1960s— that is, for 30 years—was resolved in less than 30 hours.

In the second example, the Saudis, the Soviets, and the Israelis, among others, didn't abandon their deep philosophical differences when Saddam Hussein invaded Kuwait; they formed ranks against Iraq—each country for different reasons—and they did it with lightning speed in the context of modern diplomatic history.

Perrier was a case of consent withdrawn. Overnight Perrier faced a product recall and, some estimate, a $70 million public-affairs issue. Neither years of a faithful public's yuppie love with Perrier nor widespread health authority assurance that the benzene contamination was harmless could give Perrier back its public consent on the scale it once enjoyed. Although Perrier boasted that its brand rebounded quickly after the recall had been completed and the product was distributed again, Perrier had in fact been missing from the shelves of many major cities for two to three months. Five months after the recall, the *Washington Post* reported that the brand was back, and I add the word *only* in 67 percent of the local bars, restaurants, and hotels that served it before the incident.[8] For a brand that once accounted for 44 percent of imported water sales in the United States, that loss of penetration can amount to only one gigantic "ouch."

If these situations are all examples of consent, what are the core differences between consensus and consent? For starters, consensus causes individuals to reflect on their obligations to one another. Consensus is the backbone of "win-win" relationships.

Consensus brings together people with diverse views, whose positions haven't hardened, with the expectation that it will take time to adjust those positions and create a broad-based accord. Consensus is appropriate when things have splintered, and there is reasonable time to put them back together.

Consensus is a process of reconstruction, which aims to restore order, often under new terms. Back in the seventies and eighties, business faced a number of what could be called slow-burn issues. No one expected that such complex problems as equal employment or quality control—as urgently as they needed resolution—could be mastered overnight. Perhaps the best example of successful consensus was the turnaround of a bankrupt New York City in the 1970s, marshaled impressively by Felix Rohatyn of Lazard Frères.

What made it work? One afternoon a couple of years ago, Felix explained it to me in this way: "When you want to build a consensus, you must first identify an overriding community of interests. Those common interests must make up for the difference in views and the great pressures of a crisis. In the New York situation, we had to convince the banks, the city, the state, the labor unions and others that New York truly faced bankruptcy . . . and that New York's bankruptcy would truly be the worst alternative for each interest. . . . It was just a series of steps. Consensus was there from beginning to end, and it involved a variety of social contracts that had to be upheld."

How different, consent. It is the leadership equivalent to "emergency powers" in government, without the backing of any official decrees. These days, a leader will find views setting precipitously, and the pressure to take positions quickly and decisively will often be irresistibly high. When the Iraqis marched into Kuwait, the world community withdrew its consent for Iraq. Although many people voted against Iraq for many different reasons, the vote was still the same.

Sometimes, the issue will fester for years, and some special interest will in a moment capture what Tony Schwartz calls the "responsive chord" causing the issue to take a sudden, unstoppable turn. Consider McDonald's and the polystyrene clamshell boxes in which it used to pack its sandwiches. In my opinion, McDonald's could never escape the momentum created by Earth Day celebrations in 1990, and their focus on styrofoam as an environmental hazard. The trade publication *Adweek's Marketing Week* reported in November of 1990 that within days of a call to McDonald's president Ed Rensi from Frederic Krupp of the Environmental Defense Fund, McDonald's dumped plastic foam.[9] No cheap decision and certainly not a predicted one, since McDonald's had announced plans to enlarge its $100 million styrofoam recycling program just weeks before switching gears, says *Adweek's Marketing Week*.

Because no common agreement on motives is needed in consent, the reader will perceive a strong similarity between consent tactics and niche marketing. Consent can be driven by genuine humanitarian motives; it can also be driven by self-interest. Sometimes it can be both, especially when consent hinges on the self-interested side of humanitarian or humanistic concerns. Consent often answers such questions as these: "Am I comfortable that this is happening in the world, even though the issue itself causes me no direct discomfort?" "Can I live with the vivid, appalling reports that I see on the television screen?"

The universe of consent is fundamentally a universe of "me" and "now," even when it's a matter of conscience—"What do I think is right?" As much as we like to claim that the "me" era is over, people are as self-interested as ever and more efficient than ever before in deciding what is in their self-interest. People are saying: Give me a specific reason to buy a decision or a viewpoint, just as they are asking for fully tailored reasons to buy a product from a manufacturer.

Although consensus will remain an important tool for leaders to forge long-term issues, such as strategy, and although masters of consensus, such as Felix Rohatyn, will be models for that critical leadership

Consent	Consensus
• Works when normal business is disrupted by "life-threatening" conditions or when people want answers	• Works in normal business situations or protracted crises
• Uses established relationships	• Is a dynamic process
• Targets individual opinion segments	• Requires agreement
• Can avert or alter a crisis quickly	• Is inherently slow
• Has clearly defined impacts	• Has subtle impacts
• Allows going over the heads of unreasonable adversaries	• Must accommodate fringe elements

Consent	Consensus
• Requires significant intelligence gathering and "information maintenance" to be kept up to date, fresh for use when attacked or when opportunity arises	• Permits gradual unfolding of facts and attitudes
• Expresses direct self-interest	• Satisfies self-interest by tending to the mutual interests of others

skill for many years to come, leaders will have to face the reality that an increasing number of issues will be triggered by consent-style opinion voting. This trend requires that more effort be spent gathering intelligence to determine when an issue is about to erupt in the public channel.

Consent has mounting force in resolving problems and setting direction because it seems quick and easy. People are exhausted with complicated decision making. A recent cartoon by Piraro shows a bewildered couple reading the label on a piece of home electronic gear in a store. The label boasts the following: "This product was manufactured in 27 different countries encompassing a wide variety of political and environmental philosophies. . . . you decide."

Even for business, the consent model has its attractions. It emphasizes satisfying "mainstream" activists rather than negotiating with fringe adversaries, who can bog down the process of consensus.

We are now in the beginning stages of the Age of Consent, and it will take years to refine its workings. Some questions are still debatable. We still don't know how thoughtful a highly emotion-charged public is about some issues, for example. Six months after Heinz's dolphin-safe proclamation, the newspaper *The European* ran an article saying "less enlightened purchasers may be confused by the label ['dolphin-safe'] and may have stopped buying tuna." This was during a recession and an analyst at Goldman Sachs quoted in the article says that "one possible explanation is that many consumers were not aware of the issue. They suddenly became aware and essentially feel confused. Their reaction may have been to curtail consumption. I do not see any other explanation. Tuna consumption usually goes up when the economy slows down because it is a cheap and nutritious way of eating."[10]

It's important for leaders to know four things about consent and consensus:

1. To divide the list of key public issues surrounding the organization and to separate those likely to be resolved by consent from those likely to be resolved by consensus.

2. To build a position file, especially for the most volatile consent issues, which puts the organization's desired outcome on record early, one that can be constantly resourced in an ensuing debate.

3. To install some kind of monitoring system—as simple as regularly scanning thoughtful newspapers and magazines or as complex as outside intelligence-gathering—to detect emerging issues and those issues that are gaining critical mass.

4. To limit the energy and time invested in building consensus to the most crucial, long-term topics, because most organizations simply lack the time and resources. It is better to have quality consensus on a few specific issues than to pursue aimless and frustratingly unsuccessful consensus on a broad agenda of issues.

NO GENERAL PUBLIC

Individualization and the acceptance of various lifestyles have annihilated the concept of a general public. As they craft their agendas and the communications plans to implement them, leaders must realize that the largely homogeneous society we once knew has ceased to exist. Today all marketing turf, as probably the best example of wooed publics, is a contest for niches and mini-niches. A short while back, *Advertising Age* reported on manufacturers' pursuit of the shredded-wheat market. Shredded wheat is a $300 million slice of a $6.9 billion ready-to-eat cereal market. But the contest isn't just over shredded wheat.[11] The market is divided into bite-size versus full-size, sugar-coated versus natural, stuffed-with-fruit versus plain, and on and on.

What goes for preferences in shredded wheat goes as well for religion, politics, and insurance. For those wanting to influence us, each of us has more reality as individuals than at any time since the beginning of modern, industrial civilization. We are also becoming more finitely branded as parts of thousands and thousands of subgroups.

What should this mean for the leader?

1. *Each individual in an organization is really an amalgam of different affiliations.* That network requires the leader and the organization to deliver something special if it is to influence and merit a loyalty surpassing the competing ties.

2. *A leader cannot arbitrarily expect a certain "style" of person to be part of an organization.* People are much more heterogeneous than in the preceding decades of this century, and society endorses that diversity.

3. *A leader must accept the variety of people in the organization or in contact with it and their different uses for the organization and its products.* Some employees want promotional opportunities, others, job security. Some customers prize convenience, others, diversity of product offering. All must be satisfied.

NO ROAD TO A GENERAL PUBLIC

Even if a leader wanted to reach a general public, the road to that public no longer exists. Television is the best example of a universal avenue that has been interchanged into thousands of different, individualized roadways.

In less than 50 years, television has grown from the novel to the indispensable. If television seems pervasive now, it will only become more so. A. C. Nielsen reports that children spend about 28 hours a week in front of television screens. We see the world the way we watch television. Each succeeding generation will have its vision more intensely trained by the time it logs in front of the set and by the growing sophistication of the medium conveying its message.

While we are watching more television, it is becoming less the case that we are watching the *same* television. Most of America would once congregate around the "Ed Sullivan Show" or "Monday Night Football." There is no network show—not "The Cosby Show," not "The Simpsons"—that commands anything similar to that kind of saturation today. Cable television and videotape recorders have changed our video landscape. The *Channels Field Guide 1991* reports: "The penetration level for VCRs . . . brushes 73 percent, according to Arbitron data from July [1990]. Basic cable [stands at] 58 percent."[12]

Television has ceased to be a national institution molded around three networks. In the past ten years, network television's share of prime-time viewers has tumbled from its zenith of 92 percent to 63 percent in November 1990, and the networks' skid is far from ended.[13] Armed with our remote switches, we reject commercials, we speed through boredom, and we stalk the channels for interesting moments.

Television is the best indicator of what is happening to communications as a whole. With tremendous increases in the power of high-speed computing and reductions in the real cost of information, it makes more and more sense to reach individuals directly than to pursue them randomly. Even toothpaste makers and cracker bakers, through the powerful data banks and analysis capabilities of the large packaged-goods firms, are increasingly able to reach customers one-on-one.

What does the absence of universal channels mean to a leader in an organization:

1. *Messages will have to be tailored to each key audience.* People increasingly expect that every message they receive, from a direct-mail flier about cosmetics to an appeal for the United Way, is tailored for them.

2. *The input coming back to the leader will be more diverse and therefore harder to cipher than in the past.* In the past everyone was expected to talk to the boss in the same respectful way. Not so any more. Leaders will have to understand the frame of reference of the different inputs. Does it come from the executive suite or from a disadvantaged employee on a job-training program? That diversity demands that leaders be more culturally aware than in the past, because management experts tell us they will be continually bombarded with messages from all parts of the organization in the scenario of the future.

3. *Leaders will be compelled to unify routinely the enormous diversity in their organizations to give the people a common purpose and identification.* Otherwise, the organization ceases to give the necessary meaning that makes work, growth, and a future all possible.

7

MOVING
THE NEEDLE
*Mastering the Clutter
and Catalyzing the Message*

M Y FIRST REAL UNDERSTANDING OF THE COMPLEXITIES OF
global competition came when I was a young man working
on the steel industry account for Hill and Knowlton. Back in the early
seventies, I would go through central Pennsylvania and Ohio visiting
editorial writers at papers such as the *Marion Star*, the *Toledo Blade*,
and the *Pittsburgh Post-Gazette*. My mission was to explain why the
steel industry needed import quotas—at a time when they could have
made a difference. The case we had developed for American steel was
airtight, and the editorial writers invariably agreed. They would write
positive, reasonable editorials, and nothing would happen. The truth
was they had nothing energizing or sexy to write about. They made a
good case for common sense, but common sense doesn't win trade
wars. To move the needle on the meter, you have to say your message
boldly enough to register an impression.

Representing the American Iron and Steel Institute catapulted John
Hill to fame. This was one of his first and most important clients during
the beginning years of the business. When the industry was at the peak
of its power, Hill drew on that power in the appeals he created for steel.
In 1953, Hill said in a speech: "Facts [must not be falsified] but they

THINKPOINTS

on How

Leaders Master Clutter

☐ Recognize the pervasiveness of clutter.

☐ Transcend clutter with proper emotional appeals.

☐ Cultivate loyal core supporters.

☐ Make positive messages visually rich.

☐ Make one adviser your alter-ego for clarifying messages.

☐ Use feedback loops to ensure that messages register.

☐ Speak to niche audiences through meaningful voices.

☐ Understand how clutter can be a shield in tough times.

---

should be dramatized; made understandable; clearly interpreted. . . .
The emphasis on integrity . . . does not mean facts must be dull." By
the time I was on the steel account, the communication landscape had
changed: The Information Age was dawning and people were being
besieged by data they could neither absorb nor manage. Concurrently,
Washington had made big manufacturing firms phobic about anything
that smacked of monopolies and price-fixing and had driven Big Steel,
among other industries, to a low profile at the wrong time.

In crafting messages about steel, I argued most intensely with the
lawyers, who were trying to delete the emotional appeals in speeches,
cases, and press releases. Appropriate to their mission, lawyers want to
measure words logically in a factual sequence. Corporate lawyers in
particular disparage adding the human appeal that gives the case life.
Their legal training compels them to back off and say to themselves:
"This should be enough to persuade a logical person." For thoughtful,
logical people, it may be, but not necessarily for the folks watching
"Mr. Ed." or "I Love Lucy." And the case for American steel slowly
sank below the public consciousness.

On the other hand, the Japanese know how to sing to the heart. The
Japanese grow rice on incredibly inefficient, small family farms. While
exports are beginning to trickle in today, Japanese consumers pay six
times what Americans do for rice, which is far more a staple in Japan
than it is in the United States. The difference is that the Japanese
agricultural lobby has for decades identified and used pointed emotional appeals to protect its interests. The U.S. steel lobby did not,
neither did the U.S. shoe industry. The Japanese agricultural lobby
realized that Japan's dependence on a foreign country, such as the
United States, for its key food staple was abhorrent to a people who
still remember the postwar deprivation of 40 years ago. But the domestic shoemakers and steel mills wouldn't prick the right nerves in the
United States.

Midway in the seventies, one of my colleagues staged a parade for
the beleaguered American shoe industry. Legions of shoe workers
marched down the main street of Wilkes-Barre, Pennsylvania toward
the Town Hall, an uprising reminiscent of the compelling "Les Misèra-
bles." Leading the parade was one ten-year-old boy—barefooted. The
demonstration made every network newscast, and the wirephoto hit
every daily in the country. Unfortunately, when the shoe lobby finally
came alive to fight, the battle was already over.

Today, no one is loathe to use emotional appeals to break through
clutter. Lobbyists will roll caskets into the Capitol rotunda to protest

bills about to die from neglect. The save-the-dolphin movement was catalyzed by documentaries, showing dolphins suffocating in the purse-seine nets used to catch tuna.

Leaders communicate into a landscape littered with information. In this chapter, the goal is to brief you on how to avoid clutter to convey messages clearly and how to use clutter and to avoid the limelight when high visibility may conflict with your agenda. Using emotion and imaginative presentation to get points across is a potent response to the problem of clutter. Concerning clutter, a leader must understand:

1.   How to determine its extent and pervasiveness

2.   How it affects operations as well as messages

3.   How to rise above clutter

4.   How to use clutter as camouflage.

THE SEA OF CLUTTER

Clutter engulfs us on an overwhelming scale. Advertising people are the most sorely tested by it. The United States has 6 percent of the world's people and 57 percent of its advertising. The networks each churn out 18 prime-time messages per hour. Consumers see a thousand ads of all sorts each day. The clutter in messages is matched by the clutter of consumer products themselves. The average supermarket product assortment has jumped from 9,000 to 24,000 items in about a decade.

The biggest advertising problems are, of course, in television. In the mass media eras of the sixties and seventies, advertising could create demand. Today, because of clutter, advertising is just one part of a highly intricate marketing program, using public relations, sales promotion, and special events. Getting messages across means penetrating clutter effectively—that is, studying modern marketing's most successful tactics.

HIGH-FREQUENCY MARKETING:

A leader must understand the relationship between timing and clutter. In any channel where messages vie for attention, the volume of communication ebbs and flows like an ocean tide. The temptation is to add to the clutter by investing money in promotion at the time of highest demand. Firms skilled at high-frequency marketing know better. They understand that many products—lip balm is a good example—have a core, high-frequency user. Other customers are seasonally or promotionally motivated. But the core user, the most loyal and profitable user, is always out there buying. The key in brand management is to amass and retain the biggest group of core users possible.

The trough of the annual sales curve is when high-frequency marketers promote heavily and try to raid their competitors' core customers. They will work hard to switch them over, to sway habitual users over to their brand.

Many airlines try to build business during the off-seasons, focusing largely on price to create a business that has the same volume as their busiest season, which is in the summer. After Labor Day, airlines do their heaviest discounting until December 14. After the first of the year, they discount again until Memorial Day. Most corporate travel departments are wired to recommend the lowest fare first. Reservations are therefore constantly shifting and constantly chasing price.

Shrewd airlines study the habits of the high-frequency business traveler. The choices of corporate travel departments do not necessarily reflect the preferences of business airline travelers. Studies show that business travelers tend to fly those airlines in which they enjoy V.I.P. lounge privileges. During the off-season when all the carriers are footballing price, the best airline competitors offer extra inducements in their lounges or in their frequent-flier programs.

The concept works for ideas as much as for soaps or for travel tickets. To penetrate clutter, focus on cultivating the heavy user, not on harvesting the heavy time of use. Rarely will a leader craft the marketing tactics for the business, but leaders should always insist upon demanding marketing plans that differentiate their messages and propel their organizations above the clutter, a plan that requires understanding techniques such as message timing.

MAKING SMALL BEAUTIFUL

The heart of economic and job growth in the United States is with small- and medium-sized businesses. Although these small, entrepreneurial businesses can catapult themselves overnight into huge companies, most heads of these companies know that their businesses often get lost in the clutter of business coverage. What happened to Nike, Lotus, Apple, and Microsoft did not happen by sheer accident. Their success was the result of offering desirable products, astute positioning in the markets, and planning fundamental communications.

Small companies often need to be noticed to raise capital, to attract employees, or to draw quality vendors. But size *is* a limiting factor in reaching such constituencies as the press: coverage of the big firms freezes out the little ones because only so much space is available. The *Wall Street Journal* and the *New York Times* have guidelines of size, restricting who can be covered in earnings reports or "Who's News" (the *Journal* column that reports on executive appointments). If you try to force your way in, nearly always futilely, reporters remember it with bitterness the next time around.

Magazines such as *Business Week* are thoroughly tracking growth companies, because the publication knows that's where the economic action will be for the foreseeable future. The bibles for growth businesses, however, remain *INC* magazine and *Business,* a publication in the United Kingdom. Analysts of U.S. industry are now studying the *Inc.* 500 as aggressively as they are the *Fortune* 500 list. *Inc.*'s list tallies the 500 fastest growing private companies with sales between $100,000 and $25 million. Many of these companies devise attractive strategies for expansion, and are then acquired by bigger firms as growth vehicles or go on to public offerings themselves.

A number of companies are dedicated to giving communications service to the high-tech firms clustered around Route 128 outside of Boston. Over the years, they've studied those companies and their special needs in rising above the clutter of present business coverage. Here are some general principles.

GETTING THE SMALL, TECHNICAL ORGANIZATION NOTICED

Visualize the Vision. Many high-tech products lack the visual interest or understandability necessary to get coverage by the broader press. Because only a few people grasp the significance of these wares or services, making the product accessible to the lay person, or even the lay journalist, becomes a formidable challenge. Companies that get ahead draw compelling word and visual pictures to capture the imagination. Comparing MS-DOS to the Latin of medieval monasteries, both being the basic information languages of their respective times, would be one example.

Cultivate the Support of Third-Party Endorsers. This is good advice for any leader, but especially for the heads of small, technical organizations. The financial analysts who follow emerging high-tech firms are particularly aggressive, bright, and hardworking. Because the subject can be so complex, journalists lean more heavily on these analysts than on those in many other industries. If you're the leader of an emerging technology business wanting to get the word out, respect the analysts' power. You should know all of the lead analysts, and you should spend time with them.

Anticipate the Problems Success May Bring. Companies verging on a major leap of growth should study what happened to other businesses that have gone through the same boom. Because these businesses make the transition from small to big or from private to public so quickly, they have a hard time adjusting to the sharper public scrutiny. Companies at the doorstep of success look at their position as a "high-grade worry"—something to be dealt with later, if they make the breakthrough. Often it's too late. If a company is successful, the press will want to know how the business will protect its entrepreneurial strengths while resolving the problems accompanying growth.

The rate of change is so strong in technology there is a tendency to go with the flow. As a result, the strategic identity of most high-tech firms looks like the blurred photo of a sprinter in motion. The companies that stand out fine-tune their picture and their image continually.

These same techniques for combating clutter can work for a think tank or a specialized laboratory. They also work for universities, where size is less the limiting factor, but "stature" can be the imposing boundary. A success story of a university rising above the clutter and getting noticed has been Emory University in Atlanta. Emory declared its vision of making itself a world-class institution and was able to translate it in a way endorsers and benefactors could understand.

Emory took bold steps and then publicized them. According to the *New York Times,* for example, it lured a good portion of the French department and graduate students in French at Johns Hopkins to

Emory.[1] It changed its menu, the *Times* points out, dumping dentistry and library science and adding anthropology. Through favorable publicity, it attracted even more money to build its programs. The University of Chicago Business School is another institution managing to break through clutter by presenting a fresh agenda to potential contributors.

For the redefined university, the emerging gene-splicing firm, or the small skunk-works business, the core communications challenge left to the leader is making the vision intelligible and exciting for outsiders, differentiated enough to draw the needed attention. Only then can the momentum of outside support be put into motion.

THE ATTIC

Clutter isn't just "out there." The same information clutter infesting the outside world can be found within our world at home. People will curse the clutter the world throws at them, but the worst excesses—the stuff we collect—will be found in our own attics and garages. Too many organizations collect clutter. Too many live in it every day, conducting business out of a mental rabbit hutch.

The worst kind of internal clutter I see regularly is what my former Hill and Knowlton colleague Don Deaton has called the "Tower of Babel" surrounding today's leader, especially the contemporary CEO. Most often, the Tower of Babel rises up when the leader faces a tough decision. Lawyers, bankers, and technicians of every stripe are coming at the leader from different directions. Sometimes, leaders compound the chaos by creating competition between their advisers. Adversarial work among members of the staff, pitting one adviser against another, can improve their work; it can also congest their input to the CEO and lead to enormous clutter. Often, too, the leader lacks that one critical advisory voice, the communications "traffic cop," who can assess how all the individual input will affect the vision of the organization and its direction.

One CEO I once worked with wanted to change the identity of his company, a major utility. He put his advertising agency to work on it. His market research firm tried another angle. His public relations firm prepared a third approach. In the end, the CEO was overwhelmed with an array of logos, a sheaf of names, extensive supporting research, and all kinds of typefaces. He was lectured on the psychological, practical, and financial aspects of each option. How should he decide? Having no communications adviser to counsel him, he took the choice to his board one afternoon, a board made up mostly of internal managers. They did not know what to do either. The arguments for the various choices seemed convincing. In despair, the CEO got up and walked into one of the anterooms while the board waited. He came back in with his secretary. "Doris, what do you think?" he asked. She picked the name and the logo, and that was that.

A wise leader will have a single, primary communications adviser to help with problems such as clutter. Whether that person should be the leader's secretary, of course, is a decision based heavily on the size and goals of the organization.

CLEANING HOUSE

Many organizations have implemented a host of internal communications devices—newsletters, videotapes, magazines, announcements—and have created an endless barrage of uncontrolled messages. These multiple channels are desirable and valuable. The problem often is that they are poorly coordinated. The messages must have editorial consistency and follow the priority of the vision and its agenda. This is the critical overview necessary for internal communications, one in which leaders can give enormously valuable guidance.

Leaders have to stay in touch with those persons or firms with whom the organization wants to communicate. In the consumer world, the senders, those mail-order firms, don't understand the junk-mail problem. It's you who understands trying to open the stuffed mailbox in the evening. The same is true in companies. It isn't the contributors to the clutter who become oblivious to messages, but the individuals who must weed their way through the clutter who simply become immune to them.

The majority of American workers and managers work away from their corporate headquarters. As a result, they receive a steady stream of communication from the home office. When they receive the memos, magazines, and company newsletters, most say, "So what?"

When I was at Hill and Knowlton in 1972 a major supplier of utilities across the nation asked us to study whether their company's internal communications made a difference. Traveling around their system, we found that nearly all their mailings sent out centrally were piling up for months, even for years, in a corner of the managers' offices.

When we asked the managers the reasons for the accumulation, they said three things:

1. This stuff is boring.

2. It doesn't relate to me or my employees.

3. Nobody is making me act on any of it.

I still remember one manager saying to me, "This stuff is all very nice, but what does it have to do with Kentucky?"

We reported to the firm's management. In our opinion and in the view of the firm's top people, something had to be done. These field managers were acting as gatekeepers who had cranked up the drawbridge on communication from headquarters. None of it was getting through to the people, an event not uncommon in companies. Far worse than simple waste, field apathy can derail an entire company's direction. If communication doesn't reach its ultimate target, the most enterprising vision imaginable or the most vibrant possible agenda means nothing at all.

The simplest way to fix the problem, and the way in which this firm overcame theirs, is to create a feedback control when information is sent out. A few monitoring calls to the rank and file do wonders: Call up the personnel administrator in Santa Fe or that crack repairman you met on your field trip to Kansas City and ask: What do they think about this new policy or that new benefit? The best way leaders can keep their organizations free of clutter is to make sure that key messages are regularly being received and understood.

VOICES FOR NICHES

All parents know that they can tell a kid something a thousand times, and it won't register. But if the right outside voice carries the same message: Bingo! When the War on Drugs started, Nancy Reagan was a spokesperson in public service announcements. It was a terrible mistake. The have-not kids in the slums, who needed to hear about crack and angel dust, hated Nancy Reagan and everything she represented. But when Whoopi Goldberg delivers a message on AIDS to the same group, she hits the mark.

Skilled leaders often bring in outside authorities to address their organizations, selecting voices to reinforce an important internal message that doesn't seem to be registering inside. When assembling an agenda for a major internal meeting, think of the credible outsiders you can invite to speak, not just to stimulate the thinking of your employees but also to lend persuasive support to the chosen agenda.

CROWD CONTROL

In media relations, crowd control means staging crowds in a video event so that supporters and endorsers receive maximum exposure, and detractors and demonstrators get minimum coverage. Crowd control is a way of reducing negative clutter, but it doesn't always work. Early in 1989, President George Bush spoke at a ceremony on the steps of the Stock Exchange in Manhattan, commemorating the 200th anniversary of George Washington's inaugural. The event was a classic of poor crowd control.

The outdoor audience was by invitation only and predictably friendly. Bush's security and communications people failed, however, to inspect the camera angles the networks needed to use to frame the President with the proposed audience seating arrangement. Prochoice forces did a much better job with their homework. The wide-panning angles ensured coverage of 5000 prochoice protestors, skillfully positioned two blocks away, well beyond the security barricades. Through the eye of the wide-angle lens, the demonstrators made themselves visually as forceful as the president himself.

Challenge your staff to make sure they have a logistics plan that focuses clearly the agenda and goals that you want to achieve through a communications event. Paying attention to clutter, and to wanted and unwanted breakthroughs of clutter, is one aspect of this.

CLUTTER AS COVER

Whales on the surface may be harpooned. Sometimes, it is as smart for a leader to stay below clutter as it is to climb above it. Understatement can embroil a leader in as much trouble as overstatement can. In the middle of controversy, any leader who speaks or behaves in a way different from what is expected will attract attention.

According to Press Association Limited, when the chief of the British Department of Transport's aviation security testified before a public inquiry on the destruction of Pan Am Flight 103 over Lockerbie, Scotland, he characterized this department's delay in issuing copies of a warning photo on a bomb such as the one that destroyed the plane as "unfortunate." He declined to describe it as "intolerable," saying, according to the service, that it was "unfortunate, most undesirable."[2] The coverage projected him as sounding callous.

When Neil Bush, President George Bush's son, raised eyebrows for being a director on the board of Silverado, a failed savings and loan association in Colorado, Neil Bush compounded the problem by describing a loan he received as "incredibly sweet,"[3] rather than "very favorable." When a leader is in the middle of trouble, one way to ensure the continuing glare of public attention is to be too quotable. *Note:* This is not the same as not being available to the press. Be available as appropriate, but there is no need to do the press's work in institutionalizing one's own flaws.

Neil's father George is much defter in managing clutter. One day, when reporters were hounding him about the lack of U.S. support for Lithuania's attempts to liberate itself from the Soviet Union, he managed to maneuver the topic to how broccoli had been served at a recent dinner and that he hated broccoli passionately. One reporter commented: "He knew we could not ignore what he was saying. So he offered a tiny glimpse of one of his own personal idiosyncrasies, with emotion, and we turned it into a major news story. It was the biggest thing since pork rinds."[4] The next day, broccoli was sweeping the media; Lithuania was not.

Clutter is used all the time, especially by governments. An airliner crashes, and a controversial government appointment is announced. World attention was riveted on the Middle East, and the Soviets moved their Black Berets on the borders of the Baltic republics. A prime minister resigns and the papers write of little else, while a ten-year litigation is settled for millions of dollars—and receives coverage verging on a back-page footnote.

Leaders are best advised to steer away from the gamesmanship of manipulating clutter in public forums; it's a tricky business. Their focus instead should remain basic, breaking above the clutter when messages must be heard and avoiding obtrusiveness when the organization and its leader are advantageously outside the center of attention.

CHAPTER

8

FIRST ON THE SLATE
Pacing Communication

IN 1982, WHILE ADVISING PREPA, THE PUERTO RICAN ELECTRIC POWER Authority, the importance of responding swiftly to a situation hit home to me. Puerto Rico's abominable electric utility service worsened with the growing popularity of air conditioning on the island. The Power Authority decided to build a new power plant to keep up with the demand. The tourist industry was a strong advocate of the new plant, but many locals and environmentalists were not. The most desirable location for the plant, logistically and commercially, happened to be Aquadilla, one of the most popular surfing areas in the Caribbean.

As part of their strategy, the utility asked the U.S. Navy to grant the utility a parcel of land to build the plant, but their approach was poorly planned; it smacked of horse-trading: You give us the land we need, and we will continue to be accommodating to your needs for a military base on the island. You can't carry on politics in Washington the way you do in San Juan. PREPA didn't get the needed land, and this widely publicized piece of news set a negative context for everything happening afterward.

The core problems were those of public opinion. Puerto Rico has

THINKPOINTS

on How

Leaders Control the Speed of Events

☐ Write first and clearly on the slate of public opinion.

☐ Analyze key sectors of opinion before taking major steps.

☐ Act on predictable trends of opinion before you are forced to.

☐ Condition the organization to today's compressed timeframes.

☐ Manage any crisis in the context of its phases.

☐ Isolate problems and communicate rapidly to beat the clock.

☐ Seize positive crises with the same urgency as negative ones.

2700 political factions sorted into three major political parties, but the coalitions are always shaky. The power plant was an emotional issue. Labor was generally opposed to the plant, and when labor is opposed to something in Puerto Rico, keep your eyes open. Several years ago, a hotel was torched during a strike, and over a hundred persons were killed. In this case, the arsonist was simply irrational and the union was absolved of involvement, but labor problems can have volatile side effects.

Consumers also opposed the PREPA plant, despite a rash of recent brownouts. Environmentalists had inaccurately convinced them that the plant would cause acid rain. In addition, the consumers were concerned about utility rate hikes. The controversy escalated, and some existing plants were sabotaged and even bombed.

Playboy's CEO Christie Hefner says that, if you are to prevail, it is essential in influence and opinion campaigns to write on the slate first. By the time we arrived in San Juan, there was no room to write on the slate. The opposition had already jammed it with messages. Approaching PREPA's yellow sandstone building downtown, a colleague of mine and I encountered angry demonstrators. An armed security force surrounded the building. The crowd was agitated, and some fights had already broken out. We were passengers in a black midsized car, which was an obvious mistake. Almost all the cars in Puerto Rico are compacts.

It was early March, and I was wearing a three-piece Brooks Brothers' suit, having come to Puerto Rico without notice. Here the temperature was 100 degrees and the humidity, 97 percent. A barrage of rocks, bottles, and signs rained down on the car, which was speeding along with us squeezed on the floor of the back seat. Leaving the building later, that time in a compact car, we crouched down with a tarp over us.

The meeting was fruitless. Although a coal-fired plant was ultimately built, the road to its construction was a tortuous one. The key issue was the utility had waited a month between its announcement that it wanted a new plant until the time it launched a program to cultivate the needed support. The order of events should have been reversed, with a sounding out of major interest groups on their general views before the announcement was made. This approach would have helped greatly to pinpoint support and opposition, and the utility could then have developed specific programs to spur the endorsement of allies and to answer the objections of opponents. PREPA wanted to move ahead too quickly with the announcement and had neglected the necessary research.

In any public affairs issue today, an organization will lose if it enters the ring late. Moreover, it shouldn't be in the ring at all unless it has been "in training" and has a well-researched battle plan. A pivotal element in that plan is a clear timing-and-action calendar, not just some hypothetical program. The plan must accurately describe the time an organization has to resolve an issue.

This chapter outlines how leaders can master the pace of events, especially in confronting challenging situations or impending crises.

CLOCK WATCHING

Organizations lose critical time because they fail to pay attention to the issues. Fast-food chains should have switched from animal fats for deep-frying years ago, and they should have eliminated styrofoam packing long before they decided to. The trend line of opinion against these practices was overwhelming and would not subside. Because they act too late, firms spend hundreds of millions of dollars trying to earn back lost goodwill rather than being able to use those dollars for building the business.

If lumber companies had started creating sanctuaries for the spotted owl the moment that issue blipped on the screen, 28,000 jobs in the lumber industry would not be at stake now in the United States. The public expects big organizations to have a plan, and when the spotted owl appears on the front page of newspapers and magazines, there is little time to reverse the situation.

The spotted owl isn't the only symbol of what seems to be the lack of meaningful planning in the lumber industry. Traveling down the highways of the Pacific Northwest, you often see a barren land where the trees have been hacked down by gypsy lumbermen, a landscape that seems to be plundered forever. In contrast, as you drive down the foothills of the Cascade Range in Washington or near the White Pass, north of Mt. Rainier, you will see Weyerhauser tree farms with signs such as "This forest was harvested in 1951 and replanted in 1953. It will be ready for its next harvest in the year 2000."

Weyerhauser's low-key road signs are a product label announcing the firm is in control of the time agenda. They are the Burma Shave signs of the future, and people feel good about them. Weyerhauser has written on the slate first.

You have to measure the pulse of opinion constantly. Quiet crises can become roaring crises overnight. When the liberation of Eastern Europe took place, the ministers of countless Third World countries boarded planes for Washington, London, Bonn, and Paris. Overnight, in many cases too late, these officials realized that foreign aid once earmarked for central Africa and the Asian subcontinent would now be going to Hungary and Czechoslovakia. Those Third World countries that had excelled in preserving their share of the pie and had been constantly nurturing their relationship with their benefactors also showed up at the critical time to reinforce their case, but with far better results.

THE COMPRESSION OF TIME

The speed of events that leaders must face, especially in crises, is set by the media. Until the 1970s, all media were a derivative of print, and the acceleration of "media time" in recent years has been astonishing. The conventional wisdom is that Vietnam, for example, was the first television war, but that view is false. Film footage in Vietnam had to be shipped from the battlefield to Saigon and then to Hong Kong for transmission to New York, a journey that took days. The first real television war was in the Persian Gulf, where videotape, computers, and especially satellites permitted instantaneous transmission from the battlefield to the home.

Technology has compressed time. With today's instant global communications, the system of deliberation in news organizations, in think tanks, and in the analysis units of big securities firms has dramatically changed. These arbiters of opinion are organized to react much faster.

People may complain about "instant analysis," but it is here; it is going to accelerate, and it will shape viewpoints even more in the future. Only the exceptional organization today has adjusted its own decision making to match this pace. When events transform an organization into a media subject, most organizations are chasing to catch up with the first story and few succeed.

CRISIS AS TIME MANAGEMENT

No organizational situation tests the strength of leadership as much as a crisis does. Many leaders fail to manage crises well because they don't understand the nature of the clock against which they are measured. Not seeing a crisis as a series of distinct phases, sometimes phases in rapid-fire sequence, too many leaders lower their heads and charge forward in a tunnel-visioned way, neglecting the broad network of contacts they should leverage in a crisis. They are oblivious, most of all, to the generic sequence of events that organizes a crisis in the minds of the people watching and interpreting it.

THE FIVE PHASES OF A CRISIS

Crises almost always unfold in stages and generally follow this cycle.

Phase I: Losses and Rescues. At the disaster site, news media have arrived. Officials, other than emergency personnel, have not. There is chaos. Sometimes people are hard-pressed to identify what exactly has happened. The news media has a single-minded goal: to discover what happened and to report the damage, especially in human life.

The priority in Phase I is to give up-to-the-minute data on casualties and major damage. Get it out as quickly as possible, respecting, of course, the privileges of the bereaved. In 1985, as Marion Pinsdorf, a leading independent communications consultant, has pointed out, when a Japan Airlines plane crashed and 520 persons were killed, the airline reported the precise loss of life nearly immediately. By contrast, after the Lockerbie crash in 1988, Pan Am just couldn't get the death toll right. It turned out that they counted the crew twice. Admittedly in this case, casualties on the ground made tallying the count harder, but poor credibility at the outset triggers lingering doubt that will make the entire crisis more unmanageable.

If it's a major disaster, expect direct calls from public officials and community leaders to individual top managers, but channel all media calls to your spokesperson. Identify quickly whom or what was saved from destruction through quick thinking and effective planning and be prepared to comment on this as well.

Phase II: Damage Control and the Search for Causes. Attention shifts to why the crisis happened and how people are affected. The media begins to frame the event in terms of "human costs." "Who's to blame?" Sensing their vulnerability, officials and authorities start weaving their defense. If it's a truly serious incident, and increasingly in lesser cases, the media will call in outside experts to assess damage and blame. "Why did it happen?" The press of course will want to know this right away, in a matter of hours. In fact, no one will know why it happened. Lawyers will be all over you telling you that you can't say why it happened, even if you have a good guess. You must respond. The most reliable answer is "We're looking into why this occurred and we hope to have an answer as quickly as possible."

Because of the unavailability of facts, and especially for loss of life, senior managers should stay out of the line-of-fire as much as possible. They should be poised to go to the site immediately and may go there in advance, even though they are not yet spokespersons. As time passes just saying that you're working on understanding what went wrong falls flat. You must continue to act and to recite all of the specific measures to demonstrate that you are working on finding the cause and fixing the problem.

The media ritualize crisis at this stage. Watch the morning news-talk shows the day after a crisis strikes. If it's similar to the Challenger disaster or the bombing of the Marine barracks in Lebanon, the on-air journalists will be wearing dark suits or dresses with conservative ties and scarves. They may dispense with the sprightly morning theme music. During the Gulf War, for example, networks actually created "war" logos and theme music. Crisis spokespersons must respond with a sensitivity that matches the media's behavior, because the media set the visual standard.

Phase III: Bereavement. If loss of life has occurred, the media personalizes the grief of friends and families at individual funeral and memorial services. This fuels public anger and stokes calls for reprisals and/or restoration. Officials demand investigations. Special interests shake their heads and say, "You see, *this* is what we were warning you about." Advocates who see the incident as a way to raise consciousness about an initiative, special safety seats for children on airliners or drug-testing for railway workers, mobilize around the crisis. Even if no lives are lost, bereavement still takes place as the media dramatize handicapping injuries, the loss of jobs, or harm to wildlife.

During Phase III, keep praising the individuals working on the project. It's never in your best interest to criticize the officials who are handling the crisis or to complain that the authorities are not accomplishing more. If there's a real problem, you may want to quietly backchannel to these people through a responsible, discrete emissary and ask officials to step up their efforts. Publicly attacking them will only polarize them, and probably the press as well, against you.

The best strategy is to put people in the field quickly to see what can be done to resolve problems. When Ashland Oil experienced a major oil spill several years ago, it dispatched officials to the major cities along the affected waterway to analyze the problem, map out the clean-up measures, and endorse local efforts. In short, they unleashed a network of concern that followed the path of the spill, a farsighted move.

Phase IV: Pinning Blame. The reality of the crisis then begins to recede, usually clouded by a series of conflicting positions concerning who was or was not responsible. Everyone calculates: careers and personal pride are at risk, not to mention the threat of serious potential civil and criminal liability.

In our culture, we resist accepting blame. Other cultures are more demanding. In Japan, the CEO of a firm experiencing a crisis or scandal is expected to offer to resign. Expect that leaders throughout the world will increasingly be asked to accept blame for what goes wrong on their watch. In the West, this trend suggests that leaders who are not quick to assume the proper responsibility will more likely be hounded out of office by an angry press and citizenry.

Phase V: Boredom and Confusion. Crass though it may be to say, interest fades, especially if a new and different crisis appears. Unless someone is personally touched by a crisis, passion will wane. Interest also dies out when assigning blame becomes so complex that the public cannot follow the nuances. Regrettably, firms will sometimes consciously use this complexity to dig themselves out of crises.

Occasionally there is a "Phase VI," which is the revelation of systematic and clearly provable cover-ups, but these are getting more difficult to document and dramatize. Although they are rare events, the participants in the cover-ups are less prone to leave careless, damaging evidence scattered about. Watergate was perhaps the last federal "Phase VI" event. The Challenger disaster and Irangate ultimately proved impenetrable for the media and the public.

Many people think that communications is a top-level skill only in a crisis. The truth is that crisis magnifies the communications strengths or weaknesses of an organization by bringing them under intense scrutiny. If the crisis becomes a landmark—a cause—it can besiege a leader for years.

PRODUCTS AS MURDER WEAPONS

Business leaders should realize how crucial a swift response can be to product tampering, which is no longer confined to manufactured goods. A bomb in an airplane, cyanide in a pharmaceutical, a virus in an air traffic controller's computer—all three of these are examples of product tampering and all of them can be lethal. With a few minor adjustments, almost any modern product, and an increasing number of services, can be rendered into a murder weapon.

In the event of dangerous tampering—no matter if it is to a product, a decision, or an agenda, because unauthorized tampering with decisions and direction can be as lethal to an organization as a plastic explosive is to an airliner—a skilled leader will take three steps:

1. Isolate the problem.

2. Monitor the media and/or grapevine to determine public perception of the problem.

3. Set up intense communications with the channels that distribute the tampered goods.

In one product tampering case I know of, a fire department paramedic had purchased an individual beverage container in a convenience store. He opened the bottle and took a swig of it while leaving the store. He instantly felt ill and dropped to the ground. A colleague who was with him picked up his radio transmitter and called in the emergency, mentioning the name of the beverage. Since media were monitoring the emergency bands, reporters were on the scene immediately. Because the store was part of a chain, it activated a phone network and within an hour pulled the product from the shelves of all its stores in that state.

Other parts of the chain in neighboring states reacted the same way. Within three hours, the media had sounded the alarm in a 13-state alert. By the next day, the incident had become national news, and the manufacturer and bottlers faced a demand for massive recalls. An intense investigation was conducted. Within the critical first 48 hours, the problem was isolated: a disgruntled truck driver in the delivery system decided to get back at the company by urinating into one of the product containers and then carefully resealing it. Within a day, the paramedic recovered; the problem was contained and the recall averted.

Scientific findings questioning the safety of a product can come from internal tests as well as from outside sources. If the findings are internal, a leader will have to weigh the risk of exposing the company to criticism and worse before there is any outside requirement to do so. In some cases, companies will take a risk and alert the government to their own tests only to find the government incapable of giving clear guidance.

Not long ago this very situation occurred in a case involving listeria, a potentially deadly microorganism that can contaminate processed food. On the eve of a holiday ushering in a particular food product's peak sales period, its manufacturer discovered that some of the already-shipped product could be contaminated with listeria.

The firm notified public health authorities. The bureaucratic response was a sleepy "mañana" attitude: "Perhaps it would be better to wait and see before alarming the general public." The manufacturer was taken aback by the regulators' evident indifference and geared up for a major recall. In a sudden reversal, health authorities ordered a total-product recall just hours later.

Within 24 hours, the company's 2,000 wholesale and retail customers had received an air express package with news releases, background information, a question-and-answer briefer and a pledge from the company's CEO to maintain communication. As this incident demonstrates, organizations must know how to reach their network of suppliers and customers on weekends and holidays. Information management during a crisis is an around-the-clock requirement.

Another organization with which I'm familiar held a major meeting for reviewing expenses. Participants, and all of them were senior level, were challenged to come up with provocative options and to air them behind closed doors in a highly confidential setting. One document circulated at the meeting detailed a scenario outlining what would happen if the company shaved 5000 jobs. A day later that document landed in the hands of a Wall Street arbitrageur. From there it traveled to a business columnist with a flair for the sensational. Despite company denials, employee confidence was shaken, the public's eyebrows were raised, and the company's stock took a beating. In an age of instant information, the leak of misleading data can be, in effect, an exceedingly dangerous kind of product tampering.

MINOR CRISES

The same principles I have outlined work in minor crises as well as in national-scale disasters. Aspiring leaders will internalize these principles of crisis management and apply them systematically when trouble arises. Acting urgently and intelligently to prevent brushfires from turning into uncontrollable blazes is a powerful credential for getting ahead.

POSITIVE CRISES

Leaders should have the same urgency, the same preparedness to seize opportunities as to face crises. Often an opportunity is the positive side of a negative situation. Savvy leaders get their people to regard opportunity as nothing more than a positive crisis that must be managed against a ticking clock. The chemist Dr. Samuel P. Massie gave a speech in Detroit commemorating Dr. Martin Luther King and reminded us in the audience that the word *crisis* "has two roots, danger and opportunity." We tend to forget or overlook the important opportunity often locked up in crises.

In the sixties the Japanese turned the crisis in product quality of American automobile manufacturing into a cornerstone of their economy. Similarly, if Ford had not learned from the Japanese and had not made quality its priority, it would not today be the country's most profitable automaker. Had Wal-Mart not reacted to the growing pressure on disposable income in America, it would not now be America's largest retailer. If Philips hadn't capitalized on the continuing energy crisis, it would never have designed and marketed its increasingly popular extended-life light bulbs.

According to *Business Week*, the president of Revlon, Sol Levine, has come up with a new system to make "tiny, disposable makeup samples for lipsticks and eyeshadows."[1] With the paranoia about sharing makeup samples triggered by the AIDS epidemic, the system is guaranteed to be a success and is another example of a positive response to a crisis.

For an organization to seize a crisis and make it positive, the leader must provide the added conviction and determination needed to move individuals to act, as they often lack the motivation of fear found in crises perceived as negative events. But organizations with a zest for positive crises are formidable. As Sun Tzu writes in *The Art of War*, "Opportunities multiply as they are seized."

9

NATIONS
AND NICHES
*Developing
a Transnational Framework*

LEADERS BEST LEARN THE REALITY OF OUR TRANSNATIONAL WORLD the first time they deliver the same message to audiences of different nationalities.

Two years ago, I gave essentially the same speech on global marketing to audiences in Minneapolis, London, Paris, Rome, and Osaka. All five times, I spoke English. If you scanned my written notes for each speech, you would conclude that the message in each of the five talks was the same. Had you attended the actual speeches, however, you would have left with the impression that these talks were distinctly different.

In Minneapolis, my delivery was staccato and upbeat, with many allusions to sports. I gave the three or four most quotable phrases particular weight, because they would be repeated in the press release about the speech. Also, Americans, trained by watching the evening news, are poised to hear the "sound bites" in any kind of talk. The speech concluded with a call to action, since an American audience usually asks itself, "What am I supposed to do with what you just told me?" It should also be noted that America is the least homogeneous of the five countries where I spoke. Had I given the same speech in

THINKPOINTS
on How Leaders
Guide Organizations
Toward Transnational
Effectiveness

☐ Create transnational agendas country by country.

☐ Respond to media in an essentially local way.

☐ Respect the immediate global access of all media.

☐ Abandon the "think globally, act locally" nostrum.

☐ Let dominant local markets lead.

☐ Foster global awareness.

☐ Forge global alliances to leverage strengths.

☐ Be a visible transnationalist.

Washington, I would have had to include more public policy references. In Boston I would have needed more learned citations, and so forth.

In London my speech opened with two jokes. In the United Kingdom a good opening piece of well-rehearsed humor is a decided advantage. Following the jokes were remarks punctuated by a sophisticated multiprojector-slide package. The British prefer both humor and polished theatrical flair in their presentations.

In Paris I purged the talk of examples and slides and presented it almost totally conceptually. While I delivered the comments in a conversational way, I emphasized the structure of the argument. Being factual and down-to-earth matters little in France; being rational, articulate, and witty matters a lot.

In Rome the group I addressed convened at a restaurant along the Villa Borghese. Italians treat a speech as an after-dinner entertainment, even for speakers far more prestigious than myself. The speech counselor who coached me in the essentials of Roman oratory said: Talk with dramatic gestures and great emotion, use punctuated words and short sentences, and make your talk as provocative and controversial as possible. Judging from audience reaction to the Italian rendition of the speech, my counselor proved to be absolutely right.

In Osaka I began by apologizing for my lack of knowledge of the subject and expressed regret for using up the audience's valuable time in presenting my remarks. I avoided both controversy and rhetoric and developed my position with subtlety—subtle, at least for a Westerner. I limited the number of points, and I stressed the importance of harmony as a world goal, principally because the Japanese are infatuated with creating harmony as the overriding objective of management behavior.

All of these speeches were successful, but each would have failed without the proper "cultural" translation. I am convinced that every aspect of communications in different countries, and often in different regions, must be approached in this way. Because leaders are acting on the global stage more often, they must increasingly internalize this sensitivity. My recollecting the different speech audiences has been an easy and effective way for me to do so.

My goal in this chapter is to offer leaders productive ways to think about the world of transnational business and to show them how to steer clear of oversimplified solutions in managing global situations.

NO GLOBAL AMERICA

More and more leaders understand that organizations must think in multinational terms. Because English is pervasive as a lingua franca in business and because we see Pepsi-Cola and Holiday Inns at airports around the world, many American leaders, however, still tend to think that they can transact business and advance agendas in the same way the world over. That notion is misleading and dangerous. In marketing and public affairs, especially, it can be fatal. There are regions of the world, for example, now emerging as important markets, which did not evolve in the context of American mass-market brands.

Recently, Landor Associates studied and ranked the popularity of brands in three Eastern European countries: Hungary, Poland, and the Soviet Union. This study generated three "top-ten lists" for brands in these countries. Of those top 30 names, only 5 mentions were American or American related. According to an *Economist* report on the survey's results, Ford was on all three lists. Fanta and Pepsi accounted for the other two mentions. Mercedes-Benz, Sony, Volvo, and Adidas—German, Japanese, and Swedish brands—received the strongest overall recognition. In this report, McDonald's ranked 17th, Coke's ranking was 14th in the Soviet Union, and IBM's best showing was 49th and that ranking was in Hungary.[1]

American brands are second-string in many parts of the world now poised for economic expansion. Compounding the problem, national differences the world over appear stronger each day, as countries and companies fight to preserve national economic self-interest. Even in a world shrinking through communications, technology, and mobility, *global* is a dangerous word. Leaders who don't use it cautiously can mislead their organizations into believing in a nonexistent worldwide uniformity of ideas and viewpoints.

What is true for product brands is equally true for political concepts. The Japanese practice democracy, but it is not at all the same kind of public give-and-take democracy seen in Westminster and Washington. Japanese democracy is often achieved through a series of quiet deals cut in back rooms. The economic democracy of German codetermination is generally negotiated over a boardroom table, away from the videocams of intrusive reporters. Democracy in the People's Republic of China is still an unsettled and evolving concept. Ideas such as those underpinning political systems translate far less predictably and successfully than words do. American leaders traveling abroad must have a clear idea of the cultural context and their desired goals when preaching a "democratic solution" in a foreign country or when advocating any philosophical concept.

Although I use "global" freely in this book, *transnational* is a more accurate description of what leaders must focus upon, as it accurately suggests that ideas and products must be translated from one nation to the next, one nation at a time.

THE TRANSNATIONAL AGENDA

Roger Enrico, former CEO of PepsiCo Worldwide Beverages and now head of PepsiCo's Frito-Lay division, is a master of transnational thinking. He understands how to translate the vision of Pepsi all over the world. His success, in my analysis, comes from getting Pepsi to focus on five ingredients:

1. *Market potential:* Given the economic and behavioral trend lines, what is the potential for our product in this market? How well are the needs of each market understood and how—and how quickly—will those needs change?

2. *Staying power:* How much time and money will be needed to build a desirable market position in this country?

3. *Adaptation:* How must we adapt our brand, our product, our distribution, and our messages to make sense in the marketplace?

4. *Access:* What must we do to create a credible beachhead? What political, social, and competitive forces would oppose our establishing a position in the market?

5. *Consent:* Which interests and regulators must we satisfy to sustain the goodwill that will let us do business?

A 1989 issue of *Forbes* provides a fascinating case study, in an article entitled "How Pepsi Broke into India." Here are the highlights: In 1977, the Indian government directed Coca-Cola to surrender its "proprietary syrup formula to an Indian subsidiary." Coke refused, as you would expect, and abandoned India. The company's departure has left the Indian soft-drink market—now a market of 850 million consumers, 150 million of whom are now emerging as a new middle class—in the hands of sluggish domestic competitors.

Pepsi wanted a crack at the Indian market. Years ago, you'll remember, Pepsi positioned itself in the Soviet Union and is now the foremost U.S. consumer brand there (according to *Fortune.*) It took Pepsi ten years to get into India, but they succeeded in late 1988. Pepsi began by helping their local partners educate Indian consumers, explaining how the closed market was keeping soft-drink prices artificially high.

When Pepsi examined the Indian public-affairs agenda, it saw that India was still in need of modern agricultural technology. The *Forbes* article reports that Pepsi pledged "to establish a research center to develop new varieties of fruits and vegetables that would be better suited to India's climate and soil conditions [than some current crops]. Pepsi also agreed to set up two processing plants for fruits and potatoes." (Remember, PepsiCo is also the largest restaurant operator in the world.) To create grassroots support for the governmental initiative, Pepsi mobilized the farmers in the state of Punjab to support the program. The new technology, Pepsi explained, would put these farmers on the cutting edge of Indian agriculture.

In Enrico's own words: "[The people in the Punjab] understood the politics of India, understood how to construct a deal that would be seen both substantively and image-wise as being of great value to India and which politically would be very difficult to walk away from."[2]

No doubt about it, Pepsi is in India because it fashioned and implemented a sophisticated transnational strategy. It also shows Enrico's facility in thinking through an agenda on multiple levels and with various time lines. It may take 10 to 20 years for Pepsi to realize the fruits of their strategy in India, but they have done their homework as a leader should, at a level far beyond their competition. Pepsi addressed effectively the critical niches to set up shop in India. Whenever a leader contemplates entering a new international market, the list of key niches should be the first item on the five-point agenda that addresses the following:

- Market-potential

- Staying-power

- Adaptation

- Access

- Consent

This agenda can be used by any leader considering transferring an organization's vision from one nation to another. It summarizes both the significant costs and benefits, as well as the risks and the terms under which the new adaptation must be achieved.

The whole key to any organization's transnational strategy is to think things through *one nation at a time*. *Reader's Digest* now has 15 international companies in 54 locations worldwide. "We number our customers in the millions," emphasizes the *Digest* CEO George Grune, "but we never forget *we serve them one nation at a time, in their own language.*"[3] Grune understands that no products are more closely tied to a culture than its publications.

NO GLOBAL MEDIA NETWORK

Because we see Sky Channel, Super Channel, and CNN—especially since Peter Arnett's coverage of the Gulf War—more often in travels around the world, it's tempting to assume that leaders must address a media world made up of global monoliths. That's not the case.

Rupert Murdoch has a real handle on global communications. Murdoch owns the Fox TV network, Twentieth Century Fox, *TV Guide*, the *South China Morning Post* in Hong Kong, the *Times* in London, and Sky Channel, a network that reaches throughout Europe. You would expect Murdoch to be absolutely sold on globalism, but he isn't. He has some important reservations.

In a *Forbes* interview in 1989, Murdoch said, for example, that "there is no such thing as a 'global village.' Most media are rooted in their national and local cultures." As to magazines, he said he didn't "see any global audiences for magazines" at this time.[4]

As Murdoch suggests, one has to be careful about assuming that the media have a global structure. When a story is presented to Reuters in Vienna, it is different from pitching Reuters in New York. The same press release may be interpreted quite differently by the *Times* of London and the *Boston Herald*, even though they are both Murdoch papers. Although we are seeing great global media companies emerge, no systematic editorial umbrella surrounds each of these firms.

Some business publications are trying for the "global" view. Perhaps, the most successful are the *Economist* and the *Financial Times*. When the newsletter *TJFR* (The Journalist and Financial Reporting) interviewed Rupert Pennant-Rea, the editor of the *Economist*, Pennant-Rea offered substantial insight regarding the reasons that the *Economist* is ahead of almost everyone. He said that "business life is becoming international. I don't see how any business publication can take a parochial view, by which I mean segmenting its coverage in purely national units."[5]

Most business writing is still segmented in that way. Little is written from the viewpoint of the global business reader. Although the *Economist* strives to find the global context, it also, in my opinion, is astute in the way that it projects purely national events in that context. It carries articles about the American educational system that compare it with other systems in the world and relate it to global economic competitiveness. It also reports on medical research studies in Colombia and Gambia because it knows these findings will be of interest to drug makers in Switzerland and Canada.

GLOBAL EXPOSURE

While no organized global network for information now exists, leaders have to assume that local talk has global exposure. This is a threat more than an opportunity, and a force against which leaders should protect themselves and their organization.

We call this axiom "Local talk can lead to global risk." Consider the tiff that the Sony chairman Akio Morita and Shintaro Ishihara ignited with their paper (and later book), "The Japan That Can Say No!" Published only in Japanese for a Japanese audience, bootleg translations became a Capitol Hill best seller within days of the document's appearance in Japan. In no time at all, controversy erupted across the media worldwide. While opinion leaders in the United States appreciated Morita's insights, Morita himself chose to remove his name from the American edition.

The global exposure facing most leaders will have far more mundane roots. In a growing number of cases, what the local plant manager in Cairo says to the trade press in Egypt may well end up in the hands of a Wall Street financial analyst or a union steward in Cleveland. In Yokohama, Japanese managers will decry the educational levels they find in lower-income neighborhoods of U.S. cities and, the next day, find their descriptions characterized as racist by newspapers in Chicago and Miami. Leaders must dramatize this reality to their worldwide management teams and must understand transnational impacts before they talk locally.

GLOBAL POWER CENTERS

Kenichi Ohmae, who heads up McKinsey's practice in Japan, has written an insightful book called *The Borderless World*. In one provocative chapter titled "The Equidistant Manager," Ohmae writes: "Even in companies that have operated internationally for years, most managers are nearsighted. Although their competitive landscape often stretches to a global horizon, they see best what they know best: the customers geographically closest to home . . . words like 'overseas,' 'subsidiaries,' and 'affiliates' are used to distinguish their home operation . . . a symptom seldom observed in a truly global firm."[6] Even in the finest companies, I would question if such an advanced transnational outlook still exists.

No matter where "headquarters" may be, power in organizations will always gravitate to the site of the most powerful division, and leaders know well the truth of how power and influence are positioned. Oftentimes, real power will not be in headquarters but in the dominant world market. Thomas Stewart wrote once in *Fortune*, "When it comes to power, the bottom line is the bottom line." In that article, Heinz CEO Tony O'Reilly makes a good point about the reality of power within the global business. Twenty-five years ago, 85 percent of Heinz's profits came from their U.K. subsidiary. Back then, Heinz's power base was in the United Kingdom. As O'Reilly put it, "The authority that flows from performance—which is real power—vested itself automatically in the English company."[7]

"THINK GLOBALLY, ACT LOCALLY": A TREACHEROUS THOUGHT

That prescription, which every leader today has heard before, perhaps countless times, simplifies a complicated problem, doesn't it? The maxim has some fundamental truth, but too often it is used by international business leaders to justify a universal program that is unjustified.

The "think globally, act locally" marching orders, taken alone, can be dangerous and can get leaders into considerable trouble. Too many of them think that if they "get it right" globally, the rest is inconsequential. As the Unilever CEO, Michael Angus, said at a Conference Board symposium: "Ineffectiveness in dealing with . . . local problems can easily swamp all the advantages that one gets from global economies."[8]

Globalization is not a universal blessing. There are multiple agendas at work in any global business. As a general rule, globalization is a great thing for headquarters managers because it seems to simplify the process of program development and central monitoring. For local managers, globalization is just as often an intrusion. Certainly, the local managers read the articles of Harvard guru Ted Levitt on the gospel of globalization, and they have been taught the inevitability of global business. When everyone is done singing Beethoven's Ninth Symphony and celebrating world brotherhood, however, the fact remains that globalization is often a pain in the neck for local managers, because they generally have less control, less initiative, and less autonomy.

You should empathize with your managers abroad, making sure that central programs are not sent out with arrogant directives that seem to say: "Here, localize this for us!" This is as true for strategic plans and vision statements as it is for marketing programs and internal communications. Even when it's not done heavy-handedly, many businesses fail to research local conditions carefully enough. In many cases, the weight of individual, local objections can overwhelm a seemingly brilliant global idea.

One global food company I know was determined to mount a program on global nutrition. That goal sounds high-minded, but think about it. How can this be done? Some countries are fighting for more calories; others are struggling to cut calories back. Some are striving for more meat proteins, others are stanching the flow of cholesterol. Product labeling standards worldwide are a bewildering maze. Even product labeling standards among the U.S. states have become so hopelessly complicated that manufacturers are today pleading with Washington to be federally regulated so that they face just one standard.

This firm thought they were launching a harmless global initiative, but food and nutrition are, in fact, part of ingrained cultural customs stretching back for centuries. Ultimately, the company dumped the global nutrition program. The firm now looks at nutrition as a stage on a continuum that factors in culture, economic development, and geography. Nutrition is still an important theme. In each country, however, the nutrition issue is tackled so differently that you could hardly call it a global program. Their experience points out the homework you must do: If you want to avoid bad central decisions about global communication, or anything else, you must get into the heads of local managers. It was the local managers who presented the sound, contrary evidence in the case of the food company, evidence that reshaped the direction of the program.

Some headquarters managers are convinced that remote market managers are just bred to be obstinate. The man in Caracas or the woman in Brisbane is trying only to make life difficult for the central staff, they think. In fact, headquarters is much more likely to be making life difficult for them. If you're from headquarters, ask local managers for their reasoning on issues. Have them help you by monitoring information and trends in their local communities. Similarly, if you're in the field, recognize the enormous number of cultural factors a headquarters manager must keep in mind and how easy it is to overlook any one detail.

Not long ago, futurists were projecting a melting-pot world, mostly speaking English, chowing down convenience food, and sporting Walkmans and Nikes. Now that landscape is not as certain as before. Plenty of bruised marketers have learned that "acting locally" is not simply a matter of respecting a few quaint customs. "Acting locally" is considerably more than just "fine-tuning."

This again is where leaders can help by being alert to the big trends. In their book, *Megatrends 2000*, John Naisbitt and Patricia Aburdene point out, to cite an instance of a counter-global trend, how vehement some of the emerging national movements are. For example, Quebec's Bill 101 demands that French be spoken at work. The province has even created "language police" to enforce this. "When two employees of a fast-food restaurant were overheard speaking English, the government sent undercover agents to investigate possible violation of the French-at-work law," the *Megatrends 2000* book reports.[9] By 1992, Quebec may secede if it isn't given "exclusive jurisdiction over 22 areas, including environment, education and language" as recorded in the Allaire report and as reported in *Maclean's* magazine.[10]

Comparable attitudes are emerging throughout the world. Estonians are busily tearing down expressway signs printed in Russian. Belgium continues to simmer in conflicts between Flemish- and French-speaking citizens. Singapore, strongly committed to Mandarin as a national language, is curtailing the use of English. There is no clear consensus that the world is homogenizing. In fact, if you look at Moldavia, Silesia, Croatia, and Azerbaijan, it looks as though the world is going in the opposite direction.

Another weakness in the "think globally, act locally" formula is that it makes the global role sound lofty. *Global* is big-picture and heady. *Local* may be important, but it's just arms and legs. That's misleading. Surely, we are dealing with a world economy; an economy with transnational dimensions, however, doesn't mean we have global values. A great deal of thinking must happen on the local level for the arms and legs to work. When top managers emphasize the "think-global" theme, I have noticed that many managers around the world translate it to "think headquarters" or "think American."

Part of the confusion comes from world financial markets, which should not be mistaken for the local market for products and services. As Peter Drucker puts it: "Everybody talks about the 'world economy.' It is indeed a new reality. But it is quite different from what most people—businessmen, economists, politicians—mean by the term." On the financial side, Drucker describes the "almost autonomous world economy of money, credit and investment flows . . . organized by information [and] no longer [knowing] national boundaries."[11] Products and services move in a way different from that of the financial markets, and as any leader soon discovers, ideas, products, and services move far less fluidly across borders than money does.

DEVELOPING THE LOCAL MARKETS

Rather than thinking globally, managers invest time more wisely, in my opinion, by examining the markets with the best-developed competition in a particular product or product line. On this theme, I recommend a *Harvard Business Review* article by Kamran Kashani titled "Beware the Pitfalls of Global Marketing." It richly illustrates how global marketing programs can go astray. Kashani concludes that "the way global decisions are conceptualized, refined, internally communicated, and, finally, implemented in the company's international network have a great deal to do with their performance."[12]

Kashani assails "managerial complacency toward use of market information" and "overstandardization." He talks about the costly "absence of a communication channel for sharing and building on subsidiary experiences." He tells a great tale about how Lego Toys, based in Denmark, initially refused to sell its toys in buckets in the United States, preferring its traditional prestige packaging. Typically American parents, and as it turned out, most parents, like buckets for picking up and storing the toys. Without buckets, Lego lost important share to competitors. Two years later, Lego went to buckets and now Lego uses them for its toys, not just in the United States but worldwide, with great success.

One observer cited in the article attributed Lego's sluggish response to their global marketers operating on automatic pilot. I don't know, but it *is* evident that one local market can set standards for other markets. For many products, there's much to be said for a "lead-market" approach, which, again, is very different from purely local action.

The Lego example points out what you learn when implementing a plan. Global business is waged in the trenches, not cooked up as some centralized dream. Too many people visualize the epitome of global marketing as some slick New York ad shop, putting together a 30-second spot that will strike "the responsive chord" in people in 160 nations without a single change in image, without a word of translation. It just doesn't work that way. Still, some firms spend enormous sums trying to identify *the one right way.* Trying to capture each market by pursuing its individual characteristics is far more sensible.

Moreover, because a brand has global presence doesn't mean the product in the package is universal. Preston Townley, head of the Conference Board, has pointed out: "If you want to taste every single variety of pea soup sold by Knorr across the world, you had better set aside a full day. . . . Fanta orange drink tastes tart in Italy, but sweet in Germany."[13]

LUXURY'S SINGLE LOOK

There are exceptions to the mandate to tailor products locally, notably in what I call "standardized luxury" products. If you want to see a real-world catalog of standardized luxury, look at the shelves of the duty-free shops in airports around the world. These are the brands that everyone who can afford luxury goods knows the world over. It's important for leaders to understand the symbolism of such luxury, since giving these goods as gifts, for example, is often the way in which leaders are shown respect and the way in which they show respect to others.

Understanding this international "luxury standard," many manufacturers of luxury goods try to impart a single standardized look worldwide. While basic consumables must be sharply tailored to local market tastes, it's important for many luxury products to have a single, albeit a cosmopolitan, look. The cosmetics giant Estée Lauder yields a good example of that: Up until 1989, the face for Estée Lauder advertising was the American model Willow Bay. Lauder CEO Leonard Lauder explains why Lauder switched models: "[S]he's an all-American girl and half our business is now overseas. She looked so American that we were losing out competitively in France, Germany and elsewhere."[14]

Lauder replaced Bay with the Czech model Paulina Porizkova, who starred on two consecutive covers of the *Sports Illustrated* swimsuit issue. Her look is considered more "international." In general, luxury products in the up-market have to create consistent images worldwide. The Lauder look is one example, the Gucci bag, another. These products and images have considerable global consistency.

BEYOND LUXURY

Global luxury brands also represent safe decisions. Take something as simple as a gift one international leader gives another—for example, a Cross Pen—a gift intended to make a positive impression. At a higher price tag and to make a deeper impression, a leader may choose to give a Mont Blanc fountain pen, which is a beautiful pen but a conventional expression of taste, at least in the world of luxury.

For a unique impression, a leader must transcend the statement of "conventional" luxury: For example, to commemorate the visit of two distinguished financial analysts to its offices in New York, a senior manager of a leading investment firm gave each of the visitors, both of whom spoke English fluently, a multivolume boxed set of U.S. economic history. He also arranged for the books to be shipped to Japan. This gift sent a message that eclipsed the standardized "luxury" gifts now so commonplace in upper management.

When entertaining foreign visitors, I know firms that will buy a fine vintage of Chateau Margaux or exquisite Scottish salmon or Maryland crab. These items make an impression surely, but they convey that the firm is engaging in "safe statements." On the other hand, I have seen firms go beyond the luxury idiom, serving truly local fare, but displaying a flag of the visiting dignitary's nation along side the American flag in the lobby. In my opinion, the latter statement is the more evocative and memorable one. Caution: If you make a mistake, it can also be memorable beyond your expectations. I once welcomed a guest from Italy with flags from Ireland. Their flags are nearly identical, except the last panel of the Italian flag is red, not orange. The polite smiles left no doubt that my faux pas would not be soon forgotten.

GLOBAL AWARENESS

How does a leader begin to understand all the complexities of transnational leadership—this global backdrop of nations and niches within nations? There is no substitute for direct personal experience. If you don't actually peek inside a family refrigerator in France, you won't know how important fruit juices are as a beverage for French children. If you don't see the size of a German refrigerator, generally pretty small, you won't understand why certain package sizes won't work in Germany or why ultra-high-heat preserved milk, which requires no refrigeration, is so popular.

Sometimes you need to initiate some international detective work. Jim Manzi, the CEO of Lotus, gave me some valuable insights into what may have slowed the initial market acceptance of personal computing in Japan. Jim and his people went over and studied the workings of Japanese offices to discover ways they could spur acceptance of PCs in this critical world market. Pretty quickly, two things became apparent. First, Japanese office space is much smaller per employee than that of the United States. Personal computer workstations are not feasible. High-powered laptops, however, could function as PCs, and that alternative is working successfully today.

Second, workers in Japanese offices sit close to one another. Part of the Japanese culture is that workers have a strong professional pride and are embarrassed to make mistakes in front of others. The software being used in Japan "beeped," as it does in the States, when the user made a mistake. This sound caused a loss of face with co-workers. Lotus's simple solution was to de-program the beep.

Would a checklist ever have caught the peculiarities of Japanese office space or the "beeping" problem? Most likely not. Not even a sophisticated local market analyst could have explained the problem, without a detailed cultural background, to headquarters in Massachusetts. The most effective way to penetrate global issues is for a leader to experience them directly. Experience abroad will obviously not give you all the answers, but it will suggest the right kind of questions to ask.

THE GROWING IMPORTANCE OF GLOBAL ALLIANCES

Leaders should not assume that they or their organizations should try to be global forces just by using their own resources. Too many companies believe "thinking globally" means "thinking globally all by yourself." Ironically, the biggest companies understand their own limitations better than some of their smaller counterparts do, but a growing number of large companies are joining forces with partners in other countries. We have recently seen giants mate, and the biggest cross-border deals are yet to come. Renault and Volvo are teaming up, as are Mitsubishi and Daimler-Benz. We are seeing mergers, partnerships, restructurings, joint ventures and other kinds of collaborations that go beyond traditional formats. We will see deals we once considered scarcely possible.

In the auto industry, Ford's new Escort was engineered by Japan's Mazda.[15] Ford is also using Japanese robots and engineering as the best way to reach its own domestic market in the United States. That practice is hardly "acting local." In this case, Ford is using global resources to enhance its position and is behaving like a leader, leveraging its strengths and shoring up its limitations.

Networks are multiplying between the United States and Europe, too. The Dutch electronics giant N.V. Philips wanted to secure a powerful position for itself in the appliance business in the Common Market. They are determined to create that position in advance of the 1992 market integration. Philips had a few smaller brands in the highly fragmented market of European appliances, but no real dominance. Whirlpool, the American appliance giant, had a powerful market position and expertise in the United States but not in Europe. In 1988 Philips and Whirlpool concluded a joint venture that will put the Philips Whirlpool brand in households all over Europe. Adding in the new market economies of the former Warsaw Pact nations yields an appliance market of four hundred million people in the various national markets!

The important point is that Whirlpool didn't merely decide to "go global." Hitching up with Philips gave Whirlpool an established distribution system, decades of marketing experience, and an association with a highly respected European brand. On its side, Whirlpool connected with massive regional power to put forward its global interest. Philips's former CEO Wisse Dekker sums it up well when he says: "There are no second chances for companies that fail to win a share of the world market quickly."[16]

Communicating positively about global partnerships may require a change of attitude. There are still plenty of old-style, ham-fisted decision makers who like to boast, "We will do it by ourselves, by golly!" Pure self-reliance, even the laudable Korean self-reliance mentioned earlier, is giving way to an enlightened cooperation between the world's leading firms. When Philips aligned itself with Whirlpool these companies celebrated their arrangements both within the organizations and with the press and vendors.

The decision to marry wisely is a sign of strength. It is an arrangement that must be carefully explained throughout a global organization. Leaders, at all levels in a company, should be able to describe how these partnerships work and how they earn valuable respect from the world financial community.

VISIBLE TRANSNATIONALISM

A leader can encourage an organization to think transnationally by setting standards for transnational behavior and attitudes. Healthy transnational organizations, led by internationally oriented executives such as Rainer Gut at Crédit Suisse, Jack Hennessy at CS First Boston, Bob Greenhill and Dick Fisher at Morgan Stanley, or Dick Mahoney at Monsanto, adopt the following measures:

- Welcome input and recommendations from international subsidiaries with the same enthusiasm as if the ideas were to come from Zurich, New York, or St. Louis.

- Move managers through international assignments early in their careers.

- Visit international locations often and insist that those visits be rigorous, not just dress review of the troops.

- Teach their organizations the importance of adjusting products and communications to match the tastes and characteristics of local markets.

- Create a strategic awareness that focuses on meaningful competition, wherever it may be.

THE CANON OF THE
COMMUNICATIONS
LANDSCAPE
Conclusion to Part II

LEADERSHIP MUST ACHIEVE GOALS IN A COMMUNICATIONS REALITY that is fragmented, cluttered, and high-speed—a reality that's becoming increasingly transnational.

DIVERSITY

Leaders must be able to pinpoint messages in a diverse and highly fragmented landscape of viewpoints and values. They must also be able to differentiate between those issues requiring the consent of individual niches versus the strategic goals requiring a thoughtful consensus among several parties or groups.

The leader must recognize that each person is a composite of different subgroups and that these multiple "memberships" have an impact on their viewpoint and their loyalty. Leaders must be astute in tailoring their communications, listening to various groups in different ways, and addressing effectively the concerns of particular groups.

CLUTTER

Leaders recognize the pervasiveness of clutter. They focus themselves on cultivating loyal core supporters and transcend clutter with proper emotional appeals. They learn how to make positive messages graphic so that those messages will rise clearly above the clutter. Leaders must also understand how to use clutter as a shield in difficult times.

Since clarity is pivotal in overcoming clutter, the individual leader will wisely rely on a single, principal communications adviser. To ensure that messages register clearly, the leader uses effective feedback loops.

SPEED OF EVENTS

Because events happen so quickly today, leaders recognize that they must write first on the slate of public opinion. Before taking any major strategic steps, a leader will also analyze the attitudes of key sectors and act on the trends of mounting opinion before they are forced to.

Leaders manage crises in the context of their phases. Leaders also isolate problems quickly and use advance communications to "beat the clock" governing public opinion. The most effective leaders also pursue with great urgency and fervor the opportunities that crises may present.

THE TRANSNATIONAL CONTEXT

Leaders know that all organizations must increasingly act in a global context. They are also perceptive enough, however, to speak to each country and region in a way that is uniquely local.

Smart leaders don't make "headquarters" a mental Rome, a geographical command center for the organization's thinking. Rather, they foster global awareness, letting dominant local markets lead in each of the organization's businesses and implementing transnational strategy market by market.

Although they avoid such oversimplifications as "think globally, act locally," they also recognize that local media throughout the world now have global access.

Finally, leaders look for ways to leverage the organization's strengths through international partnerships and set an example by acting in ways that encourage global openness and effectiveness throughout the organization.

III

THE
COMMUNICATOR'S
TEMPLATE

There is a powerful drawing that depicts God operating a compass to design the universe. Part of the drawing's impact for me comes from the reality that leaders must use resources to realize a vision. You can't just *think* a plan into reality.

There are different views regarding what belongs in a leader's tool kit. Some think it should have a carrot—and a stick. Others believe leaders must work with smoke and mirrors. Still others feel that computers and yardsticks are needed to obtain the most precise possible measurement of results.

For me, the tools of leadership are more generic; and they all have to do with communications. In my view, the four most important tools are:

1. Information about issues and trends

2. Intelligence and research

3. The formulation of agendas and plans

4. The proper use of advice and staffwork.

Taken together, these four tools form what I call the "communicator's template," which you could consider a "leader's template" as well. Before examining each aspect of the template in more detail, let me share with you a story in which the use of these tools played a particularly important role.

In January 1984, a prominent Chicago CEO was asked to join the board of directors of Continental Bank. At the time, I headed Hill and Knowlton's U.S. operations out of Chicago, and so I ran the largest public affairs shop in the city. The CEO called me for advice. Should he accept? As I normally do, I conducted a series of "soft soundings": confidential conversations with opinion leaders, who are asked to assess an individual or a company without necessarily knowing the reason why. I called up bankers, senior government officials, journalists, and analysts and asked them for their opinion of Continental.

The responses were forthright. My sources characterized Continental, then the largest bank in Chicago and the eighth largest in the nation, as "aggressive" and "freewheeling." They pointed out that Continental was a major buyer of energy loans from the ill-fated Penn Square Bank, but felt that Continental seemed to be withstanding that mistake. They spoke unenthusiastically about top management, however. Again and again, one word was used: "arrogant." I duly reported my findings back to the director candidate, who ended up turning the offer down.

In the months that followed, other events brought me into contact with Continental in a different way; indeed, the company became for several long weeks the center of my professional life. The Continental Bank building lies in the heart of Chicago's Loop, forming a triangle with the Federal Reserve Bank and the Chicago Board of Trade building at the intersection of LaSalle and Jackson Streets. The geography of that intersection hardly seemed coincidental, for both the Fed and the CBOT, the largest commodity market in the world, were fated to factor in the crisis that struck Continental during those weeks. At the height of the crisis, armed guards literally stevedored bailout money from the Federal Reserve Bank across LaSalle street to the Continental so that Continental could cover its daily transactions.

The Continental crisis was the first piece of dramatic proof that we had entered the age of the 24-hour global financial market. On Wednesday, May 9, 1984, Jiji news service, the Reuters affiliate in Japan, broke a story that Continental might be facing insolvency. Because of the source, the Japanese banks had an initial leg up. According to James McCollom, "the Japanese banks—others too, but mainly the Japanese—had withheld a billion dollars in CD renewals."[1] At The Sign of the Trader, a financial district watering hole, a rumor erupted that a CBOT clearinghouse officer had pulled $50 million off deposit at the Continental. Major European and U.S. banks started yanking deposits too. By Sunday, news of the impending crisis had reached the general public. The syndicated news program "The McLaughlin Report" featured speculation about a possible Continental collapse. The run on Continental turned into a gallop. On Friday, before the Sunday broadcast, the bank had lost $3.5 billion in overnight deposits.[2] For perspective, consider that the largest previous bank run in U.S. history had been the $1.5+ billion drain on Franklin National Bank.

At one point Continental stood to default about a billion dollars. This might seem a piddling sum compared to the $400 billion bailout facing the savings and loan industry today, not to mention other bank problems since. At the time, however, it loomed as the worst threat to the banking system since the Great Depression. Until Continental, the public and most of the experts had thought of the banking system as a Rock of Gibraltar: now, they weren't sure. Continental was primarily a commercial bank, and commercial accounts were its lifeblood. When the industrial community voted no confidence, the ensuing run on deposits resulted in the largest bank failure the United States had ever witnessed. By July, Continental had in effect been "nationalized"— taken over by the FDIC.

Arrogance had a lot to do with Continental's plight. It caused the bank's management to ignore issues and trends, intelligence and research. It caused them to formulate superficial plans and to reject advice from leaders in the banking industry and the Chicago business community. When Continental became a client of Hill and Knowlton in July 1984, employees told me that the bank had virtually no internal communications. Top managers disdained talking to their people.

In addition, while the members of Continental's hot-shot loan department may have painted themselves as the superstars of banking, the regulators in Washington were enraged over the bank's fast and loose loan tactics. The *Wall Street Journal* caricatured the top energy lender at Penn Square as a man "known to wear Mickey Mouse ears and drink beer from his boot."[3] Chrysler president Lee Iacocca remarked in a speech at the Chicago Economic Club that had he known how easy it was to get money from Continental, he would have gone there for a bailout instead of to the federal government.

When Continental finally tumbled, people were waiting in line to pummel the fallen giant. One banker confided to me a sentiment widely held in financial circles. "This Continental situation is a terrible affair," he said, and then he added wryly, "It couldn't have happened to a more deserving bank." Employees, hungry for news, took to inventing their own. The destructive leaks and misinformation that resulted only hurt the bank further.

Until my colleagues and I worked with the bank, Continental had never solicited outside communications counsel. Unfortunately, the top management lacked the communications skills that might have enabled them to do without such advice. And their overconfident management team had no knack for the skillful use of power. Taken together, these factors had led to the unseemly undoing of a major money center bank. Things had to change, and the appointment of new management was the first signal. (Offices were set up for the former top management in a remote wing of the bank, christened by one wag as "Sleepy Hollow.")

The new CEO, David Taylor, who has since gone on to a remarkably sucessful career in the London office of Chemical Banking Corporation, knew he would probably serve only for an interim period. Taylor was a different kind of manager from the top executives who ran Continental during the go-go years. He and his president and chief operating officer, Ed Bottum, were long-time bank employees. Coming from the trading division, they were untainted by the energy loan scandal. On the urging of several outside directors, Taylor and Bottum decided they needed outside professional help to save the bank's reputation.

Gene Croissant, the administrative head who worked for Taylor, and who is now one of the top executives at RJR Nabisco, called me up and invited us to a preliminary discussion at the bank. At 6:00 P.M. on July 12, 1984, I went with four colleagues to one of the bank's private dining rooms. We dined on beer and salami sandwiches in a setting once known for haute cuisine. The bank was beginning to adjust its attitude.

This was my first real encounter with Taylor, and he impressed me with his levelheadedness. He explained that he was headed to Washington the next day to discuss the bank's rescue plan with William Isaac, then head of the FDIC. Taylor said he wanted a communications strategy to support the plan. (It later became our view that individuals inside Isaac's organization had used selective leaks, which contributed to the horror headlines that drove depositors away.) After listening to Taylor's plan, we talked about what it meant for communications. We discussed both Continental's current results and their longer-term problems. They were expecting, it was now clear, to lose a billion dollars in their second quarter.

Less than two days later our counseling team laid out a proposed communications plan for Continental:

1. To restore confidence, the bank had to regain control over the information being released about it. It had ceased to be a credible source; its official releases were written in "legalese" and usually came out after an unofficial channel had already sprung the news. For the "real story" on the bank, the public and the papers were relying on leaks and innuendoes from employees. We knew we couldn't restore Continental's external communications credibility fast enough to make a difference. Instead, we decided to prune the grapevine—to equip it with accurate information and begin using it to our advantage. Any internal communication in the bank would now be written with the assumption that it would be leaked to the press. In this way, we began feeding the grapevine a steady flow of credible, candid information. Since the public was only believing "inside" information about the bank, we made "inside" info the same as outside.

2. Since no one believed what the bank was saying, we had to tighten up the credibility standard for anything that went out on bank letterhead. Thus, from now on, whenever we showed a press release or a background paper to Taylor, he would always ask, "Does it pass the chuckle test?" By that, he meant: Will people just laugh into their sleeve when we send out this serious communication, or will they believe us?

3. We would get all the remaining bad news out fast. In the next three weeks, we knew we would be announcing the bailout plan. At the same time, we would also drop a strong hint about the upcoming earnings problem. We wanted to be candid about the bad news, but we wanted to minimize the number of bad-news moments.

4. We would separate the "good bank" from the "bad bank." As much as possible, we would isolate the energy loan problem and all other problems that could legitimately be made separate, and

then pin those problems on people who were no longer with the bank. After all, their lapses *had* brought about the trouble.

The plan was implemented in an aggressive way. It turned out that the outside directors, two years earlier, had commissioned a prestigous Chicago law firm to study Continental's problems and prepare a confidential report. We urged the bank to release this report, for it would show that Continental had recognized its own problems early and had begun taking action. Releasing the report would also demonstrate the bank's willingness to share information with the public.

Once we had printed copies of the report, we made them available at commuter rail stations frequented by the wealthy and powerful of Chicago. The reports were stacked up like a community newspaper. Judging by the rapt attention of the readers, however, it was as if we had just published the memoirs of the Happy Hooker. Walking down the aisles of the commuter trains that morning, all you could see were people reading the report. The tactic opened eyes to the change in management attitude that was taking place at Continental.

On July 26, we engineered a series of satellite broadcast communications that ushered in the new Continental. We knew that Isaac would be announcing the FDIC rescue plan in a news conference in Washington. A government official in Isaac's position might easily seize the opportunity to attack Continental, especially if he felt he was talking to the nation in general. After George Glazer, Hill and Knowltown's electronic media whiz, had diagnosed the situation, we arranged to have Isaac's press conference viewed in-house at Continental.

We lit up Continental like a Christmas tree, putting video monitors everywhere. We made sure the local Chicago press was invited into the bank to see the reaction of the employees to Isaac's message. We knew that they would be there with action cams and mikes to capture the employees' responses. Suddenly Isaac had to contend with a whole new constituency of 13,000 riveted Continental employees. This may well have had a leavening effect on his comments. Isaac's remarks were followed in direct succession by a Taylor-Bottum press conference and the introduction of John Swearingen, the former chairman of Standard Oil of Indiana, as the new CEO of Continental.

It was at that point that the crisis began to pass. Continental successfully made a transition in its leadership and is today, under Tom Theobald, a different and far more successful bank. Fundamental changes in banking practices helped secure the changes, but it was a basic adjustment in the management of communications that allowed the leadership changes to take place. By respecting the grapevine, by making credible inside information the source point for outside information, by forcing communications staffwork to pass the "chuckle test," and by disarming the regulators so they couldn't make Continental an object lesson, Continental regained its footing with the safety rope of communications.

The Continental experience is a modern classic of a business problem that more and more leaders will experience—a crisis set into motion by a gap between external and internal realities, a crisis that can only be resolved through the skillful use of communications tools. The next four chapters outline how leaders can use the communications tools available to them not just to stay out of trouble but to seize opportunities as well.

CHAPTER

10

SEEING
AROUND CORNERS
Unearthing
Issues and Trends

INFORMATION IS ALL AROUND US. MORE AND MORE, IT HAS AN IMPACT on every kind of organization, and moves with accelerating speed. Organizations will often manage the internal flow of information from their data processing systems with huge staffs and considerable investment. External information—the kind gleaned from newspapers, magazines, newsletters, television reports, and casual conversations with people who have expert insight—is rarely treated with much seriousness. But this is exactly the type of information upon which the Japanese, for one, rely heavily in charting their strategic course. And it is this kind of information that is the focus of this chapter.

The effective use of external (or "soft") information is no passive exercise. Mastering information is the first and one of the most formidable communications tools available to the leader. Leaders are responsible for seeing that relevant information is gathered and analyzed. Most of all, they must place external information into a context for the organization and show their people how the achievement of their goals is connected to relevant external events.

I recall one CEO who visited the People's Republic of China just after that country opened its doors. Upon returning, he pulled all of

THINKPOINTS
on How Leaders
Make Information Actionable

☐ Guide the tracking of external information.

☐ Create connections between goals and external events.

☐ Foreshadow events to help realize goals.

☐ Dispel groundless accusations early.

☐ Consume media intelligently.

☐ Take public rankings seriously.

☐ Read and see *for* the organization.

☐ Scan entertainment and humor for emerging issues.

☐ Sift shreds of data to identify new megaforces.

☐ Constantly weed out old—and new—preconceptions.

---

his people into a room and briefed them on China. I happened to be in the building on a client visit and was asked to attend. The CEO talked about the greasy food, the people on bicycles, the Great Wall, and the armies of bureaucrats in government ministries. At first, his account appeared to be no more than an interesting travelogue. The officers gathered in the room began to wonder what these verbal reminiscences meant. You could see it in their puzzled faces. "Why are we being told this?" they were asking themselves.

As the meeting dragged on, I made the casual suggestion to the CEO that he write to all his company's customers, explaining and interpreting what he had experienced. That seemed to register; the group began to discuss how the findings of the CEO's trip related to customers. The information now had a purpose, a context. It became a way of furthering an agenda and took on a viewpoint. You could tell that the group was both relieved and energized with this connection now in hand.

More leaders need to learn to play the interpretive role well. During the recent wave of mergers and acquisitions on Wall Street, the leaders of corporate America did a poor job overall of interpreting the meaning of those events to rank-and-file employees within their firms. When employees saw evening news stories about mergers and acquisitions leading to the loss of jobs and livelihoods, they would have benefited had managers taken the initiative to explain those events. Managers could have done a great deal, from talking about the broad issues of U.S. competitiveness to preparing workers for organizational changes that would take place within their own businesses. Most, however, ducked the issues, and some seemed only to surface as the benefactors in lush leveraged buyout schemes. This failure to foreshadow events served to tarnish management credibility and to amplify the lack of trust between organizations and their leaders.

Recognizing the critical role leaders play in interpreting and using external information, this chapter outlines how leaders should view information as a communications tool.

FORESHADOWING EVENTS

Although leaders are rarely prophets, they can often foreshadow events—especially positive events and initiatives—for their organizations. Since leaders control budgets and plans, it should be no surprise that they can exert this kind of positive influence; however, too many leaders allow direction to trickle down into the organization in a haphazard way. Especially where topics on the public agenda are concerned, leaders rarely assert themselves and give information the proper shape and direction.

Before the year began, Monsanto CEO Dick Mahoney identified five broad issues that he thought would be important in 1990. These included chemical wastes in the environment, genetic additives and the milk supply, and the changing face of distribution in the international chemical industry. After digesting, screening, and analyzing a wide range of information, Mahoney and his staff had converged on these particular themes. Why?

First, the issues were high on the agendas of opinion leaders and major public segments important to Monsanto. And second, the issues were wrapped up with marketing and product initiatives that Monsanto was pursuing. Through speeches, articles, and videotapes, Mahoney and his team schooled the Monsanto organization in the public affairs priorities facing the company. This helped people in the Monsanto organization interpret newspaper articles and news broadcasts they saw in an intelligent way. As a result of Mahoney's foreshadowing, Monsanto had a very clear direction for the year—not only operationally, but in the way that its people combed through and digested information on their own.

Issue identification can prevent problems and wasted dollars in marketing programs. A soap manufacturer doesn't want to spend half of a 30-second commercial talking about the recyclability of their packages, but the company may have to if a lack of research into public sentiment marks the manufacturer as environmentally insensitive. With enough of an early warning, a detergent manufacturer can create an information program based not on smoke and mirrors but on tangible evidence that it is fulfilling all its commitments to environmentally sound packaging.

A smart manufacturer will not only take positive actions but will hold press conferences in the news or environmental arena to address those issues, enabling it to devote more of its marketing program to selling its cleaning power or convenience. The great packaged goods firms are masters of this concept, as proven by their ability to liberate a large percentage of their high-cost marketing dollars for use on direct selling of product attributes. Such firms are running parallel track campaigns.

Organizations must be able to see around corners—to effectively analyze the flow of information surrounding them, interpret that flow, foreshadow how the company will be a part of the information itself, and, finally, become part of the news in a positive way that enhances their agendas. This thoughtful, systematic approach to information happens only in organizations where the leaders take an active hand. Leaders must ask such questions as, "What on the political agenda or the news beat could prevent the cash registers from ringing, or would force us to close our doors this year?" and "What are the issues which will help us sell more and expand our business?" In conducting this review, leaders should pay special attention to loose accusations reverberating through the marketplace, no matter how groundless or capricious the claims may appear.

ACCUSATIONS TRIGGERING ACTION

When the EPA banned phosphates and nitrates in laundry detergents back in the early seventies, laundry detergents became a key target of governmental regulation. The entire scenario was brought about by the detergent industry's failure to take the accusations of environmentalists seriously enough. Detergents were presumed to be a major cause of environmental pollution; in fact, they were not. Independent scientists retained by the detergent industry ultimately proved to the regulators' satisfaction that groundwater pollution from nitrates and phosphates resulted almost solely from the use of chemical fertilizers in agriculture. The heaviest pollution stemmed from spillage of chemicals into the water supply as a result of farmland runoff.

Yet the industry was also forced to remind the public and the press why phosphates and nitrates had been used in detergents in the first place. The predecessor of these additives, lye, had caused many serious burns and disfigurements in children who had come in contact with detergents. At one time every laundry detergent had contained lye. The EPA rescinded the ban just a few months later. The entire disruption could have been avoided had the detergent industry been monitoring the information pulse of the country. The leaders of the industry would have seen much sooner that detergents were being set up to take the fall for nitrate and phosphate pollution.

THE LEADER'S MEDIA DIET

Because leaders must be able to see around corners, their media diet—the public information they take in to spot threats and opportunities—is very important. Just as all of us are eating more fiber and less cholesterol, more complex carbohydrates and fewer processed sugars, the media diet of leaders is changing.

To some extent, leaders can still rely on staples like the *Wall Street Journal, Business Week,* the *New York Times,* and *Fortune* to give them basic information. These general publications are continuously retooling the kind of coverage they offer as trends and issues change. Some media channels, however, are becoming significantly less or more important as information sea changes take place. Here is just a smattering of them.

HOW THE LEADER'S MEDIA NUTRITION CHART HAS CHANGED

1980s	1990s
General interest news magazines *(Time, U.S. News, Newsweek)*	Electronic news briefings (CNN, FNN, MacNeil-Lehrer)

Reason: Leaders need information faster and in a more concentrated way.

Business financial publications *(Institutional Investor, Trusts & Estates)*	People-centered business publications *(Harvard Business Review, Fortune)*

Reason: Workforce leadership is displacing aggressive financing as the number one business topic.

Local business pages (as reporters of national business news. Important to note: local business pages will be redoubling efforts on local news—leaving national news to others.)	Regional business journals, international business publications (such as the *Financial Times,* already one of the most influential publications in the United States)

Reason: More and more business news is being absorbed by electronic media; print media specialize in in-depth analysis, and few local newspapers can afford the staffs that would allow them to compete in the area with the *Wall Street Journal* and the *Financial Times.* The latter, in turn, have growing importance as sources for analysis of big-picture international events and trends.

The press is also becoming much more active in ranking the performance of leaders and organizations. More and more, leaders are getting marks similar to the approval ratings traditionally reserved for the President of the United States. Leaders will do well to read these polls and figure out why certain individuals and companies are approved or rebuked, because that will have a great deal to do with the consent or disapproval their own businesses face. Endorsements such as the *Good Housekeeping* Seal of Approval or a high ranking from *Consumer Reports* have had powerful effects in the consumption culture of the last several decades. *Fortune's* annual list of the Most Admired Corporations has effectively become the leadership standings for American companies. Companies directly mentioned are obviously conscious of the list, but other companies should be conscious of the values and standards this list implies. (As with the Oscars and Emmys, judging for the *Fortune* list falls to a jury of industry peers.)

A listing of quite a different sort is the "hit list" published in *Chemical Week,* a chemical industry trade journal. A 1988 survey, comparing chemical emissions for the leading companies with those of the previous year, has blossomed into an annual media event. Inadvertently, this report has become a "hit list" for environmentalists, who target those firms with the poorest improvement or no improvement over the preceding year. The *Chemical Week* standings can thus represent a frighteningly important force for many companies, for anyone familiar with emissions problems knows that controlling the last 1 or 2 percent of problems can cost many times that of mastering the first 98 percent of the problem.

More and more evaluation lists are affecting how organizations are run and what they aspire to do. Thoughtful leaders anticipate the effects of these lists, which represent an effort to quantify and standardize public and press evaluations of how organizations perform.

A USER'S MANUAL FOR THE MEDIA

Given the sheer volume of public information, it is extremely hard to pick out the trend information, lists, and early indicators that can have a bearing on the organization. To do so well requires discipline. Another analogy to sound diet and fitness comes to mind: If you go to a gym, the staff may not let you use the Nautilus equipment unless you have been trained on how to exercise with it. Similarly, leaders must be trained on how to read or absorb media; otherwise, they may waste valuable time or misinterpret the trends that are unfurling. The answer is not speed reading; it is a matter of approaching information with the right attitude.

Practice expanded thinking. If *Fortune* runs an article on how to manage manufacturing businesses in a recession, and you run an insurance business or a hospital, mentally edit the article, focusing on what is relevant and irrelevant to your area of specialization. If you read an article on marketing pitfalls when pursuing the aging consumer, convert the emphasis in your mind to the marketing opportunities in going after the same market segment. Leaders should be ingenious, unbridled readers, chiefly because they are reading more for concepts than for facts.

Learn the media diet of vital constituencies. If certain publications shape the thinking of key audiences outside your organization—such as suppliers or special interest adversaries—their reading lists should, in large measure, be your reading list if you are to track their moods and their priorities. One retailer I know religiously sets its buying plans according to the Conference Board's periodic economic forecasts. Any major supplier serving this company will get a good idea of the retailer's probable order levels just by tracking the Board's reports and projections.

Read for the organization. A leader with a broad media diet should read for the organization. *Inc.* reports that the famous Connecticut grocer Stew Leonard, having had marginal success in passing complete books out to subordinates for them to read, now outlines and summarizes each book that he reads, then passes his synopsis on to his management team.

Vary the inputs. Always relying on the same publications or broadcast programs can dull any mind to the vast variety of perspectives available. Keep varying the diet and, if you can, read foreign publications. A leader who doesn't speak a foreign language should periodically scan the British, Canadian, and/or Australian press. In the same *Inc.* article mentioned above, Tom Peters describes himself as a reading "garbage-man of the first order," because 90 percent of what he finds as interesting "comes from someplace other than where it's supposed to come from."

I believe that leaders should make a conscious effort to include unconventional reading sources in their diet. In recent months, for example, I learned:

- that Akron-Cleveland is one of the world's 25 most important centers for money management from a Global Money Map (from a report by Technimetrics, Inc.)[1]

- how junior high school students follow current events (from a study in the *Children's Express Quarterly*)[2]

- that America's investment in science will likely be a casualty of continuing federal budget deliberations (from a *Time Bureau Chiefs' Report* newsletter)[3]

- how Porsche understands the psychographic make up of its customers (from an article in the *Delaney Report*)[4]

- that a "new concept of men in the '90s" is emerging with the softer personal styles of a Kevin Costner or a Tom Selleck (from a report by Manwatchers, Inc.).[5] (The Oscars awarded to Costner's *Dances with Wolves* would seem to bear this out, as would an article in *Working Woman* magazine describing the "neo-male" of the nineties as "aggressive yet ethical, traditional yet adventurous, intimate yet independent.")[6]

Out of context, any one of these trends might seem an oddity. If the leader can piece together a mass of these directional tidbits, however, macro-trends of great significance to the organization's vision and goals will start to emerge.

MACRO-TRENDS

Few ad people think like Hal Handley, ad and marketing guru for Kraft in the sixties. He would say things like: "America's taste preference is becoming sweeter." He was literally following the trends of what people tasted and was helping with market development. Today, people in advertising just don't do that. They may make great ads, but they don't say, "America's taste is becoming sweeter. How can we exploit the trend? Or buck it by creating a powerful countertrend?" They don't look for relationships to the women's movement, to nutrition, or to global music.

An article I read recently with the headline "WE'RE DYING DIFFERENTLY" discussed changes in mortality patterns in the United States as studied by researchers at the Southern Illinois School of Medicine. The information contained in it should be influencing the planning of hospitals and insurance companies, medical fundraisers and pharmaceutical firms.

In early 1990, *Fortune* ran an article on what consumers would want in the new decade.[7] It predicted that five principal values would predominate: time, quality, health, home, and environment. Not only are all five of these trends important, but each of them has a major news and public affairs dimension. News about each of these values will change the perceptions of customers and citizens as the coming decade unfolds, and that in turn will have a bearing on how firms manage their goals.

Time, for example, translates into the pressures on two-income families and such issues as the "mommy track" centers for care of infants and the elderly. The scarcity of time also creates a tolerant environment for automated checkouts and drives the need for delivering nutrition information to children who are increasingly buying and cooking their own meals in the family microwave.

Quality is a public obsession as well. To deliver it, businesses now recognize, they must literally reconstruct the country's public education system. That's just one huge public affairs issue tied to realizing quality as a marketing objective.

On the topic of *health, Fortune* reports that "Consumers are so preoccupied with health that in a survey of shoppers, over half said a new product should be allowed on supermarket shelves *only* if it contained little cholesterol, little fat, and few calories." Wait until state legislatures take on that cause as a legislative initiative, as they doubtless will and may already have!

If the *home* becomes more important, public spending for roadways, sound barriers, and sewer system renovations—investments that protect and improve homeowner values—may well diminish spending on social issues. A home-based society is also likely to esteem nostalgia values and "parental" political leaders. Who knows: perhaps the 1990s will see the creation of a neo-"Ozzie and Harriet."

When people do leave their homes on vacation, they are doing so with more consciousness of the *environment*. This trend will accelerate in the coming decade. *Fortune* reports fast growth for the "low-environmental-impact travel business," which lets people visit interesting natural sights without harming the local ecology.

Each of these macro-trends, and hundreds more like them, should be suggestive to the leader of potential challenges and opportunities. Any leader who doesn't spend at least a few minutes a day mulling over macro-trends is unlikely to be able to lift the organization's reach beyond the day-to-day grind of existence.

ENTERTAINMENT TONIGHT, POLICY TOMORROW

The output of the entertainment industry is a rich source of information about attitudes that influence leader behavior. The movie *Wall Street* and the novel *Bonfire of the Vanities* and such TV shows as "Dynasty" and "Dallas" have far more influence on what the public believes to be the reality of business than any article in *Business Week* or *Fortune*. Not long after the collapse of the Berlin Wall, Sylvester Stallone predicted that Rambo's future battles would be directed against environmental abusers rather than communists. As ideological issues become less important in world affairs, it's certain that economic controversies will rise to fill the void.

Johnny Carson's opening monologue on "Tonight" was a barometer of public dissatisfaction for decades. Popular humor usually is. After members of an airline cockpit crew were found to be intoxicated while on duty, the company became the butt of cynical jokes nationwide. "How many pilots does it take for this company to fly a plane?" asked the straight man. "Four . . . and a fifth" was the response. The *Chicago Tribune* interviewed me, asking how seriously such humor could affect the image of a company. I responded that the damage could be serious indeed, and could start in apparently harmless ways. There's a mathematical multiplier, I said. The joke on late-night TV becomes the 9:00 A.M. joke at the coffee machine.

During the war in the Persian Gulf, editions of a paper carrying the comic strip "Doonesbury" were banned in parts of the Middle East, presumably because of the strip's outspoken commentary on the Middle East situation. The prime-time cartoon series "The Simpsons" crossed swords with the nuclear power industry for depicting nuclear power plant workers as, in the words of one industry group, "bungling idiots."[8] Humor is often tied up with volatile public issues. Every month, I scan a humor magazine called the *Funny Times* to see what newly identified targets of dissent and humor are on the horizon.

In January 1989, *The American Spectator* published an insightful report on a small genetic engineering firm that sprayed a modified form of common bacteria on strawberries to help them resist frost. "After five years of controversy and regulatory review," the verdict was that the modified bacteria were harmless. The company was permitted to be the first "to take a man-made organism out of the laboratory and release it into the open air with government approval." When the fateful day arrived back in 1987, however: "By some whim of the California health authority, [the woman who did the first spraying] was made to wear what appeared to be a spacesuit, as if the bacteria she sprayed was radioactive or as if the field on which she stood was the surface of the moon. . . . Even today, more than two years after the fact, there are those who will say that the effect of that picture, burned into the collective consciousness the following day by media around the world, was to . . . perpetuate the superstition that gene splicing was a strange and dangerous science to be carried out only under the most extreme precautions."[9] The California authorities, I'm convinced, had an acute visual sense, and knew that the entertainment value of the spacesuitlike outfit would drive opportunistic photo journalism—which it did.

While a good publicist can often find a way to leverage a trend and place a photo or a story about a company, it happens more often that events and trends leverage organizations and create "entertaining" coverage that is undesirable and that quickly has a bearing on policy.

MEGA-FORCES

Leaders stand at the information mailbox of their organizations. They regularly receive information coming up through various avenues and channels. Some of the mail will surely be junk, but some will contain the jokes and gossip that can foreshadow new attitudes. And, given the sheer bulk of what any leader receives, he or she should be able to piece together the collective data shreds by which the organization's "map" of reality must be rewritten.

For example, leaders with a feel for the information pulse in America would be hard pressed not to detect the ever more important role occupied by California as the U.S. direction-setter. Consider some of the evidence:

- One of every eight Americans now lives in California, making it—as the *Economist* has pointed out—demographically as important to the United States today as New York was to the United States in the 1870s.[10]

- Last year California wanted to advance the date of its presidential primary to a week after the New Hampshire primary, giving it far greater power in creating the slate of presidential candidates for the nation. In the coming decade, such a change is quite possible. Election campaigns for state officials in California now run easily over a hundred million dollars.

- California's contribution to the GNP has reached a level 30 percent higher than that of New York. In fact, the trend lines for the two states now run in opposite directions.

- California's governor has appointed the executive vice-president of the World Wildlife Fund to become secretary of the state resources agency, a cabinet level post. This move will surely set expectations for similar appointments nationwide.

- *Forbes* has reported that Los Angeles is now the manufacturing center of the United States, with 1.2 million jobs in that sector— more than twice as many as second-place Chicago.[11]

- The *Los Angeles Times*, with a circulation of 1.2 million, has bypassed the New York *Daily News* to become the biggest metropolitan daily newspaper in the United States.

- In a *Washington Post* article titled "America's Asian Destiny," the authors argue that America must realign its primary center of gravity away from Europe and toward Japan and Asia, which, of course, makes California more important, as the U.S. gateway to the Orient.[12]

- California continues to grow in significance as the lead bellwether state for referendums on public policy issues.

If a leader's organization has a stake in the United States, this is more than an interesting array of trivia. If California were once an 8 on the scale of importance assigned to the nation's geographic locales, it is now probably closer to a 10.

A leader in agreement with that reading would naturally want to watch California more carefully. Perhaps California would merit more of a listening post, or should be visited more often. If a leader's organization makes lawn products, the regulators in California may have a very direct influence over the kinds of herbicides that will be sold in South Carolina or Ohio. If a leader's organization is a school system, policies on teacher hiring and qualifications could well be set in Sacramento even though the school system is in Brunswick, Georgia, or Bangor, Maine. A Southeast Asian maker of fashion apparel would definitely want to know the pulse of Rodeo Drive and Wilshire Boulevard.

California is one mega-force. The attitudes and spending habits of the post–Baby Boom generation are a second, Eastern Europe, a third, and the multiple impacts of Islamic Fundamentalism, a fourth. Mega-forces will differ according to the goals of various organizations. And while mega-forces often have a trend component, they are not really broad trends. The power of California is less a trend than it is a fact. It is important to look at the transferable, extendable facets of California, and not to be caught up with its idiosyncrasies, such as new wave music or holistic health. Instead, look at California's significance as a trade center, its importance to the Japanese, or its role as a source of new legislative initiatives.

Overall, it is the leader's job to keep amassing information—to determine the locators of the important geographic and conceptual epicenters that could affect the organization and then to apply the organization's ear and brains to those critical points.

PRECONCEPTIONS

A leader sifting through information should always have one eye open for preconceptions and should challenge them aggressively. Readers may find the following "preconception checklist" useful in hunting down assumptions that conceal both risks and opportunities. Keep these thoughts in mind, particularly as you page through your industry's trade journals:

- The industry's typical approach has been . . .
- Industry consensus is . . .
- Industry leaders (or experts) agree that . . .
- Historically, customers have said this is unimportant . . .
- It's been tried before, of course, but . . .
- Statistical evidence shows that . . .

Federal Express would never have been born had Fred Smith not challenged preconceptions about what the business public would tolerate from the U.S. Postal Service. On the other hand, the mass manufacture and distribution of Fax machines would never have become a reality unless—as someone in the Fax business recently put it—"express mailings absolutely, positively couldn't get there until tomorrow morning." Preconceptions change all the time.

II

THE UNIVERSE
OF 25,000
Mastering
Research and Intelligence

A BOUT A MONTH AGO, I CALLED HOME FROM THE GILT-AND-INLAY splendor of a hotel room in South America to talk to my wife. It was my first night in the country. My goal was to negotiate a contract to represent the tourism program of this county, and I was a guest of the government. During the phone call, I raved about the exquisite lobster and prawns that I had eaten for lunch in a restaurant at a coastal seaport.

Later that night, I went down to the hotel restaurant for dinner. After the maitre d' in the dining room seated me at an excellent table, he told me, with obvious pride, that the menu tonight offered superb lobsters and prawns of the sort to which he understood I was partial. I felt like I was in Casablanca! Needless to say, I postponed the call to the State Department scheduled for later that evening.

From bugged telephone conversations to exhaustive surveys of public opinion, everyone is doing much more listening these days. While leaders need to listen to the drumbeat of trends and issues in publicly available information, they must also commission their own studies of information through research and intelligence. Some information must

THINKPOINTS

on How

Leaders Should Apply Intelligence and Research

- ☐ Enlist the Universe of 25,000 to win influence wars.

- ☐ Reach opinion targets discretely through the Audience of 1.

- ☐ Be research-literate, but don't tamper in process.

- ☐ Know the "baseline" of how you are perceived.

- ☐ Use research to enhance message-delivery skills.

- ☐ Change the reality along with the image.

- ☐ Help important outsiders do research about you.

- ☐ Maintain the information file in advance of crises.

- ☐ Avoid "binder-heavy" intelligence.

- ☐ Scour public data with focus and energy.

- ☐ Investigate your business associates thoroughly.

- ☐ Detect opportunities through positive debriefings.

be gathered in a way that is tailored to the organization and the needs of the leader.

Intelligence and research are powerful communications tools. This chapter describes how they can be used for optimum results.

THE UNIVERSE OF 25,000

To my mind, the most important single marketing concept for any leader is the Universe of 25,000. Its foundation is research, and it is the quintessence of niche marketing, but it goes far beyond marketing products to include gaining acceptance for ideas of all sorts.

I began thinking about the the Universe of 25,000 in 1988, and first used it while conducting several global strategies in 1989. I learned I could generally carry the day if I could get a well-defined appeal into the hands and minds of about 25,000 opinion leaders: investment bankers, analysts, government officials, think-tank researchers, portfolio managers, journalists, and others of this sort. With fax machines and today's telecommunications network, reaching an audience of such a size is not very difficult.

In one respect, this is a niche strategy, because it targets a very narrow universe. In another sense, however, it is exactly the opposite. The people in this universe are the gatekeepers to the global mass market, at least as far as finance is concerned. Sometimes you need reach only these people themselves. On other occasions, the Universe of 25,000 is the avenue through which you reach everybody else, because their views are the views that will dominate the press and the media.

My success with the Universe of 25,000 in the financial arena started me thinking about parallel universes in other disciplines. Sure enough, I learned there is also a universe for occupational safety. It is much smaller—perhaps 15,000.

There are thousands of similar sets and subsets, and the challenge is to identify and court the special universe you need. There is a global ecology niche and an ethics niche and universes that belong to both. I'm sure there is also a catalytic convertor niche and a candy bar niche . . . which represent serious business if you are trying to design proto-types for "global" consumer products.

The universe theme is especially powerful for leveraging public-affairs issues. For example, only so many Americans can affect the dialogue with the Japanese. Call them what you will—some are sages, some are Nippophiles—but this is a very short list, containing such names as Pete Peterson, Mayor Tom Bradley, Les Thurow, former New York mayor John Lindsay, and Ambassador Gleysteen (who runs the Japan Society)—but not Dick Gephardt, whose protectionist positions are just not taken that seriously in Japan. By reaching and persuading a well-chosen list of a thousand people who *do* affect the dialogue with Japan, you could move an issue with the Japanese in days. Classical communications tactics would take months and still probably fail.

In addition, every society, every government has its core power universe. That universe *in* Japan is relatively big—several hundred. For Paraguay or Thailand, the core universe of people who must be persuaded is smaller, but it does exist and most people in such a core have at least a vague idea of who the other members of the core are.

Research is the cornerstone of the Universe of 25,000. Once you find out the names of the constituents who must be reached, all the rest becomes a routine job—although at times a very challenging one, involving message formulation and communication.

The Universe of 25,000 points to a much broader trend. We are going to see very sophisticated mailing lists in the future. Mailing, by the way, is really a misnomer. It implies the sluggish shoveling of third-class drop pieces into mail boxes. We are talking instead about immediate, electronic access to influence lists.

When George Bush used the metaphor "a thousand points of light" in his presidential nomination acceptance speech, what flashed in my mind was somewhat different from what Bush intended to express. Instead of beacons of light expressing widespread optimism and common purpose, what I saw was a world of flickering lights, flashing on and off, voting yes and no. These are the thousand points of light that govern world decision making. This light board may one day become two-way communication as world opinion leaders sit in a perpetual electronic referendum on the vital issues in their specialty or their profession.

THE AUDIENCE OF ONE

Sometimes the Universe of 25,000 reduces down to the Audience of One. I was once approached by the directors of a corporation who wanted to sell one of its businesses. The directors had researched the universe of likely buyers and were sure that one person—the principal shareholder of a privately held conglomerate—would be the ideal purchaser for this subsidiary. A direct approach to this individual, however—either by the directors or through an intermediary—would nearly guarantee a lower sales price, since the purchaser would not have initiated the deal.

A little inside background on the potential buyer said that he had a voracious appetite for intelligence and an outstanding network that combed for information. I advised the directors to issue a news release across the Dow Jones broad tape, giving a general update on their corporation. Toward the end of the release, it was suggested, they should mention casually that the potential sale of the division in question was being considered, but the decision was by no means final. In fact, the division might also be significantly expanded. (That was the unfortunate truth as the directors saw it. They would either have to grow the business to make it competitive—an alternative they would rather avoid—or get out of it.) Within 30 minutes of the release crossing the wire, the targeted buyer called the CEO of the corporation that wanted to sell. Within six days, a very favorable deal was consummated.

Good intelligence may tell a leader that the best way to reach another leader—a very important Audience of One—is sometimes just to talk to the world at large in a very subdued way.

RESEARCH LITERACY

While the need for research may be spurred *by* creative questions and may lead *to* highly creative questions, conducting research is itself a very technical and analytical business.

While leaders don't need to know the technical details of conducting research, they must be intelligent consumers of research products. For example, they must know if the research being reviewed or considered is rigorous and projectable, or simply descriptive and provocative. Many leaders don't make that distinction and start projecting the most imaginative idea aired in a focus-group interview as their own best hunch about what customers or concerned citizens are thinking.

In key aspects of the research process, creativity can be a dangerous liability. The most creative and ingenious study can be worthless if the questions, for example, are not posed by the researchers in a dispassionate and systematic way. Local-level political research is especially prone to this distortion. The people doing the research are often so partisan that they can't put aside their loyalties to ask objective questions or report neutral results.

The kinds of research tools relevant to individual organizations differ so greatly that it is pointless to try to speak of them in a general way. Spending an afternoon with a skilled technician, however, will school the leader in the art and a science of data gathering.

One general rule is true. Leaders have to endorse rigorous sampling and analysis techniques. An organization can buy the most sophisticated analysis in the world, but if its people believe that the business is run by seat-of-the-pants intuition, that's how they will always behave in making and implementing decisions.

Leaders must also help factor international differences into the way research is interpreted or conducted. Their capacity to do this grows as they become familiar with the behavior of other cultures. Phone research for example, is a relatively recent phenomenon in Japan. In the past, it was considered rude to call people in their homes and to ask their opinion about things. And up until recently, all types of consumer research in the former Soviet Union were unreliable, because the research was conducted through a wing of the KGB, and people knew that they were talking at least indirectly to the government. Although this is no longer the case, research there still has progress to make before it reaches Western standards.

Beyond knowing the basics of research techniques, standing behind dispassionate sampling and analysis, and giving insights into foreign or special cultures, it is better for the leader to stay out of the way of conducting research. Too many leaders I have met like to tamper in the research process. As keepers of the vision, many leaders think that they are naturally gifted in breaking the code of the Rosetta Stone of research. This is rarely the case. Because statistical methods and research processes are so well developed these days, it is unproductive for leaders to attempt to play with the raw data unless they have strong statistical skills. A leader should periodically see a focus group in operation, however, because in a focus group, one can hear the way the respondents articulate certain reactions or particular feelings. Leaders should understand, however, that although the findings of focus groups can offer instant insights, they are nearly impossible to generalize over a broad population. This point is made strongly in Ken Clancy and Robert Shulman's book *The Marketing Revolution.*

THE BASELINE

Understanding the baseline is the starting point of all research related to leadership. Before any special situation or crisis intervenes, you should have a clear idea of how your organization is perceived. The reason is simple. When any special situation arises, the key question is: How much has the event *disturbed* the way we are seen?

Knowledge of the baseline helps leaders ensure that they don't underreact or overreact to situations that arise. Baseline studies should be conducted at a time when the organization has a low public profile for an organization of its type or size. Shielding the organization's identity in a control group, researchers will ask about: its reputation, its management, integrity, financial strength, customer service, quality, and so on.

Knowing the baseline can save time and enormous sums of money. It can also help enormously in making the right communications decisions. For example, a major consumer products client of ours, which had conducted methodical base-line studies over the years, experienced a terrible product-safety incident. Their past reputation was so solid, however, and the company acted so quickly to attack the problem, that people actually felt better about the company after the crisis than they had before it occurred. That's a very unusual result. But if the company hadn't had the baseline study data, they wouldn't have known the impact of the crisis and would probably have overemphasized their reaction to it, keeping the topic in the public eye far longer than it needed to be—and losing their own credibility in the process.

MESSAGE DELIVERY

Leaders will be spending more time on how they deliver messages and less time on the content. It's not that the content is less important; rather, the more we learn about messages, the more we learn that how messages are delivered determines if any of the content is received. As Jim Granger, president of the Wirthlin Group, observes: "It is clear and provable that a good message poorly delivered is no better than a bad message delivered well or a bad message never delivered. Because so many CEOs are trained in public speaking, they think that they are good at message delivery, when in fact they are not." They don't adjust their messages and their style when speaking to particular audiences.

Research allows leaders to determine how messages and appeals must be shaped and presented to reach particular audiences. Many leaders do a lax job of message delivery when they speak to audiences within their own organizations, yet research is every bit as important when speaking inside the organization as it is when talking outside of it. Too many leaders think that their messages will be accepted because of their position as leaders. That strategy works for fewer and fewer internal audiences.

IMAGE MOVEMENT

It is possible for an organization or a leader to move an image using research. With a baseline study in hand, organizations and leaders are able to frame messages and create delivery vehicles so they can move images in the direction that they would like.

If the baseline is known, a leader can both set expectations and change them if necessary. Both presidential candidates used this tactic in the 1988 campaign. Baseline research for the Dukakis campaign was clear: Michael Dukakis was perceived to be a weak public speaker. The Dukakis staff was publicly apprehensive about how well Dukakis would deliver his convention acceptance speech. The media in turn created a low expectation level. When the talk—a mediocre one at best—was actually delivered, it came across as an oratorical triumph because expectations had been so low.

Bush insiders, in the same campaign, leaked fears that Bush would be clumsy and rigid in a stand-up situation and would be lucky to survive the two debates, and his basically acceptable performance, because it so far surpassed expectations, may have earned him the presidency.

These two examples are colored by the actual manipulation of the baseline expectation—a practice I don't recommend. In the world of politics, it is much easier to manipulate images than in, let's say, the world of business. In addition, political campaigns are tent shows that fold on Election Day, whereas ongoing organizations must live with the reputations they acquire, and it is not healthy to have a reputation as an image manipulator. Still, the illustrations show that baseline awareness can be a powerful advantage in setting expectations and delivering messages.

If a business leader wants to move an image, that person had better be working equally hard to change the underlying reality. To understand this better, take a look at a copy of a competitor's recent management presentation to the financial analysis community. Then read the report on that presentation by the most demanding and perceptive analyst who follows your industry. Chances are, you'll see how a keen analytic mind cuts through the rhetoric and illusion.

OTHER PEOPLE'S RESEARCH

Some leaders and organizations are preoccupied with their own research. They forget that the research done on them will be far more influential in establishing public expectations of how they are regarded than the research they do themselves.

Reporters, for example, have limited time and limited resources. In a crisis such as a takeover, a player in the game can actually be a reliable source of information for a reporter, provided that person has established credibility in the past. An insider can provide, for example, a file of all the key public documents—negative as well as positive—although license may be taken to highlight the passages and viewpoints considered important to the source's cause. By being a convenience—and a fair-minded one—the organization generally improves its chances of being treated fairly.

INFORMATION MAINTENANCE

Information maintenance simply means updating the information found in the public record: newspaper articles, brokerage reports, government documents, and court filings. It isn't just what *you* know in advance of an emerging crisis that is important. It's equally necessary that you study what is available for others to know about you.

The public record, as embodied by your organization's or industry's file in databases such as Lexis/Nexis, becomes your character reference and your credit rating in a public opinion war. Through information maintenance, you stand to gain some often vital control over the public record. Accordingly, information maintenance has become a prerequisite for organizations operating in the Age of Consent.

Organizations should constantly be carrying out risk analyses to determine where the consent they need to do business might be withdrawn. For example, let's say that you are in the confections business and you learn that chewing gum is going to be a major public issue in six months. (There isn't a scintilla of evidence that chewing gum *is* going to be controversial, but let's pretend that it will be.)

Your researchers have concluded that some congressional oversight committee plans to attack chewing gum for a preposterous reason— that it distends the muscles of the jaw, or that all chewing gum includes some ingredient only available in countries hostile to the United States. The emotional appeals that this committee will use are going to scare people, which could severely damage your industry and your business.

How does a chewing gum company prepare for a dark day like this?

BRACING FOR AN ASSAULT ON CHEWING GUM

1. You study the files and determine what general attitudes are toward chewing gum.

2. You profile your strongest supporters and adversaries and chronicle their respective positions as best you can. It can be extremely valuable to pinpoint the demographics of your most loyal supporters, as well as their reasons for supporting you. Consider the case of saccharin. Before the days of NutraSweet, certain health activists tried to ban saccharin because lab experiments had shown that massive doses of saccharin caused cancer in rats. Saccharin supporters won the day, though, by mobilizing diabetics and the overweight—people exposed to far more serious medical risks from the use of sugar.

3. You analyze the emerging issues and project their impact on supporters, adversaries, and that vast body of people who are totally indifferent to the issue of chewing gum today.

4. You look for potential supporters who could be mobilized when the issue erupts. These could include people in secondary industries, or members of special-interest groups—antismoking advocates,

perhaps, who see chewing gum as a harmless alternative to smoking cigarettes in public.

5. You launch an information initiative. Smart firms anticipating an issue will try to angle a definitive article in an opinion-leading journal, for such a piece may well become "the source" for much of the ensuing debate. If a major story isn't written, companies can get position papers directly into the Lexis/Nexis data banks, bypassing the press positioning step.

   You must disseminate information *before* an issue arises. Information released by firms after a controversy begins fully raging is often dismissed as propaganda or viewed with considerably more skepticism than data already on file. The building blocks for gaining consent through information maintenance must be in place long before crisis or controversy strikes.

   Leaders should recognize the distinction between information maintenance and disinformation. Disinformation seeks to distort or manipulate the truth. Information maintenance tries to set the record straight before someone else tries to upset or distort it. In this sense, information maintenance is like keeping your résumé or credit rating up to date before events may cause you to have to show your credentials.

INFORMATION THROUGH INTELLIGENCE

While the dictionary distinguishes intelligence from research by saying that intelligence deals with *secret* information, I don't think that distinction still holds today. In my opinion, intelligence is best differentiated from research as information gathered in a more opportunistic and less systematic way. A survey constitutes research, but finding out that such a survey exists and determining what it could portend—that's intelligence. Looking at your competitor's house organ or periodically having dinner with the staff director of your trade association are other forms of intelligence gathering. Intelligence is generally more focused: When you gather intelligence, it's not like conducting a random sampling, because you have a pretty good idea of who or what the source of information will be. That information may not be "secret," but it can often be hard to get—or to recognize.

While most people assume that intelligence means cloak-and-dagger spying, the majority of intelligence work involves analysis and sifting through reams of public data. Consider the brilliant astrophysicist who was assigned to track down a 75-cent phone bill account problem at the Berkeley physics lab—and ended up busting a KGB spy ring in Hanover, Germany.[1] He did it not by donning a trenchcoat and playing secret agent but through novel and exhaustive hacking. He never even saw the people his tactics caught.

Forget the cloak-and-dagger approach. When you need intelligence to be gathered, tap the brightest analytical minds for the mission—not people who are devious or manipulative.

BINDER-HEAVY INTELLIGENCE

The Conference Board recently published an excellent study on competitive intelligence. In it, there is a sound caution from Juliana Simmons, the market research director at Searle Labs. She advises firms to steer clear of "binder-heavy" intelligence.[2] Don't simply collect reams of intelligence without a clear focus on what you are seeking. Sometimes the more intelligence organizations collect, the more they are crippled in using what they know. The sharpest competitors are those who emphasize the utility of what they learn. Managers should be rewarded not for the intelligence they gather but for the intelligence they put to work. Throughout the organization, leaders must constantly challenge whether the intelligence is fresh, whether it moves through the organization quickly, and, most of all, whether it is used.

The swift pace of today's marketplace makes intelligence gathering critical. Not only do trends change, they can change very quickly. Take, for example, "green marketing," or making environmental claims for products, a trend that is sweeping the United States right now but could well have peaked by the time you read this book. The idea originated in Europe, and 18 months after it had taken off in the United States, I was already reading surveys that found the importance of environmental issues to European voters had fallen off dramatically. In March 1990, the *Economist* printed the results of a survey conducted by MORI, a market research firm, stating that "the proportion of voters listing the environment as one of the most important political issues fell by half between July 1989 and February 1990."[3] A month later, the *Economist* published an additional report discussing "a survey of 1,400 British shoppers carried out quarterly by Jones Rhodes, a

Nottingham-based research firm . . . indicating that 56% of those surveyed are now suspicious of claims that products are environmentally friendly."[4]

Because the ruling Conservative-Liberal coalition in Germany did such a good job of launching environmental initiatives, the West German Greens lost their seats in the first all-German parliament. That was another indicator of the significant rethinking taking place on environmental issues. As a reflection of the environmental agenda, green marketing is in for trouble, and firms considering this path should tread very carefully. Consider that in 1990, many firms spent time and money trying to develop biodegradable packaging, despite the fact that environmentalists, in their caucuses and local newsletters, had been lining up against biodegradability since October 1989. As a Sierra Club official put it, "We're concerned that biodegradable plastics like diapers will leach toxic chemicals into the ground and water. . . . We think we might be better off after all if plastic *is* stable."[5]

THE PUBLIC RECORD

So much vital information is tied up in the public record, but it is often difficult for otherwise intelligent people to believe that this source holds anything worthwhile. It's even harder to persuade citizens of the value of the public record in autocratic societies like the former Soviet Union. The former KGB agent Victor Orlov has written, "[Soviet intelligence officers] disbelieve [public records] can be genuine. That disbelief is supported by their performance evaluation system, largely based on how impressively the information they obtain is classified as secret. Sometimes, in fact, a classification stamp is put on an otherwise nonclassified document 'for the common good.' It is a common good indeed. The agent gets paid better . . . and the customer [the Soviet government] is happy with 'reliable information.' "[6]

A careful tracking of the public record can also result in victories in court. One large consumer products firm that experienced a problem with one of its brands was insured against *transfer damage,* or damage to the profits of the product or group of products caused by adverse government action or media attention. Several of this company's brands suffered a loss of sales when state regulatory agencies ordered their removal from store shelves, an event widely reported by the media. The company's insurer's refused to pay its claim, contending that the magnitude of the damage was far less than the company claimed. The company sued the insurers and won a $50 million judgment, in large part because of evidence entered that gave the results of comprehensive monitoring. Used five years later, news clippings and video reports compiled over a four-month period helped prove the magnitude of the company's case to the jury.

Don't assume that you can just go back and collect such information at a later date. Even such a prestigious organization as the BBC doesn't keep a videotape record of much of its daily news broadcast material. If the case is a potentially serious one, intelligence must be gathered proactively, with a clear eye to its potential use. Because the time frames for this kind of collection are long and the discipline needed is rigorous, this job is rarely done diligently unless the leader's active backing is evident. If as a leader you have a well-grounded suspicion about possible future need, this is an area where your vigilance can reap great dividends.

NEGATIVE PR

The heart of negative PR is intelligence. Leaders should be aware that bright, unscrupulous people may want to use negative PR against leaders and their organizations.

Negative PR is often an instrument in takeover deals, in which the press is manipulated into acting as an agent in the deal rather than simply a reporter of events. The following incident was called to my attention by Dean Rotbart, editor of *TJFR* (The Journalist and Financial Reporting) newsletter.

A firm based in Luxembourg was trying to buy a large British mining company in a hostile takeover. Opposing forces hired a negative PR specialist to come in and try to undermine the deal. Knowing that upsetting the confidence of bankers is the surest way to undercut any deal and that bankers are generally responsive to public opinion, the specialist investigated and discovered that the firm in Luxembourg had interests in South Africa.

One of the backers of the takeover was a prestigious New York bank, which has a major block of its stock held by the City of New York's pension fund. The fund's management rules stipulate that companies with stock held by the fund must not invest in South Africa. A tipster thus called a network television station in New York City and rang the alarm bell, announcing that the bank was investing in South African businesses.

Morally, I hasten to add, the specialist and the tipster were both on the side of the good, but one must recognize that the specialist's motive in the disclosure was to break up the deal, not to make a statement about apartheid. The disclosure did not in the end prove to be the decisive point in the deal, but it could easily have been. Incidents such as this show how crucial it is for leaders to demand that their organizations do business only with parties having impeccable credentials. Reputations can easily be stained through back-door associations, which a determined intelligence effort is bound to turn up.

HAPPY INTELLIGENCE

In addition to the combative uses of intelligence, there is also what I call "happy intelligence": the use of intelligence to detect opportunity. One of the best practitioners of happy intelligence is Gillette, which has been engaging in it for years. The company routinely asks U.S. executives assigned abroad and their spouses what European products they would miss most upon returning to the United States. In one instance, the answers led Gillette's shampoo division to launch the industry-revolutionizing category of herbal shampoos. (The detergent industry first learned about concentrated packaging in a similar way; overall, European countries have much more dramatic disposal problems for packaging waste.)

When VCRs were first introduced into the United States, manufacturers targeted the early adopter and the yuppie. Yet today senior citizens, who are less likely to go out at night and stand in line at movie theaters, are one of the largest single groups buying VCRs. The development of this market would never have happened had intelligence findings not driven the industry to demystify the operation of the equipment and to use larger type on the operating controls and in the instruction manuals.

With customers, contributors, natural allies, or anyone on whom the organization's future survival relies, leaders should constantly be encouraging the gathering of positive intelligence that will maximize opportunities for the organization.

12

GUIDANCE CONTROL
Setting Agendas and Making Plans

L EADERS MUST PATROL THE HORIZON FOR WHAT THE FUTURE MAY bring. They have to combine what they learn about future probabilities with their knowledge of how the people in their organizations adapt to change.

Quaker Oats' CEO Bill Smithburg once drew an interesting analogy for me between today's corporate leader and a fighter pilot. "One of the key functions a CEO performs," he said, "is that of guidance control. He is constantly scanning future factors that could affect the organization, like a fighter pilot speeding over the landscape. These could be any important force—competitive threats, legislation, or emerging technology. At the right time, the manager has to lock on to the target and start applying the company's resources to meet the individual upcoming challenges."

The trigger may be external, but the communications resolution will increasingly be internal. How well the inside is marshaled will depend on the leader's ability to deal with the situation. The tools the leader must use to achieve guidance control are agendas and plans. This chapter explains how leaders combine agendas and plans with their own judgment and perceptiveness to help achieve the vision of the organization.

THINKPOINTS
on How
Leaders Exercise Guidance Control

☐ Scan predictables for their effects.

☐ Lock onto targets before dedicating resources.

☐ Create agendas to map out forward motion.

☐ Endow agendas with staying power.

☐ Create the communications flipside to each step in the agenda.

☐ Behave in accordance with the agenda's prescriptions.

☐ Limit back room agendas to constructive goals.

☐ Patrol the horizon for conflicting agendas.

☐ Support the annual planning rhythm.

☐ Plan better to give customers more choices.

☐ Plan to withstand disruption effectively.

SETTING AGENDAS

It's said that, rather than carousing on New Year's Eve, Richard Nixon sits down with a legal pad to map out his annual agenda—the nine or ten things he wants to make progress on in that particular year. A newly elected President of the United States communicates his agenda in his inaugural address. Companies, too, can and do have agendas. Few design them well, however, and even fewer communicate them effectively.

Nations can also have agendas. Many Americans believe that Japan is very secretive about its agenda, but that is simply not the case. Just by reading the periodic statements of Japan's powerful industrial ministry MITI in the *Financial Times* or the *Wall Street Journal,* it's relatively easy to stay abreast of the Japanese agenda. Back in 1983, Wisse Dekker—then chairman of Philips—said, "Japan's MITI . . . publishes what it wants to do—and nobody bothers to read it except us."[1]

The agenda is a leader's personal plan for any institution or organization. It is not simply a business plan in the conventional sense, however. Instead, it is a set of themes or topics requiring action or progress—forward motion—in a particular year. From my experience working with leaders in drafting their agendas, I'd recommend confining the number of points on the agenda to four or five.

When the agendas of different parties collide, either serious dialogue or conflict may result. Any organization's agenda will shape and be shaped by the agendas of suppliers, community groups, regulators, special interests, industry trade associations, and countless others. Adversaries surely have agendas, but it's not enough to say that an adversary "has an agenda against you." What exactly is it and how and why does it affect you? Leaders must know how to examine the agendas surrounding them, extract what is meaningful, and factor what they learn into their own agendas and plans.

The agenda's elements are neither financial goals nor objectives to be met and discarded. The agenda is not a mission statement, nor is it a code of behavior determining how the company will do business. An agenda guides the direction of the organization's short- to medium-term behavior in the realization of its vision. For a U.S. firm with a vision of being an important force in the Japanese market, penetration of the Japanese distribution system would be a plausible agenda item, while making the next quarter's sales goal in Japan would not be.

A leader's agenda should spin other agendas into motion. If leaders are effective in doing this, they will find that their agenda becomes the agenda of the organization. Over five or ten years a plank of the agenda may shift, but overall the agenda must have great staying power. As Bill Smithburg told me, agendas from year to year "are more similar than different."

A well-crafted company agenda can be a powerful competitive weapon. Several years ago, the CEO of a major Far Eastern consumer products firm (the name of which I cannot reveal) told me that his company had crafted its agenda along four key themes:

1. Intellectual property rights (such as patents)

2. Technological innovation

3. A grasp of consumer behavior in developing countries

4. The maintenance of open trade in world markets.

Quietly, the company went to work over about a decade to realize its agenda and to be recognized for its achievements. Today, it harvests the fruits of that investment. Nearly every week, an article in a major business publication describes how this firm continues to make headway in each of these four areas. On intellectual property, the company will have defended an important patent or copyright. An unexpected new product will bolster the firm's reputation as an innovator. A marketing journal will extol the way one of the firm's divisions is creating and selling inexpensive but durable products to build brand loyalty in a developing market. On the trade front, its lobbyists will be busily at work on the Washington Beltway or at Berlaymont, the European Community headquarters in Brussels, to protect the company's positioning in global markets. Each week, the stories will be different, but the themes will reappear again and again with the regularity of a well-developed fugue.

AGENDA COMMUNICATIONS

From the business agenda grows the communications agenda. Many leaders stumble because they don't understand that communications is the linkage for *everything*. Every element on the business agenda has a communications flipside that will allow that aspect of the agenda to be achieved. Leaders need to understand and activate the relationship between each part of the agenda and its corollary in communications.

There are many ways to communicate an agenda. Printing it up and sending it out is a harmless and often necessary step, but that won't sufficiently "communicate" the agenda. If quality is a focus of the agenda, this can be communicated by the number of intense and thoughtful meetings the leader spearheads on quality and how much higher the leader holds the quality standard than the profit target, despite pressure from Wall Street. (Henry Schacht is achieving the long-term positioning of Cummins Engine in this way.) If risk taking is on the agenda, the treatment of people who take intelligent risks and fail communicates the agenda on risk. In sum, leader behavior is far more important in communicating the agenda than any written or videotaped message can be.

BACK ROOM AGENDAS

As the official, public agenda is advanced, there will always be back room agendas which require attention as well. These are not always devious, under-the-table dealings; often a back room agenda calls for the exchange of legitimate favors. A leader's back room agenda may be to evaluate a young executive's handling of a crisis. Occasionally, the back room agenda will be more important than the public agenda, but this is risky, because it can confuse the organization. Leaders must control the back room agendas as skillfully as they articulate and guide the achievement of public agendas. They should also limit the number of back room agendas, or the organization will soon be awash in palace intrigue.

SURROGATE AGENDAS

When the University of Notre Dame decided to tear down its field house, a wild uproar arose among the alumni. The place had been a workshop to greats like Knute Rockne for seventy years. The alumni agenda was to revere the feelings the building evoked. But the structure was totally out-of-date and had to go. The administration's agenda was to make way for the future.

What Notre Dame needed was to find a way to memorialize the passing of this field house. So a plaque for the new field house was created, stating simply: "For seventy years, here's where they shook down the thunder." Now, when alumni walk by, they are moved by the message—perhaps as much as if the old building were still there. The plaque and its inscription became an effective surrogate agenda for the field house. Leaders often must use their creativity in devising surrogate agendas whenever they must implement significant change.

INFORMATION AGENDAS

Some agendas, like that of the Notre Dame alumni, are purely emotional. Others can be quite subtle. Recently, I spoke with a consumer behavior researcher who was bemoaning the slump in her field. With bar codes in widespread use on consumer products, manufacturers rely increasingly on the hard behavioral data they can glean from the checkout register. As a result, many have lost interest in consumer research. In so doing, most are compounding a serious setback they have suffered as another group—retailers—has effectively advanced its information agenda. Many manufacturers still don't realize that by agreeing to the UPC system, they have given up enormous power to the retailing industry. Manufacturers may have thought they were helping retailers to lower labor expenses in marking and cash-registering merchandise. Yet at the same time, retailers were also shifting the balance of power in information in their direction, away from the manufacturers. While retailers were quite conscious of this larger agenda, manufacturers failed to see it coming.

Don Schultz, a marketing consultant in Chicago, describes the reality quite well: "In the next decade, retailers are going to begin holding manufacturers hostage. You see, most packaged-goods manufacturers don't have any idea who their customers are. They sell to the retail stores and the chain stores, but they don't really know who their consumer is. They must rely on the retailer to make contact. But, as the retailer gets more and more powerful, he will control the shelf, and the manufacturer has no way of influencing his own consumers. Additionally, packaged goods manufacturers are having difficulties integrating the behavioral and attitudinal data they are collecting."

This confusion is being amplified by reductions in research in the name of short-term cost control. The behavioral data coming from cash-register records doesn't always mesh with the traditional attitudinal research being done, especially by firms that are skimping on their budgets for attitudinal research. Taking up the slack created by manufacturers cutting back on research, the European supermarket industry is at the cutting edge of the new information power. Because of the proliferation of new products and the limited amount of space in most stores, more and more retailers are only giving shelf space to the top two brands competing in any one area. In this way, the retailer excludes all but the most powerful manufacturers.

Leaders should always look at the agendas of neighboring organizations and examine how those agendas—whether for suppliers, key customers, or similar companies—might be used to disturb the parity that an organization enjoys today. The hidden (and sometimes hostile) agendas of other organizations will not always be information agendas, but they are increasingly agendas that relate to information, because, quite simply, information is growing in importance as a component of power.

MAKING PLANS

Planning is a detailed—and usually documented—way of looking at the future, which should always be carried out in the context of both the organization's vision and its primary agenda. More and more planning can effectively be decentralized, however, because of advances in processing data. A leader who understands this unusually well is Dick Bartlett, president of Mary Kay Cosmetics, whose concept of human resource information systems has effectively redrawn the Mary Kay organization chart. All the decision-making authority is now placed at the point of contact with the customer, while the leader is positioned at the *bottom* of the chart as the key supporter and facilitator.

Styles of planning differ radically from organization to organization, and planning is more a technocratic than a leadership concern. It is important, however, for a leader to make sure that the planning process can accommodate three factors:

1. A regular annual rhythm

2. Diversity

3. Disruption.

Rhythm. Protecting the annual planning rhythm—making it reliable and thoughtful—is an important ritual duty of leadership. While leaders should set an energetic pace within their organizations, and should punctuate new events in a way that causes people to stop and take notice, they must nevertheless strive to maintain an even, largely predictable planning cycle. That cycle should match up with the important strategic events of the year—be they new product introductions, plant openings, or annual meetings—as well as the internal communications of the organization. These communications should generate an awareness of and excitement about the company's progress, as well as a sense of anticipation—just as people look forward to the Fourth of July picnic or the December holidays.

Diversity. A characteristic of the new technologies of information delivery and robotics is their capacity to deliver personally tailored products. That may not be the case in the supermarket, which is increasingly an "automat" for a predetermined number of choices. But it can be true of something as simple as a home-delivered magazine: In November 1990, *Time* personalized its subscription magazines with the names of its individual subscribers as part of the cover art. And it is certainly the case for nearly everything that constitutes a major purchase.

The Japanese, who are now making more than a million cars a year in U.S. factories, "are changing the rules of the contest—again" according to a 1990 article in the *Economist.* "Norimasa Furuta, Mazda's president, has told his people to produce cars that are more luxurious, that have more 'individuality' and that meet a wider range of consumer tastes. That is why Japan's carmakers are investing heavily in 'flexible' rather than mass manufacturing, so they can build several models on the same production line."[2]

In the 1980s, leaders encouraged their organizations to focus on the few things they did well. In the 1990s, a countertrend is already emerging—to provide as much diversity as possible under a single focused umbrella. The Japanese are already doing this kind of planning, and doing it well.

Disruption. I first learned that Saddam Hussein had invaded Kuwait as I was being fitted for a suit at Brooks Brothers. My tailor, Charlie Goldstein, handed me the phone, and I got the word from sources in

Dubai. My first instinct was to order two more suits that would travel well in desert climates.

Saddam's invasion did more than change my wardrobe planning, however. When he crossed the Kuwaiti border, plans at virtually every business in the world changed—from the pricing of products to the way companies moved their people around the world and how they prepared for the possibility of terrorist attack. In our unsettled times, leaders should do more than plan for contingencies. They must ensure that their organizations are prepared for disruption. Most planning is preoccupied with "most likely" cases. More companies, I contend, need to think about what they would do in the event of real catastrophe, not just a 5 percent shortfall in sales. There is already a monthly magazine solely devoted to the subject of crisis and catastrophe planning in the world of data processing. Such thinking needs to be extended to topics such as external relations, governmental affairs, and even employee relations. The 1990s will most likely be a time of massive disruption, and leaders and organizations must accustom themselves to thinking in terms of the large-scale impacts that will probably result.

13

THE EARNEST EAR
Soliciting Advice and Staffwork

RECENTLY, I MET WITH THE TOP THREE EXECUTIVES OF AN IM-
mensely prestigious Fortune 100 company. My role was an
awkward one. The two executive vice-presidents—robust, athletic guys,
both with Harvard Business School diplomas, and both with at least 25
years of operating experience and personal net worths easily exceeding
$10 million—were scared to death of the CEO, who was a bespectacled
little dropout from an agricultural college. The CEO had held onto his
job for fifteen years chiefly because he had learned to play his board
of directors like a violin. He was a master of using the Executive
Committee to keep his key people "in line," through intricately laced
golden handcuffs that were tied around his own personal agenda.
Slowly, however, the company was losing market position, because
people were afraid to bring up the innovative new ideas called for by
a dramatic new time filled with change.

As the meeting progressed, I said that the company deserved better
and fresher ideas than it was getting—and that there seemed to be an
awful lot of fear in the room. The two EVPs shifted around nervously
in their chairs, while the CEO boasted that fresh ideas and bold risk
taking were exactly what he was looking for. After I had raised the topic

THINKPOINTS
on How
Leaders Get the Best from Their Advisers

- ☐ Enable advisers to bring you forthright advice.

- ☐ Practice intensive, noninterruptive listening.

- ☐ Invest in "good fat" staff.

- ☐ Balance creativity and pragmatism in staffwork.

- ☐ Don't delegate leadershipwork to staff.

- ☐ Expect speech preparation to advance the inside agenda.

- ☐ Require each speech to have one to two memorable messages.

- ☐ Accept platforms that further the organization's agenda.

- ☐ Expect written plans for important phone calls.

- ☐ Seek closure in each meeting and on each agenda item.

- ☐ Demand personalized, action-oriented written communications.

three or four times, no one seemed ready to confront the fear issue. The meeting was inconclusive, and as I left I wondered whether real progress had been made (even whether it could be made).

Many leaders either succeed or fail based on the quality of advice and staffwork that supports them. The purpose of this chapter is to outline how quality staffwork and advice can reliably be obtained.

DON'T TRY TO SCARE OUT THE TRUTH

For reasons no more complicated than the simple show of power, many leaders cut themselves off from one of their most important leadership assets: the honest counsel of their best advisers. At United Technologies, CEO Harry Gray was brilliant at running the business, but he was so powerful, so imperious, that people were afraid of him. Ideas that reach the CEO in this kind of environment are distilled and massaged. Some leaders don't understand that when ideas lose their juice coming up the line, it is the leader who is put at risk.

David Johnson at Campbell's Soup is the opposite: a magician at dispelling fear. He enjoys the intellectual back-and-forth that leads to the formation of his own ideas. George Fisher of Motorola shields his people from the tyranny of quarterly earnings and genuinely encourages their innovation. He is investing in his businesses as a Japanese manager would. Both Johnson and Fisher represent a model toward which future leaders should groom their behavior.

NONINTERRUPTIVE LISTENING

I have a friend by the name of Dan Boland, who is a Ph.D. and an ex-priest, and who recently wrote a paper on the priest as leader. In it, he describes the skill of "intensive, non-interruptive listening. . . . Listening intensely and supportively, without judging or criticizing, without intruding or correcting, is difficult (if not unthinkable) for many priests who exert control and believe that preaching is more important than listening." (It's easy to substitute "leader" for "priest" in that characterization.) Boland argues that "maintaining intense, riveted, unwavering interest (even with uninteresting people) is indeed a mildly heroic enterprise [but] effective leaders listen *intently, uncritically and constructively—without interrupting, challenging or defend-*

ing—until they understand not simply the words but the deeper inner meaning of the speaker."

Over the past 25 years, I have seen plenty of staffwork hit the desks of CEOs and other leaders. Some leaders regularly receive superior staffwork. Others must rely on mediocre analysis and recommendations. In fact, the quality of the work has much less to do with the quality of the staff than with the attitude of the leader. Those leaders who are "earnest ears"—who truly want to be engaged by other quality minds and listen intensely—are the ones who get the staffwork capable of fueling an organization's future.

THE CONSTRUCTIVE ROLE OF ADVISERS

Advisers are a resource for leaders to preserve their power and achieve their objectives. I could give you all kinds of self-serving reasons why leaders should use advisers, especially communications counselors, but in truth, there are really only three good reasons to do so:

1. To get an objective view from somebody who is able to face you squarely and act as a strong sounding board

2. To unburden the leader's calendar from the details that often enter into staffwork

3. To give leaders a fresh and expansive range of options.

Leaders who couple a focused view of staffwork with intensive listening are likely to receive staffwork that will measurably improve their own performance and the performance of their organizations.

GOOD FAT

Of course, some leaders, through overzealous expense control, have placed untenable limits on the simple *amount* of staffwork they receive. The late Hedley Donovan, who was editor in chief of *Time*, had a productive way of looking at the issue of staff support. He distinguished between *good fat* and bad fat within a staff organization.[1]

American business will likely miss much of the staffwork capability that it has trimmed out of its organizations. Information systems are not always an effective replacement for people. While PCs can produce data, they cannot produce deliberate advice that presents meaningful options thoughtfully. I was deeply embarrassed at one recent U.S.-Japan business conference at which the Japanese outstaffed their American counterparts to the point that the CEO of Nissan urged us Americans to "do more homework." The staff sacrifices we make for short-term profitability today will probably cost us gravely in our pursuit of long-term positioning.

When I visit the Common Market's research consortiums or the offices of MITI in Japan, I see no shortage of well-trained planners looking out for respective industrial futures. Tom Peters has argued for the advantages of "the fleet-footed organization," and there are many, but in seeking to achieve this ideal, American industries may come up short on thoughtfulness and the capacity to present their thoughts. This could be deadly at a time when long-term economic policy is being shaped by other world industrial powers more accustomed to thinking in terms of the long term. Dealing with the coming shortage in intellectual capital is one of the great challenges facing U.S. industry today.

THE POLITICAL MODEL

As business staffs have been cut back, White House and congressional staffs have grown immensely. All leaders facing their staffs tend to compare themselves with the president fielding questions at a news conference or the chairman of a congressional committee conducting a televised hearing. What can businesspeople in general learn from the staff structure and system of politics?

In general, the Democrats far exceed the Republicans in the development of creative staffwork. Bill Bradley, for example, has great staff. However, Democratic superiority in this area hasn't won the Democrats the presidency in 15 years. Young and idealistic on the whole, the Democrat staffs flow with imaginative ideas, initiatives, and provocative position papers. Yet the Democrats have historically been unable to get their individual staffs to coalesce behind one or two central ideas.

For the Republicans, in contrast, staff innovation is a lower priority, because major social change is not at the top of their political agenda. However, the Republicans do a superior job of reading their mail, which is the politician's equivalent of grassroots research. The Republicans are staff pragmatists. They focus on the demand side of the influence equation—not on all the problems that need to be solved but on the solutions most people want.

Leaders in other fields would be advised to seek staffwork that balances these two contrary tendencies: encouraging the creative staff ideas that will enable a positive future to be realized, while conducting enough pragmatic research to ensure that the company is still around to guide the future when it happens.

LIMITS TO DELEGATION

While staffwork can support leadership, leadershipwork can rarely be delegated to staff. Take the example of Bob Gilkeson, who was once CEO at Philadelphia Electric Company. Gilkeson was a wonderful fellow, but his view of leadership was just to tell people to go do something. In one instance, the legislature in Harrisburg was contemplating some onerous laws that would do long-term damage to Philadelphia Electric. Meeting to discuss the issue, we talked about how to mobilize suppliers, trade associations, and employees to fight these proposals. After listening to our presentation, Gilkeson said impatiently, "Just go do it."

"Bob," I replied, "we can just go do it, but that won't be enough. This is going to need your personal endorsement. You need to tell people you're behind it."

He never did, and as a result, the various groups never sensed his personal involvement. They weren't convinced that he felt this was important to the business or to the community. Philadelphia Electric was seen as cold and imperious. Although all of the individual staff campaigns had been mounted, they lacked the glue that an involved leader would have provided. It became easy for the legislature to vote against the vague, impersonal power company—and they did. More recently, Philadelphia Electric has gone a long way to solve these problems of perception and has significantly changed how they are regarded, through the active involvement of their management.

STAFF PREPARATION FOR COMMUNICATIONS

There are four principal kinds of communication in which staff can help leaders prepare: speeches, phone calls, meetings, and written pieces. Let me begin with speeches, because speech making is one of the most demanding uses of leadership time and deserves to earn good rewards for the time invested.

SPEECH MAKING

A speech gives the leader a chance to demonstrate brainpower in front of an audience. For the leader with growing influence, persuasive brainpower is first measured in departmental presentations. It is then seen in companywide and corporationwide talks. But the key measure of a manager's ability to influence is the outside speech—especially those aimed at trade associations, the investment community, management forums, or civic groups.

Speeches have always been used to measure effectiveness in putting thoughts together in a convincing way. History is steeped in examples: orator generals such as Pericles and Patton, orator statesmen such as Churchill and Lincoln, orator religious leaders from Buddha to Billy Graham. The ability to speak, to present a case in a clear and persuasive way, has forever been a test of leadership.

Only those leaders at the very top of any organization have the luxury of support from a speech writer. Still, the relationship between speech writer and executive speaker is a good one to study for the aspiring leader who wants to prepare for the future. The process of writing speeches and critiquing them can be internalized as a personal discipline, and this frame of reference can be valuable even for the leader of the future who is just beginning to make public speeches.

A leader should recognize that any speech made outside the organization probably has more value internally than it does externally. Speech writing drives organizational policy. It is an instrument to make something happen. As a result, the speech writer can be seen as both management consultant and midwife. Landon Parvin, speech writer to Ronald Reagan, certainly believes this. "Often times," he told me, "a manager will have an idea or a concept, but it will lack focus and shape. As such, it's useless to his organization. When he shapes and delivers the speech, the idea becomes clear."

Leaders should study political speeches, but only those by *modern* political leaders. Speeches today differ from the days of Roosevelt and Churchill. "Any politician who used purple prose the way Douglas MacArthur did would be laughed out of town," Parvin told me. Parvin believes that every modern speech must be reducible down to one or two memorable statements—a necessity born of the evening news sound bite. "If you don't have the lines, you don't get the coverage in politics," Parvin says. "Now people expect those key lines as an essential element of any major speech whether it will be on the evening news or not." Those lines become the "take-home"—the quick message summary people use to recall the speech.

Lastly, (and this is another piece of advice I owe to Parvin) leaders should spend more time choosing their own speaking opportunities, rather than responding to outside requests. It's easy to be flattered if you are invited to talk, and hard to say no, but such responses won't serve the goals of the organization. Instead, leaders should figure out what message they want to get out. Then the staff should zero in on the best way to deliver that message and anticipate how it will be received and covered.

TOUCH-TONE POWER

Most leaders spend between 20 and 30 percent of their time on the telephone. Although phones have been an integral part of business life for nearly a century, many leaders still don't know how to conduct a well-managed phone call.

Phone calls are a very serious business. Often, problems must be solved by thinking through an integrated strategy of telephone contacts, rather than just placing a single call. When the hostilities that led to the Gulf War were brewing, the ministers of a Middle Eastern country were prepared to sell half a million barrels of sweet crude oil to a major oil company. That's plenty of oil, and most companies either couldn't take it in one gulp, or weren't hungry enough to build the consortium needed to divide up the stock. I was called in and had to act quickly and that required a convincing phone strategy.

My first step was to call the State Department and confirm that the U.S. government would approve of liftings taken out of the country in question. They would. Next, I looked in the *Oil and Gas Journal* and called contacts I had at *Platt's Oilgram*. Without disclosing my mission, I created a list of three current names for each of the major oil companies—those in and outside of ARAMCO. The three names were those of the CEO, the communications officer, and the crude oil trader for each firm.

My first call let the communications head know that I would be calling the CEO, and that there was no cause for alarm (in other words, I was not bypassing the communications person to make a pitch about agency work to the CEO—or, in fact, calling about a communications matter at all). My mission in calling the CEO, I explained, was a confidential one on behalf of another client that could present the firm with a significant business opportunity. I was only permitted to conduct the discussion with the CEO directly.

Had I not taken this first step, my call to the CEO might well have been bucked to the communications head for handling. Instead, I was free to personally schedule calls with the respective CEOs through their secretaries, specifying the time I would call and explaining that I couldn't discuss the details, but that my call represented a possible major opportunity for their company. When the appointed time came, I placed the call myself, avoiding the status contests that so often result when administrative assistants place calls to executives through their counterparts.

Upon reaching each CEO, I first reassured him that the State Department approved of the liftings, since I knew that this would be the CEO's first concern. The CEO's second impulse in receiving such a call is to identify to whom the project could best be handed off for evaluation. In each case, I was quickly able to suggest that he might want to hand the assignment off to the crude oil trader, whom I referred to by name. By this point, the CEO was convinced that I had some basic knowledge of the business—or had at least done some research. For the several firms that expressed an interest, I then helped arrange the phone contacts between the country's oil minister and the crude trader. Within twenty-four hours, the deal had been struck with a leading oil firm.

Staff can be of great help in designing phone calls. Important calls deserve not just a call sheet listing names and phone numbers, but written objectives: What result do I want? How can I overcome the objections I am likely to encounter? What statistics or facts must I be sure to include to make the desired case?

The more important the call, the more necessary it is that there be some brief but convincing small talk at the outset to put everyone at ease. Then get to the point fast. If it's bad news or criticism, explain that the respondent is probably not going to welcome what you have to say, but that you are obliged to report it. Before you make the call, try to think of some positive way of concluding the conversation.

Phone calls from the press, special interest groups, or adversaries must be handled with particular care. In these cases, a leader must balance the desire to offer an earnest ear with the obligation to protect the interests of the organization. If you believe that the person on the other end is hostile, once you have learned what the topic is, try to shape the conversation rather than letting yourself be subjected to a series of inquisitorial questions.

Leaders have to design their conversations with other people. The higher up you go, the truer this is. And that includes your conversations across the desk or over coffee. When one has several agendas to advance, time is simply too scarce not to map out important calls and contacts.

MEETING CLOSURE

In a meeting, the leader is responsible for helping the organization to close an issue the same way a broker closes a house sale. Staff can prepare you with background for the meeting, but you will have to manage the actual dynamics of the meeting yourself. This means planning: knowing in advance what the probable alternatives will be and how they should be played out. It means listening to the flow of ideas—especially for the repetition of ideas, generally a cue that the meeting has played itself out and that control must be seized. It means one final sweep of the conference table to see that all the key opinions have been registered. It means acknowledging all the main issues involved without necessarily trying to bring closure to each. It means making sure the minutes are written to wrap things up—to get people to act, not to record a state of deadlock.

THE WRITTEN WORD

In my opinion, every letter that a leader sends on behalf of the organization must have three essential ingredients. The first is a personal tone that creates some sense of humanity and warmth. Second, an action point should clearly spell out what needs to be done. And third, there should be a mechanism in the letter that will ensure a follow-up.

The Procter & Gamble memorandum has always been a benchmark

for strong internal writing standards, but it's a dying art in the world of business. And, as I will discuss later, E-mail and computerized communication may be completely overhauling the standards for written communications in all organizations.

In the management of staff and the pursuit of sound advice, you will get the best results if you listen intensively, focus staff assignments sharply, and set standards for staffwork on communications projects that gives those projects a decided focus on results.

THE CANON OF THE
COMMUNICATOR'S
TEMPLATE
Conclusion to Part III

LEADERS HAVE FOUR PRIMARY MEANS THROUGH WHICH THEY CAN achieve their agendas and realize the vision of their organizations: the effective management of issues and trends, the commissioning of focused research and intelligence, the devising of agendas and plans, and the empowerment of advisers to provide high-caliber staffwork.

ISSUES AND TRENDS

Leaders should guide how the organization tracks external information. They must also create connections for the organization between external events and realization of the organization's vision.

Leaders must take a clear viewpoint toward external information, one that lets them foreshadow the positive events that can help the organization realize its goals. By scanning for information from an informed perspective, the leader can also identify and combat early on the "hostile fire" of looming attacks and groundless accusations.

In consuming media, leaders should use their time and energy intelligently, take public rankings seriously, and read and see on behalf of the organization. They should reflect on current entertainment and humor for emerging trends, and sift the various shreds of data they collect for new megaforces.

Leaders should also use their critical skills to identify potential public policy problems in apparent opportunities and to challenge old and new preconceptions.

RESEARCH AND INTELLIGENCE

Leaders should use intelligence in a targeted manner to win influence wars. While leaders must be "research literate," they should avoid tampering in the technical process of collecting and analyzing data.

Leaders are prudent to use research in enhancing both their own message delivery skills and the image of their organization, but must also change the underlying reality when any change in image is attempted.

Leaders should help important outsiders in their research about the organization and carefully maintain the file of public information about the organization in advance of any crises.

The intelligence activities commissioned by leaders should focus on utility and should not neglect review of the public files. The most important regularly gathered intelligence should address the integrity of other organizations with whom business is done. Finally, leaders should be sure that intelligence is used to detect opportunities as well as to help control risk.

AGENDAS AND PLANS

Leaders must scan the horizon for events that may materially impact the organization's future but should dedicate resources only after locking onto specific targets. This requires the skillful creation of agendas and plans.

Agendas help leaders sustain the organization's sense of direction as short- and medium-term goals are realized. Agendas must have staying power and each step must include an explicit communications plan.

An organization must behave in a manner consistent with the values and prescriptions expressed in its agendas. Leaders must limit the number of back-room agendas and focus them on constructive goals.

Leaders must also be on the lookout for the hidden agendas of others, especially those that could give competing organizations an advantage in controlling information.

In guiding the planning process, leaders should help sustain an annual planning rhythm, make sure plans respond to the diversity of important constituents, and guarantee that the organization has meaningful ways of weathering disruption.

ADVISERS AND STAFFWORK

Leaders must create a positive, receptive environment that will encourage staff to bring forward honest, high-quality advice. This is best accomplished by being an intense and focused listener.

Effective long-term leadership requires investment in quality staff resources. The staff should be challenged to achieve a balance of creativity and pragmatism in its work. Leaders should not delegate leadershipwork to their staffs.

Leaders should use the considerable investment in preparing speeches to advance some important internal agenda of the organization. Each speech the leader delivers should have one to two memorable and skillfully written messages. Leaders should only accept speaking platforms that will further the organization's agenda.

In day-to-day activities, leaders will improve their effectiveness if they work from written plans for important phone calls, orchestrate closure in each meeting they chair and on each agenda item discussed, and demand personalized, actionable written communications for themselves and others.

LEADERSHIP'S
GOALS

Through combining the raw materials of leadership with a sense for the communications landscape and an agile use of the communicator's template, leaders should have the ability to achieve their goals. But what exactly should those goals be? Visions are realized only over time; thus, the leader can't simply jump out of the office one day, wander through the organization, grab for its pulse, and pronounce, "We've got the vision right!"

Leaders also need more immediate goals. There are four reliable goals that, if achieved, almost always indicate that an organization is on track in achieving its vision.

These four generic goals of leadership are:

1. Creativity

2. Access to sources of power and to the minds of opinion leaders

3. Well-positioned and reliable organizational performance and growth

4. The goodwill of those forces whose consent is needed for the organization to continue to operate.

These four traits are all signs of organizational health:

1. Creativity, or the capacity to change and innovate

2. Power alliances, which multiply strength, especially when the organization is beset by outside opposition

3. Stability and reliable growth, which create the kind of organizational stamina that gives both the confidence and the tangible resources needed to realize the vision

4. Goodwill, because organizations whose attitudes are positive and that are regarded positively are quite simply the likeliest to succeed.

One organization that is well along in achieving its vision and displays ample evidence of these four traits is Ford. Indeed, Ford has a better idea. You can learn only so much about the communications program at Ford, for it is the only company I know of that regards its communications program as proprietary technology. Ford believes that it gives them that much of a competitive edge.

Ford is doing a great deal right, and experts say that Ford's communications practices are a major factor in its success. The company's communications challenge: to reach and motivate some 350,000 (mostly unionized) employees worldwide. Its response: the most intensive program of communications—especially employee communications—yet devised within American industry.

Ford chairman and CEO Red Poling and his team acknowledge that they learned much about communicating the message of quality to employees from W. Edwards Deming, the American management guru who revolutionized Japanese management practices after World War II. It was from Deming, for example, that Ford learned and invoked the philosophy of "continuous improvement." Managers should never put a cap on the quality standard, Deming believes.

Certainly, there is always room for *material* improvements, the kind that are achieved time after time and that can thereby be noted and appreciated by customers as a sign of a high quality standard. But years ago, improvements at a particular plant could easily have meant beefing up the repair pits. Instead, Ford today goes upstream. The approach is "information trouble shooting," or getting a focused quality message across that tackles problems of attitude and competence before mistakes get made. For example, a quality problem might trigger the airing of one of Ford's favorite videos: "Squeaks and Rattles," a 30-minute "docudrama," in the style of "The People's Court," in which the plaintiff pleads, "But I had nothing to do with the glove box!"

Don't confuse Ford's system with its strategy. Twenty-three staff members and a host of freelancers feed Ford Communications Network programming. The video library has miles of "B-roll" tape (background footage), allowing managers and staff to custom-assemble programs on anything from internal combustion to customer service.

Certainly, the TV network is glitzy and makes nice copy. The reason it works, however, is that there is a well-defined need and idea behind it. I have seen untold numbers of expensive company video systems that are worthless. Leadership lusted after the technology; now the gear sits in the corner like a jilted lover. Nobody has figured out how to give the medium a purpose in those businesses. The concept and the commitment must come first. The technology is just the means—in this case, an indispensable means—to an end.

The important points to note about the Ford system are these:

1. It is *creative.* Beyond Ford's outstanding use of technology, its capacity to help solve practical problems is truly innovative.

2. Ford has demonstrated its *effectiveness.* The folks in Washington know that Ford is a national treasure: one of the few U.S. companies that get the job done on quality and global competitiveness. The analysts, the press, and opinion leaders worldwide know it too.

3. Ford has achieved remarkable *dependability* in its sales and profit performance. Ford is seen in the financial marketplace as having the financial reliability of a Japanese company, and its carefully managed growth is now allowing it to invest like a Japanese company for the long term.

4. Ford enjoys impressive *goodwill.* Ford has been a groundbreaker in community-industry cooperation. Its labor relations situation is the best of the Big Three American car makers, and better than most, if not all, of the Japanese car makers doing business on U.S. soil (with the possible exception of Mazda). The Ford Foundation

has been one of the pacesetters in American philanthropy for decades.

Thus, if a leader wants to study one organization to see how the goals of leadership can be realized, I would suggest Ford. If, however, I were asked to identify one leader whose personal style comprises these four generic leadership goals, I would choose, not a businessperson, but the Reverend Robert Schuller. Since Reverend Schuller is devoted to doing good works, it may be a little easier for him to behave in such an impeccable way. (His business counterparts must often deal in the trenches of commercial reality, with all their shades of gray.) Even so, Schuller was the most significant electronic minister to have withstood the scandals of the last few years. His personal style is a model of leadership behavior toward achieving a vision.

A quick measure of Schuller against the four leadership goals shows the following:

1. *Creativity:* Without histrionics, Schuller is capable—week after week—of drawing 1.3 million American households into his ministry. He created a powerful visible symbol for the ministry when he tapped America's foremost architect, Philip Johnson, to erect the Crystal Cathedral in Garden Grove, California. He also has an acute sense for the use of sound, space, and medium, as proven by a recent broadcast in which a huge American flag was unfurled while he read a moving prayer for the GI's in the Gulf War. His ability to convert the world of current events into lessons about modern values is remarkable.

2. *Access:* In Washington, Schuller is a welcome guest at the White House and in the offices of Congress. No minister today has a better or more comprehensive rapport with American boardrooms or the American press.

3. *Positioned growth:* Schuller's message has reached an estimated 100 million individuals. His Sunday services are regularly attended by 8,000 guests. His goal is to get another 100 million individuals worldwide to recognize his message, and he seems well on the way to achieving that goal.

4. *Goodwill:* Schuller has managed to acquire and retain widespread goodwill during a time of tremendous cynicism toward teleminis-

tries. Perhaps the best evidence of the esteem in which Schuller is held was the decision by Reverend Bruce Larson, pastor of the University Presbyterian Church in Seattle and probably the most esteemed community minister in America, to join Schuller as "co-pilot" in conducting the Crystal Cathedral ministry.[1]

Schuller also has all the raw ingredients of leadership. He is a man of enormous physical bearing, exuding great presence even before his rich, resonant voice is heard. He's believable, but also energized: an idea-a-minute man, constantly looking for new ways to realize his vision.

What makes Schuller most effective as a leader, however, is his recognition of what can be accomplished in a limited amount of time. When Schuller meets with people, he radiates a sincere and intense personal interest, but when topics change or one meeting moves into the next, you always have the feeling that Schuller is reaching into his vest and pulling out his pocket watch. He seems to be focusing on the dial of his Power Clock, knowing that he is accountable for using every second to its fullest. After all, someone schedules every phone call Schuller makes, every letter he writes, every contact that occurs. When there are disruptions—as when President Bush was unable to see him in Washington because of the outbreak of the Gulf War—Schuller is immediately able to fill the gap in his schedule.

Schuller has contact with many world leaders. He recently offered to the President to organize a number of church leaders—the Pope, the Dalai Lama, the Archbishop of Canterbury—to go to Iraq to try to turn Saddam Hussein away from war. The mission came surprisingly close to fruition, but for diplomatic reasons and because of his concern about the personal safety of these remarkable leaders, President Bush finally declined.

The final part of this book deals with the generic goals of leadership—the kinds of things a Ford and a Reverend Schuller do so well. Pursuit of these goals, amidst the confusions and frustrations of everyday business, is the surest way I know to achieve the vision of any organization.

CHAPTER

14

THE KING'S SEAL
Engendering Creativity

O F ALL THE DIFFERENT BEHAVIORS A LEADER SEEKS TO ELICIT IN an organization, creativity is the most elusive to sustain. This chapter outlines proven tactics that leaders can use to draw creative thinking out of their people. Sometimes the most creative thing which a leader can do is to stay silent. Once I went to a meeting where a client took me through a presentation and internal dialogue that lasted six hours, outlining an initiative the client wanted to take. Outside of an occasional nod or noncommittal comment, I said nothing the entire time. Finally, the CEO became exasperated. He turned to me pleadingly and asked if I had anything, *anything* to say.

"Yes," I said. "Don't do it." The message registered: They abandoned the program. In my opinion, my nerve-wracking silence was probably worth far more than any amiable chatter I could have used to fill the air. My purpose was to endow a single moment with great significance and to let it reinforce a critical conclusion. Think of the movies and television, where some of the most memorable moments occur when the screen goes to black and the sound is still—when what is communicated is silence.

THINKPOINTS

on How

a Leader Generates Creativity

☐ Use silence as a creative medium.

☐ Master the pace and style of electronic communications.

☐ Encourage provocative questioning.

☐ Help people to project the thinking of others.

☐ Advocate role reversals to expose fresh viewpoints.

☐ Pose positive questions with a long-term hook.

THE SEVEN USES OF SILENCE

There are seven significant uses for silence, probably the most under-estimated creative weapon in any leader's arsenal. They are:

1. Buying time to put a response in order

2. Giving an adversary a chance to reconsider an attack

3. Giving a subordinate the chance to take a risk and grow

4. Endowing a moment with great significance

5. Announcing that there are no new messages

6. Throwing the marketplace off stride

7. Climbing above the fray.

Let me explain each in more detail.

Buying time. Every day, I see this use of silence—or the need for it—in dealings with the press. So many leaders simply fail to pause and organize their thoughts before they answer a question or make a statement. Alexander Haig's infamous and impetuous declaration that he was in charge, after the assassination attempt on Ronald Reagan, contributed to his departure from the post of Secretary of State—and quite possibly also blocked his chances for the presidency in later years.

A chance to reconsider. In the last seconds of Super Bowl XXV, then New York Giants coach Bill Parcells effectively used a device that has been tapped many times by successful coaches caught in the same situation. He called a time out to plant second doubts in the minds of the opposing Buffalo Bills before they attempted a potentially game-winning field goal. One could see the momentum drain from the face of the kicker when the time out was called. The kick was missed, and the Giants won. (By the way, some experts estimate that missed kick cost kicker Scott Norwood about half a million dollars in testimonials and endorsements.)

Leaders can use the pause for reconsideration in the creative pursuit of positive behavior as well as in outwitting opponents. If an executive is about to set out on a rash or useless course of action, cornering the executive and getting her or him to reflect for a moment can often save the organization considerable pain.

The chance to risk and grow. The most dramatic use of silence I ever encountered came under the category of letting a subordinate risk and grow. Ian Rolland, CEO of Lincoln National Corporation in Fort Wayne, wanted to be sure that his management team was prepared for succession. So, over a period of three years, he simply disappeared periodically to the heart of darkest Africa and elsewhere on personal travel. When crises arose, his lieutenants tried to phone him and telegraph him; they sent helicopters, scouts, and runners. On one occasion, they even organized a small-scale safari to try to reach him, but Rolland—like a character in a Joseph Conrad novel—would not be found. The remaining team had to make their own decisions. Management cream rose to the top. And the succession plan worked—partly, perhaps, because Rolland's board supported his approach.

Maybe fax machines and uplinks would catch up with Rolland today, but there is a lot to commend a leader's staying silent at times to see how potential leaders take the helm.

Implying great significance. My "Don't do it" advice to the client I stonewalled for six hours would have meant infinitely less had it been given in the first ten minutes of the presentation. Even though I had a good instinct early in the presentation for where I would come down, it was important to lend a *visibly* earnest ear (and it would have been possible for me to change my mind as I heard their case develop).

No new messages. I counseled Frank Lorenzo on his departure from Eastern Airlines. For a period of about a week, Lorenzo conducted an exhaustive media schedule and did a superb job of saturating the media with his story. After that, however, I counseled him to "go to black"— simply not to do any more interviewing for a while. My reasoning: First, the message was already out there for anyone who wanted to learn it. And second, continued exposure would simply gnaw away at the strength of his established messages; there was nothing to be gained for the present by prolonging his exposure.

Rising above the fray. This can be effective advice, but it has its dangers too. In Robert Caro's compelling account of Lyndon Johnson's contest with Coke Stevenson over a Texas seat in the U.S. Senate, he notes that Johnson successfully undermined Stevenson by using Stevenson's own determination to stand above the fray and his unwillingness to explain his stand on labor and the Taft-Hartley Act.[1]

In some instances, however, a silent stand above the fray may be appropriate. When Louis Austin, as president of Texas Utilities, had to address objections from a series of special interests, he taught me an important lesson: "You must get special interests in an atmosphere where you can talk off the record. Neither side can 'test' positions in open meetings. Texas Utilities once ran afoul of the League of Women Voters and the Environmental Defense Fund. We talked about how to tackle the problem, and all three groups got together along with Georgia Light and Power Company to sponsor a symposium. We leased the Aspen Institute facilities on the Maryland eastern shore." What enabled the dialogue to get down to the issues was a conscious decision by management to let the other groups say what they wanted at the outset and to be as vicious as they wished. Management was prepared to take it, and to ask only clarifying questions. "You must let them cuss at you the first day," Austin said.

Sometimes silence can be more than golden; it can be gold itself. Aspiring leaders are well advised to experiment with the uses of silence and to master the creative opportunities silence can hold—well before they reach the pinnacle of their organizations, when a steady stream of silence can easily be dismissed as aloofness from the organization and its people.

ELECTRONIC DIALOGUE.

One area in which leaders cannot afford to be silent, although many are, is electronic communications. No leader can ignore the presence of terminals and keyboards on nearly every desk in the organization, but few have adjusted their own behavior to match the new reality.

One leader who made the adjustment was the late Bill McGowan, as CEO of MCI. In a speech before the Economic Club of Detroit, he described leadership companies—truly transnational firms—as having "a management style that's geared to the fast pace of the Information Age. Their management is online. They're plugged into a steady stream of information." Indeed, electronic mail (E-mail) is changing the nature of communication and influence in countless firms.

Four years ago, MCI decided to divisionalize into seven regional territories to correspond with the domains of the Baby Bells, which were the places MCI needed to compete. At the time, MCI's top management team was all in Washington, and they used to meet regularly for breakfast each Monday morning. Today, this "breakfast" still lives, but instead of being a chalk talk over flapjacks, it has become an electronic communication conducted through MCI-Mail (MCI's version of E-mail). Each division now sends in a report for the breakfast, which is submitted in a fairly standardized way. The submissions are merged and the document is transmitted across the country each Monday. "Breakfast sets the agenda into place for the week," Bernie Goodrich, MCI's director of public relations, told me. The company supplements the E-mail wrap-up with an in-person group meeting once a month.

The revolution of E-mail at MCI doesn't stop with breakfast, however. This company estimates that they are moving a million messages a month internally through their E-mail system. The network gives employees previously unheard-of access to top management. Many people are directly in touch with the CEO. Bernie Goodrich described the impact of the E-mail revolution this way: "E-mail changes the style of verbal communications in the company. It is much terser. It accelerates the speed of decision making. You aren't constantly trying to convene meetings to resolve simple matters. E-mail also creates a relatively flat information structure. It works against people becoming repositories of information who then block the process. E-mail makes it easier to manage the information flow. You can propose a new practice or program to 15 people at once and ask them 'Does this affect you?'"

Today's leaders will have to grasp the use of E-mail in the same way that leaders in the Middle Ages had to master the art of composing letters. It must be creative and it must be fast: the electronic equivalent of the king's seal in the twelfth century. My own IBM PCs, located both in the office and at home, receive about 50 to 75 E-mail communications a day. The technology drives much of my business life, which I'm sure is becoming the case for more and more leaders. Stylistically, E-mail reduces the importance of eloquence; it demands a whole new style of communication. One must be able to answer a direct question—and answer it on the spot. As a result, electronic communications are modifying the nature of management power. The winners in decision making contests were once those who wrote the most eloquent memos, the most cagey debaters in meetings, or those who had the best appendices to their reports. Things are different today. It's the executive capable of banging out a message with the rat-a-tat of a Sam Spade who will likely win.

Of course, E-mail has its disadvantages too. Remember the damage to the quality of staffwork caused by the elimination of staff positions? E-mail, for all its speed and immediacy, may cause us to become less thoughtful and less conscious of how our decisions evolve. That's something that leaders must also be conscious of, and the most concerned will insist that the organization retain some sort of institutional memory for how it makes decisions.

LICENSE TO QUESTION.

Innovative approaches to questioning can often unleash considerable creative power in an organization. At a second telephone communications company I know, leaders regularly ask the company's ad agency to bring in change agents and to conduct off-site marketing brainstorming sessions. They have creative people who are unfamiliar with the product sit and listen to presentations. These thought terrorists complain, taunt, and make up wish lists. They raise crazy questions: "Why don't you just give them a credit card?" or "Why don't you just tell your computer department to make the systems change?" When these wild-eyed sessions lead to new policy, the policy is usually remarkably successful.

Another firm asks their top people such questions as, "If Competitor X, our toughest competitor, were to introduce Product M, what would their marketing plan be?" and "If that's what it will be, how do you plan to stop it?" In this same company, 55-year old male sales managers will play the role of 22-year-old female graduate student customers, and will then be asked to explain why these customers should care about all the product attributes listed on the pages of the company's sales brochures.

A third company holds off-site brainstorming sessions at which attendees are banned from talking about their specialties. If you are from manufacturing, you can't talk about making the product. If you're from sales, you can't talk about selling it. If you're in distribution, you can't bring up shipping. No matter what your specialty, you have to leave your official hat hung up outside before walking into the session. You are forced to think beyond your normal frame of reference, to identify the wider potential opportunities for the firm.

In all of these instances, an irreverent license to question can give the leader and the organization itself an enormous edge in creativity. Leaders themselves can set a creative standard for interrogation within the organization; I'm talking not about CEOs grilling subordinates to get at the truth behind last month's shortfall in orders and sales, but about positive, energizing kinds of interrogation.

Merck, the distinguished pharmaceutical firm, has stared on *Fortune*'s list of "Most Admired Corporations" in recent years.[2] Merck has an incredible record of bringing successful new drug products to market. Are Merck's scientists unusually insightful in the laboratory? Doubtless they are. But Merck is also relentlessly diligent about bringing a continuing stream of the highest-quality people into their organization.

Ralph Waldo Emerson used to greet his friends by asking what had become clear to them, what they had learned, since he had last seen them. According to *Fortune,* Merck's brilliant but low-key CEO, Dr. Roy Vagelos, will greet his managers with "Who have you recruited lately?"[3] Who else would think of recruiting as everyday work? Do most managers say to themselves, "I better hustle and find the company's next star before the CEO buttonholes me again in the hallway"? Hardly; in most companies, headhunting is the sole province of the personnel department. Not at Merck. And look at the results: Merck's research staff is superior to the graduate faculties of some of the world's leading universities. A creative approach to staffing has led to competitive excellence. Through the adventuresome use of communications— from E-Mail to silence, from outrageous questioning to role-reversal simulations, leaders have countless opportunities to introduce fresh viewpoints into the organization and to keep the organization's thinking agile and fresh.

15

BEYOND
THE GATEKEEPERS
Gaining
Access and Achieving Penetration

T HE MOST OVERESTIMATED ASPECT OF LEADERSHIP IS "PLAYING IN the right circles": holding a spot in the right clubs, on the right boards, and on the right invitation lists to dinners and other social events. Certainly, these "memberships" can be important, but in the end, the world of power and leadership turns on quality—quality of thinking and quality of results—just like everything else. Thus, rather than focus on the elaborate etiquette of modern power—most of which has little to do with real leadership—I have chosen instead to give a select few illustrations of how serious-minded leaders can improve their odds of reaching other powerful opinion leaders and thereby furthering their agendas. Access to gatekeepers and power brokers can be essential to your success, but effective courtship of these individuals has more to do with thoughtful planning than with personal charisma. This chapter explains how a leader can get this job done.

THE SHORT LIST

When I first arrived in New York in the mid-sixties, I was befriended by a woman named Lyn White. White worked for Norman Cousins

THINKPOINTS

on How

Leaders Gain Effective Access and Penetration

☐ Focus on quality and results before access.

☐ Learn that real gatekeepers are diverse and unexpected.

☐ Know the political agendas of leaders you dine with.

☐ Use "executive advance" to learn while you travel.

☐ Strive to speak at important forums.

☐ Radiate the effects of key talks.

☐ Use "single-story" strategies to set the public record.

☐ Cultivate promising young reporters.

☐ Educate reporters to build long-term relationships.

☐ Telegraph your leadership role in community involvement.

☐ Visit Washington sparingly and only with an agenda.

---

at the *Saturday Review,* which was then the pinnacle of thoughtful, liberal journalism. On first blush she looked more like a cowgirl than a *Saturday Review* savant. She was 4'10" tall, but not short on either money or moxie. Often she would wear a huge Texas Ranger badge on her dress.

For over two years, Lyn White took me to lunch at The Four Seasons on average twice a week. We would sit at her regular table, and she would hold court. She would greet a steady stream of New York celebrities, from the comedian Jackie Mason to Walter Cronkite and Norman Cousins.

I also met a number of significant people through John Hill, who used to have two or three parties a week at his apartment at 800 Park Avenue. His guests included investment bankers, labor lawyers, and the heads of such major companies as U.S. Steel. Hill had his own continuous symposium: a running industrial seminar in which we would sit around and discuss the issues of the day. It was quite an experience.

Power lunching is still New York's number one hobby. Visit Le Cirque at noon on a Saturday and see for yourself. Along the wall, in between the barons of American industry and the celebrities, you'll see people who may appear quite insignificant, but many of whom are actually the glue holding the power structure together.

As for me, I take in the smaller haunts; it's the only way I can keep my agenda private. Meeting people through Lyn White and John Hill early in my career helped me in a key respect: They gave me some immunity to being awed by the self-importance that afflicts so many powerful people. Perhaps these friendships also gave me the insight that the leaders who control the power switches are not always the ones with the titles and the reputations. Leaders should learn about the nature of the "short list" of people who matter to public decision making. The list itself is less important than the diversity and unexpectedness of some of the people who are on it. Above all, leaders should see that the power of access can often come from unexpected places.

In Chicago, a man named George Dunne has run an insurance agency for more than 30 years. Some may think that George just peddles policies, but he is connected to all the major power lines in that city—perhaps better than anyone else in that town. In Miami, a central figure is a PR counselor named Hank Meyer. I don't believe there's a door in Florida Hank Meyer can't open. There is even a Miami boulevard named after him. In Pittsburgh, Tony O'Reilly is the key, while in Nashville, three figures are particularly formidable: TVA chief Marvin Runyon, Watergate lawyer Jim Neal, and John Seigenthaler at the *Tennesseean.* In San Francisco, the guy who runs the show is the eminent historian Roger Starr. In New Orleans, it's Michael Read, a local lawyer who also sits on the Sugar Bowl committee. O. Mark De Michele, the CEO of Arizona Public Service, is the number one contact in Phoenix, and Tip Lifvendahl, who runs the *Sentinel,* is the person to know in Orlando. These people are not necessarily wealthy, but they are all genuine power brokers who get a certain pleasure from that. They know how to cut deals and how to put people together.

And who is the most powerful person in Washington? Frank Mankiewicz, former head of National Public Radio, tells me it's Jack Kent Cooke. Why? Because Jack controls access to Redskin season tickets and—above all—the owner's box. In Frank's words, "That is pretty powerful coin."

CEREMONIAL MEALS AND OTHER OCCASIONS

The likeliest place for leaders to encounter other leaders is at one of the dozens of banquets and luncheons that occur in every major city every day. While these are called meals, food is never a factor—even though the society pages write endlessly about the napery and the entrées. I have eaten ceremonial lunches of tofu with the likes of Ken Ejiri, the former head of Mitsui, and kosher suppers with Rabbi Arthur Schneier, head of the Appeal of Conscience Foundation in New York (and probably the most discerning host of dinner parties in all of Manhattan).

Before attending such events, the leader who wants to advance an agenda needs to research the people who will be there, mostly in order to understand their politics. At the end of the day, the one topic you can bet will be on the agenda is politics—especially on the national level of the country where the dinner takes place. It's simple. Some people want to stop ideas, others want to advance them. For every person backing tort reform in the United States, there are as many— probably more—vested interests trying to block it. And so it is with every issue.

It's not hard to gain access to the local landscape, whether in Bangkok or Buffalo, and even to get invited into the social life of other cities. In fact, it can be done with relative ease and speed—with the proper plan.

THE EXECUTIVE ADVANCE

Leaders today have to be much more conscious of the public environment around them than was the case in the past. That means knowing a lot more than what's going on in their home town or at their corporate headquarters. It is not necessary, however, for leaders to carry the agenda of a thousand different cities around in their heads at the same time.

Because so many leaders travel extensively, they have enormous opportunities to learn about the influence and power structures of cities throughout their own country and around the world. This information can make an executive more competent in public affairs, marketing, and a host of other disciplines. The trick is to know how to gather it and apply it quickly to the proper context.

Most businesspeople today don't know how to learn while they are traveling. As they race through airports, expressways, and office centers—all of which have a deadening sameness—their eyes glaze over and their awareness is numbed. The leader who can overcome this reaction gains a valuable advantage. Political campaigns—which have taught business so much about marketing, intelligence, and research— also hold the secrets of traveling to forward leadership. It's really the skill of being your own "advance" man or woman.

In my thirties, when I spent considerable time on the road, I got to know all the major—and most of the minor—cities in the United States reasonably well. Here are a few quick tips I learned in my travels that can help a leader get rapidly up to speed on any local visits:

- Before making a visit, use your information retrieval data banks to call up an article or two about major political issues in the town you are visiting.

- Use your local subsidiary office to see if there is a way to be invited to a local civic activity that coincides with your visit.

- On your arrival at the airport, pick up the local paper and scan it for issues and events of current importance.

- If you are traveling abroad, use your accounting firm, management consultant, or lead bank to give you background information on the economic context of the country you are visiting.

FINDING THE GATES

When I travel my secretary Joan Avagliano develops for me a list of phone numbers and names of people I might contact. Some kind of reference or intermediary contact is always best, but if you don't know them at all, you can still in most cases simply call their offices and say that you have heard they are people who have remarkable influence in their communities, and you would simply like to introduce yourself through a five-minute meeting. A recent casual contact I made through such an informal visit caused the other party to reach for his phone, call me, and say, "Solve my problem." It was lucrative business for our firm.

In Europe, and even more in Japan, one cannot expect a business relationship to spring up overnight. Because business is done differently in these countries, it may take one or two years instead. If you don't build the relationships first, however, your chances of doing business in these areas at *any* time will be remote at best. With a minimal investment of time and expense, every trip away from home can become a conscious learning exercise. The contacts acquired as a result can amplify the leader's and the organization's power in the future.

For the aspiring leaders, who want on their travels simply to observe the procession of powerful people, it's easy enough to stake out a watching post. If you wait long enough in such places as the Berkeley Hotel in London, the important figures in the international business community will generally come through. Same story if you stay in the Imperial or the Okura Hotel in Japan: you'll find out who is in town. The French are just beginning to have power breakfasts; their international guests are likely to be found at the Plaza Athenée or the Crillon. In New York, try the Regency, the Mayfair Regent, or the Carlyle.

As I said before, however, all the manipulation that will get an aspiring leader to the right place at the right time takes up time better spent getting a thoughtful message out to a suitable public, through giving a provocative speech or attending a worthwhile conference. Being a power groupie has few real rewards.

THE SATIN SOAPBOX

Perhaps the best way to access and penetrate powerful and influential minds is through carefully selected speaking forums. The most potent forums in the United States include the National Press Club in Washington; the Council on Foreign Relations in New York; the Economic Clubs of New York, Detroit, and Chicago; the Commonwealth Club of San Francisco; and Town Hall in Los Angeles. While a leader may not be able to land such a distinguished forum, it is wise to set one's sights on the standards required by forums as demanding as these.

For public figures, especially ones embroiled in controversy, the honoraria in some forums can soar to lofty heights. Retired sports figures, politicians, or bestselling writers can make a handsome living on the speaking circuit: Don Regan and Al Haig routinely earned speaking fees of $20,000 to $25,000 plus expenses after they left office. Ronald Reagan has made much more: a million dollars for a three-day trip to Japan. These sums can easily surpass what professional athletes, rock stars, and concert pianists earn for a one-hour performance.

For years, Wesley Johnson guided the agenda of the Detroit Economic Club as its president. This organization is typical of the very select speaking forums that most managers can only lust after. The Club hosts 37 or 38 speeches each year, with speakers divided about evenly between businesspeople, governmental officials, and members of the scientific, educational, and other specialized communities. That adds up to only about 12 shots for business executives in any given year. If each of the Fortune 500 industrial CEOs were to speak at this forum once, it would take 42 years to exhaust the list!

It is the duty of the organizers to bring in speakers who will be an effective draw for large and sophisticated audiences. According to Johnson, the number one factor in selecting a speaker is name recognition. Thus, such figures as Lee Iacocca, Red Poling, Robert Stempel, and Peter Grace are always sought after, while speakers who don't have quite that status must offer another angle. Perhaps their business is tied to an important emerging trend (such as waste management technology or superconductivity applications) or perhaps they can offer a truly innovative managerial slant, such as pioneering an important luxury market in what was thought to be only a commodity business.

Who are some of the best speakers who have appeared at the Detroit Economic Club? In recent years, member surveys have given very high marks to three people in particular: Ross Perot, who radiated a straightforward, personal charm; former Porsche CEO Peter Schutz, who was both natural and highly incisive; and, perhaps most impressive, Richard Nixon, who surprised the audience with both his spontaneity and his air of authority. What do the best speakers have in common? They don't tout their company or champion a cause. They're not stiff. They have solid content and they speak spontaneously. "They don't sound as if they are in the clutches of their speech writers," Johnson says.

Interestingly, I know of more and more speakers who may go through several drafts of a speech, polishing both the ideas and the style, only to abandon the written text when the speech is given (with all due deference to the fine staffwork that may go into preparing the talk). The stages of developing the speech present the opportunity to refine and distill the language and the ideas. In the end, if the process is effectively internalized, the written speech itself usually serves as an obstacle rather than a tool.

THE RADIATION FACTOR

Writing and delivering a speech are only two-thirds of the job. It is of equal importance that the speech have effective downstream distribution. Leaders should think about the "radiation factor" in speeches and should build into the talk downstream audiences and ways of reaching them.

Let's say that I am talking to a group of attorneys on the subject of business ethics, but I also want to reach the key heads of the construction industry on how to publicize contract arbitration. I will make it a point to contact five leading construction CEOs for their views. Invariably, these people ask for copies of the speech. Sometimes they will end up distributing it to their entire company.

THE PRESS

Another important facet of penetration is how a leader is regarded in the press. On this topic, I offer three pieces of advice: the potential importance of a single story, the power of education, and the cultivation of young reporters.

THE SINGLE STORY

Leaders facing a public problem often think that they must right the record with every journal that normally covers their beat. In truth, a single interview with the right publication can be a powerful antidote to negative press.

Many times in my career, when the first access for an in-depth story on a crisis situation was turned over to a capable and fair-minded publication such as the *New York Times,* the *Wall Street Journal, Fortune,* or *Business Week,* key research pieces have resulted that led to reasonable public viewpoints on the organizations in question. If you know the publication and the reporter have strong journalistic ethics, you have a better than even chance of being treated fairly.

YOUNG REPORTERS

One of the smartest investments leaders can make is to cultivate relationships with young reporters who appear to have potential. In the journalism profession, five years is a very long time. If someone is a major beat reporter with the *Wall Street Journal* at 25, they could well be editor-in-chief of a major publication by the time they are 40. Don't favor the mediocre writer who happens to pen a favorable article; instead, look for those who have genuine analytical skills and journalistic talent. Annually, Dean Rotbart's *TJFR* newsletter on the press identifies 30 journalists "under the age of 30 who are already on the fast track to success." It's a list well worth reading.

EDUCATION BUYS ACCESS

Neither most business leaders nor most organizations think they have the responsibility for educating the financial press. Yet in many areas—particularly those dealing with cutbacks in staff—business pages no longer have the sheer numbers of people they need to cover particular industry segments. The simple willingness to help educate a reporter on an industry can buy a leader enormous long-term goodwill from the press, even for firms in so-called "declining" industries. As Dean Rotbart has pointed out to me, when such an educational opportunity arises you can often find the chance to say to the reporter, "Don't be fooled by the decline in the industry. This industry is still larger than these six other industries which seem to be attracting a lot of attention. Here, let me show you why we are still a very important economic factor."

A CIVICS LESSON

Knowing opinion leaders and gatekeepers and building constructive press relationships are two aspects of a leader's public involvement. The third dimension is what the leader attempts to achieve in civic situations, on both Main Street and Pennsylvania Avenue.

THE PROVING GROUND OF COMMUNITY LIFE

Community life is an important proving ground for influence. One headhunter whom I know claims that a leader's status directly correlates with the "power to influence others to give money to significant charities and causes." Fund-raising creates strong rivalries, especially in large cities. Most nonprofit boards, however, are populated with just four or five true dynamos who have influence. The rest are just "association groupies" who are merely along for the ride. Community influence is one measure that can declare your true status loud and clear to the leadership peer group.

WASHINGTON

Recognition and acceptance on a local level are relatively easy. Only a very few leaders, however, maintain a powerful profile on the Washington scene. A great many leaders simply lack the proper credentials. In my view, the thoughtful leader should aspire to pursue only a moderate profile in Washington. If leaders limited their trips to Washington to those occasions that were really important, then it would be no problem to get congressmen and cabinet secretaries to spend time talking about the issues. Unless a leader has a well-thought-out agenda, the best advice is to stay home.

When the *New York Times* interviewed me about lobbying power in Washington, I told them that it was the super-sophisticated expertise of smaller lobbying firms such as Timmons and Company and Wexler, Reynolds, Fuller, Harrison & Schule that really made the difference.[1] They go beyond the stock and trade of position papers and press backgrounders. Indeed, my views on what a leader should do in Washington are simply lessons I have learned from real experts, such as Bill Timmons.

Some leaders have tried to elevate their importance in Washington by associating themselves with a single issue. Bill has told me that the issue should at least be a winnable one. If you become an expert in some issue, however, while you may earn credibility on that front, you may find that you lose credibility on others. You can come to be viewed only as "trade," or "health care," or "competitiveness."

Most leaders have never understood the motivations and crazy alliances of Washington. Business figures often fail to see that even their most serious issues are, at most, simply gambits in the overriding chess match of big-league political power.

16

FREEZE-FRAMING CHANGE
Growing Steadily and Sensibly

W HEN I MANAGED HILL AND KNOWLTON'S NATIONAL OPERATIONS out of Chicago, many a lunch hour was spent at the grill of the Chicago Club. Over the black bean soup or the delectable tail of whitefish, the conversation would often turn to the fate and future of Amoco, then known as Standard Oil of Indiana. The time was the mid-seventies and oil companies across America were rushing to diversify. The companies offered "strategic" reasons for this, but part of the real motivation was the heat being directed at them by consumers during the era of lineups at the gas station and oil embargoes. The companies wanted to make their image a little fuzzier, to present a less sharply defined target for public attack.

Marathon was taken over by U.S. Steel. Mobil had acquired a substantial presence in Chicago through its acquisition of Container Corporation and the retailer Montgomery Ward. But Amoco, under the leadership of John Swearingen, remained committed to being an oil business, pure and simple. Some people thought that Amoco was conservative, others that it was turning itself into a relic, vulnerably reliant on the fortunes of a single natural resource. But John Swearingen had a strategy and a vision. He was able to see beyond immediate market

THINKPOINTS

on How

Leaders Stay Committed to Steady, Sensible Growth

☐ Freeze-frame time and steer toward long-term opportunity.

☐ Target market fundamentals to the financial community.

☐ Market fundamentals to individuals using the grass roots.

☐ Keep valuable brand assets working hard.

☐ Help change public policy on key financial issues.

---

turbulence and the voguish conglomerates that now seem as dated as mood rings and pet rocks. Passing the baton first to Dick Morrow and then to Larry Fuller, Swearingen cultivated a unique capacity at Amoco—the ability to freeze-frame growth, to take the long view and to methodically pursue strategy step by step. That's how Amoco was able to make things happen in every area—exploration, production, refining, and marketing.

As a result, Amoco has had one of the steadiest performance tracks of any oil company in America—or, for that matter, in the world. The consistency of its performance has earned Amoco the accolade of being "the oil professional's oil company." And back in the mid-eighties as the Continental Bank crisis erupted, it was no surprise that the then-retired John Swearingen was called in to stabilize the situation. The federal government may think it bailed out Continental. In truth, it was John Swearingen's reputation and his ability to break apart a complex problem and resolve it in a series of clear steps that really restored the confidence of the business and the financial communities in the bank.

The same commitment to "freeze-frame change" and to achieve steady, fundamentally solid growth is exhibited by CEOs George Fisher at Motorola and Henry Schacht at Cummins Engine. It drives Dick Fisher and Bob Greenhill as they outline the future for Morgan Stanley, a firm successfully weathering the hostile climate currently facing the large investment banking houses. It motivates Mike Miles to steadily build industrial dominance at Philip Morris.

This chapter discusses both how to sustain a focus on steady, long-term growth as these leaders do, and how to communicate that performance message to the financial community and beyond.

A GOAL COMES OF AGE

Recall that the third goal of leadership is the need for steady, well-positioned growth. All of the firms cited above have this philosophy of growth. Most Japanese and German firms live and breathe it. While this kind of steady, long-term thinking is absolutely crucial, the American financial marketplace has been slow in rewarding it. This is beginning to change, however, making it important for leaders to understand the way the financial context in which they have been operating is now evolving.

Since the 1980s, Wall Street has been dominated by traders. A majority of the top 10 investment houses on Wall Street are run by executives who came up on the trading side of the business. This has continued even with the intervention of Black Monday and despite the controls instituted on programmed trading. As financial communications expert Tim Metz says, "If you're a CEO, and the wrong five guys end up owning your stock, you better watch out. Your company could be in play the next morning."

During the go-get-'em eighties, Wall Street hired dozens of mathematicians and economists (called "quants" in the financial firms) to design mathematical models to refine trading programs. Back in 1984, the New York Stock Exchange allowed program trading orders to be sent simultaneously to the various specialist trading posts via its electronic order delivery system, further facilitating program trading. While some have since backed away from the heyday of indexation, it remains the most powerful force in the marketplace and will be for years to come.

During the era when Michael Milken reigned as junk-bond king, the American financial markets took on the colors of Amsterdam at the height of the crazed tulip-bulb speculation in the seventeenth century. In its American iteration in the eighties, hundreds of 25-year-old kids were able to make $100,000 to a million dollars a year without having any special skill. Tim Metz describes some who would simply watch the Salomon Brothers pit trader to decide whether to buy or sell. (The Salomon trader's bright green blazer stood out in the sea of red coats on the trading floor.) The American financial markets had turned into a high-stakes game of Simon Says.

THE ROAD BACK TO FUNDAMENTALS

In the aftermath of indexation and the other numbers games, those organizations that have practiced a steady commitment to fundamentals have been rendered irrelevant. Today, with less than 500 stocks participating in market indexation, a particular stock is much more likely to be valued in relation to where it sits with reference to an index. With a few notable exceptions, and notwithstanding the bull market of early 1991, the vast majority of the remaining 5,000 public company stocks have languished. Even companies with exceptional earnings tend to be more sensitive to bad news than to good, if they are not a part of an index. Many brokers and investment houses steer clear of these kinds of stocks, preferring to buy into equities that move predictably with the indices.

Companies must move beyond value to gaining recognition for their value. Does this mean that leaders should continue to bust up the nation's businesses in sell-offs and reorganizations, just to improve their firm's odds of being recognized as valuable? No; that era is ending. Leaders should be aware, however, that two trends are replacing it.

First, more and more strategic acquisitions and ownership positions ·are taking place in the global markets, funded by bankers with deep pockets full of real money. Matsushita invests more than $6 billion to buy MCA. Sony buys CBS Records. British American Tobacco acquires Farmers' Insurance. The criteria for such acquisitions—largely because of the firms doing the buying—are going to be much more thoughtful than they were during the takeover wave of the last decade. The prospects for the United States as a global competitor grow dimmer, however, if too many of our most attractive assets are owned abroad, and we lose the initiative to be a leadership nation in the global economy.

SELLING VALUE

Companies are recognizing that they can get credit for their fundamentals, but they must view their investor relations department as more of a marketing unit than a reporting bureau mandated by the SEC. For example, the same computerization that has permitted indexation and program trading to materialize has also allowed leaders instantly to analyze institutional shareholders as a target audience for promoting company stock. If one views investor relations not as a service function but as an information-driven marketing department, the impact can be phenomenal.

Rather than having an investor relations professional waiting to hand out data kits to analysts who don't call, smart companies are practicing a very sophisticated form of telemarketing: combing the lists of institutional holdings. Let's say you are a newly restructured electric utility. You use research to find the right institutions to contact. Your financial relations professional or your investment banker calls up a targeted institution and says, "Typically, you hold 8 percent of your portfolio in utilities. Right now, you're a bit light. We've got a dandy little stock to talk to you about that can beef up that part of your basket." That's how smaller companies—who are not part of the indices—get the value they deserve today. Not, as Tim Metz would say, by waving their press releases in front of *Forbes* or *Barron's*, but through carefully engineered calls and face-to-face marketing.

Companies adopting this practice have learned that they literally cannot spend enough on this kind of marketing. You can analyze the performance of such a marketing campaign using hard numbers. You can measure the number of successful calls, identify your most receptive prospects, and reward your best communicators. Such campaigns mark a return to the era when a company's stock had to be sold one prospect at a time.

THE OLD-FASHIONED WAY

Some companies have decided to get recognition for value in an even more old-fashioned way—by putting more of their stock in the hands of individual investors. There has been an explosive growth in grass-roots marketing of equities to individual investors in order to get around heavy ownership by institutions. More and more corporations are talking to local investment clubs and regional brokerages, since a disproportionate amount of stock is always owned in the regional community surrounding a company's headquarters. This trend is likely to continue as well. While the United States is justly criticized for not having strong enough national financial policies to reward steady long-term performance, individual companies are seizing the initiative to get a fair reward for their value, and they are succeeding.

BRAND NAMES GO BACK TO WORK

During the eighties, indexation and the loss of focus on fundamentals in the financial markets also caused leaders to take some of their organizational assets for granted. After all, if a company's values seemed largely controlled by factors beyond its control, why not look for the easiest ways to be rewarded by the marketplace?

During the era of acquisitions, American business leaders drifted into believing a fallacy about the power of brands, from which they are just now recovering. Many thought that if you simply owned a strong, established brand or group of brands, that was enough. The truth is that the brand must be kept alive and must work hard to retain its value.

Writing in *Adweek*, Stewart Alter made a particularly lucid point about the financial value of brands. The "much touted romance that the client takeover world purportedly had with 'brands' was somewhat disingenuous," he says:

> In retrospect, it had very little to do with the enduring value of advertising-built brand qualities in consumers' minds, though the agency business gasped and fell for that hook, line and sinker. Rather the so-called value of brands was more fundamentally financial. An established brand was more valuable because the price of entry had skyrocketed in a mature economy. Valued brands represented products that had already made it into acceptance through the distribution system and with . . . the customer.[1]

That realization will spread and will further burn off the "marketing aura" around vast numbers of existing brands. Leaders should know that every asset in their portfolio has to be managed to realize its value. Failure to do so is almost sure to convert any investment into a fading glory—and a wasting asset.

VALUES AND VALUE

I wish I could say that the financial markets respond thoughtfully to the moral values of businesses and leaders. Idealists like to believe that companies that behave in a morally responsible way will be rewarded in the financial marketplace. The truth, of course, is that this both is and is not the case. Johnson & Johnson, Ford, and IBM, for example, have great financial strength and an enduring core group of shareholders because of their strong images as firms. In contrast, if you have plenty of float, there is generally little penalty—even if you are perceived as controversial. Between March 24, 1989 (when the *Exxon Valdez* ran aground) and December of the same year, Exxon stock moved from 44⅝ down to 42 on April 14 and back up to 51⅝ on December 12. Almost every day during this period, Exxon was a leading news item. Even as people watched the slime coat the rocks of the Alaska coast, however, the market and the indices didn't really care.

On the other hand, any given day on Wall Street finds little pharmaceutical companies or computer businesses with their share values wiped out by only a moderate blemish. The lesson for a leader is clear: If you run a large company, the market may not directly punish you for irresponsible or corrupt behavior. (Regulators and public opinion can do enough damage on their own, however, to make such behavior costly in simple, pragmatic terms.) If you are the leader of a small company, you can expect that the financial marketplace will react swiftly to any news of corruption or poor business practices.

GETTING THE WORD OUT

American's business institutions need to be far more aggressive in publicizing their views on government policies and public attitudes on such issues as capital gains, excessive litigation, and outdated accounting practices—areas in which misguided beliefs can hamper the creation of real value. Leaders should look harder for creative and intelligent ways to load traditional business vehicles with provocative messages.

The average corporate annual report costs a huge amount to prepare and mail. Some companies spend more than half a million dollars a year to prepare and send their reports[2], but the letter to shareholders in most U.S. annual reports almost never carries an appeal that will do the business any good. In 1989, Deutsche Bank's annual report included a ten-page discussion of the environment and entrepreneurism. The letter, which referred to the ideas of Joseph Schumpeter and Edmund Burke, was painstakingly reasoned.

Deutsche Bank has been using its annual report as a platform for speaking out on issues since 1980. How many U.S. reports show similar creativity? And annual reports are just one unused avenue; the opportunity for creative position-taking on everything from invoices to message slots in metered mail is endless. Yet unless the CEO takes an active interest in using all the alternative communications channels available to put company performance in perspective and to argue for public policy that supports steady, sensible growth, no one else in the organization will either.

17

GOODNESS
AND GOODWILL
Fostering Friendship

A NEW MOVEMENT IS EMERGING AGAINST BUSINESS. ITS PARTICI-
pants may simply oppose big organizations in general—a
1990s version of the antiestablishment thinking that rocked U.S. society during the 1960s and early 1970s. Yet this rising tide of animosity
is more subtle, more elusive, and more difficult to answer than any
opposition American business has yet encountered.

Time magazine sensed the negative wave in the summer of 1989,
when it printed a business feature titled "Listen Here, Mr. Big!"[1] The
article chronicled the many alleged abuses of power perpetrated by
businesses, and stated ominously that "In a Yankelovich poll conducted
for *Time* [in 1989], nearly 80% of the Americans surveyed said the
government sides too often with business when it comes to environmental issues." The environment was only the most ticklish topic of
a number for which respondents made this claim.

Indeed, polls show that in our society of a million and a half million-
aires and millions of homeless, there is growing resentment from the
have-nots toward the haves. Respondents resent the increasing information power of companies, political parties, and even charitable institutions: the ability of these large organizations to gather data on people,

THINKPOINTS

on How

Leaders Help Their Organizations Earn Goodwill

☐ Use statistical analysis to drive organizational giving.

☐ Magnify giving through identified tie-ins.

☐ Help the organization take credit for its gifts.

☐ Use the influence network to raise money.

☐ Strategize timing in fund-raising campaigns.

☐ Make courtesy a foundation of goodwill.

and to pinpoint marketing messages from the results. The alternative press writes about members of a neo-Luddite movement who instead of smashing machines with hammers plant viruses in computers and "liberate" animals from laboratories.

In such an antagonistic climate, leaders, particularly business leaders, must build goodwill. Goodwill is a precious and fragile asset, and this last chapter offers some tips on how to get it and keep it in an often cynical world.

THE GOLDEN RULES OF GIVING

Leaders stand to gain a great deal by helping their organizations take part in gracious and intelligent giving. When organizations, particularly businesses, give money, they generally get more credit for it than one would suspect. Perhaps the most striking fact about corporate contributions is how small a portion of total giving comes from corporations. In 1989 (the most recent year for which data is available), the American Association of Fund-Raising Councils reported total donations of $114.7 billion. Of that amount, $5 billion came from corporations and another $6.7 billion from private foundations, some with business roots. Although these two sources account for less than 11 percent of giving, they seem to play a far greater role. An organization can earn plenty of leverage from a few strategic contributions, if the giving is effectively managed.

COMPUTERS DO GOD'S WORK BEST

Some leaders let their passion for the ballet or their deep-seated belief in the Sierra Club drive their organization's giving program. I disagree: No one better does God's work than a computer.

Let's say you opened a new plant in North Carolina three years ago. You do a computer run on your 3,800 employees and find that heart disease is their number one cause of death and disability. You investigate the area surrounding the new plant and discover that there isn't a decent, modern cardiac care facility within a 150-mile radius. Yet there are 35,000 people living in the greater vicinity of the plant.

Your company has a very smart opportunity here to invest in building a cardiac care unit. Your employee sample is probably representative of the overall health profile and needs in this area. Grateful community members will no doubt express their appreciation when individual lives are saved. You have to make sure, however, that the investment is publicized. For starters, you can ensure that the local plant manager is recognized as the symbolic donor at the annual hospital ball.

MAGNIFICATION

Even a small organization can still look like a significant giver. Say you don't have the resources to drag the treasures of King Tut to the United States; you can still tie yourself securely to the coattails of a blockbuster project. How? Maybe a major touring art exhibition is coming to your town. The museum gift shop is sure to want to mail out a brochure or minicatalogue to the leading citizenry. For several thousand dollars, you can sponsor a project like this and get tremendous benefits from the association: a credit line stating, "This brochure is made possible by a grant from . . ." Ensuring recognition of this sort is the only way for a little fish to participate sensibly in a big program. You might sponsor a particular performance at the local opera or concert series, gaining a mention in the program. Or you could finance the building of a stage for a fund-raising rally, and earn a visibly displayed company logo on the background. The challenge for small corporations contributing to large programs is to magnify the perception of the gift, in order to make the investment worthwhile for the organization.

TAKING CREDIT

Corporations cannot afford to be humble. Leaders often confuse their own humility with the humility of their companies. Managers—unless they are also the owners—simply don't have the right to be humble with corporate money. It's important to your employees, your shareholders, and your ability to earn the entitled return on the investment in the community. The reason that corporations seem to play such a major role in the world of donations is that smart corporations know how to take credit for their role.

THE ART OF THE ASK

Giving money is one important part of leadership; raising it is another, equally important task. When a leader raises funds for the community, the power lever is knowing the prospect's personal interests. You can't just go to the prospect and baldly ask for the check, especially for a big gift. You need to test your appeal with the influence network surrounding the prospect. Use the network to build expectations that the prospect will donate. If these expectations are built properly, your prospect will not want to disappoint.

My colleagues and I once decided to establish a chair at one of the most prestigious universities in the country, to memorialize a colleague who had just passed away. The going rate for such endowments was a million dollars. We needed to find a single large benefactor to come through with a very sizable gift. We looked at the leading givers in the private sector. Among them was one man who knew our late colleague and respected what he had done for the city where both had lived. We also studied the potential benefactor's network of friends. We knew that each of them would also lend support for the chair, albeit on a much smaller scale.

We started by soliciting the largest possible gift from everyone in our target's influence network. At the same time, we made a special point of *not* asking our target benefactor. Months passed. The target was perplexed. "Why aren't they asking me to help?" he wondered. Then he actually came forward—not once, but twice—to my colleague's widow and said to her, "I'm prepared to give to this drive." She said, "That's generous, but let's wait. You already do so much. Let's see how much the others will give."

Finally, we went to the influence network and said, "We're about a quarter-million dollars short and we don't know where to get it. It looks like the project may fail." At board meetings, civic affairs and receptions, the group began to talk about the fact we could miss our goal. At that point, our benefactor could no longer be reined in. He made a point of saving the day and gave the university the quarter million. He just came up to me and said, "How much do you need, and I won't take no." He was a hero—just what we wanted him to be.

Would we have gotten the same result without all the plotting? I don't think so. We had also carefully studied the big-gift giving pattern in that community over the preceding 12 months. The real insiders said that our project would take in somewhere between $600,000 and

$700,000, but that we would need a single big gift to cross the finish line. If we wanted the chair while the memory of our colleague was still warm enough to trigger broad-based giving, we would have to wrap up the drive in six months, and we would have to engineer a single large contribution in the mix of gifts. Any other approach would have been much too risky.

As I thumb through the manuscript for this book, there are no other places where I recommend conspiratorial thinking to leaders. Perhaps this is a lapse, but since it's for a good cause, maybe it's an excusable and worthwhile outlet for those conspiratorial urges we all have.

BAD WILL

Leaders who conspire for charity may have a defense, but leaders conspiring for self-interest are totally indefensible. Indefensible, but also worth examining.

Leaders should study bad will as much as they study goodwill. Few leaders in modern history have made a worse mess of things than the former Romanian dictator and all-around Dracula Nicolae Ceauşescu. Bad leaders get what they deserve, and that's exactly what Ceauşescu got from the good people of Romania after they suffered through a gut full of agony under his reign. Ceauşescu's venality was so sheer, so direct, that if nothing else it makes a superb case study. When a Ceauşescu is exposed—and today's world of satellite dishes, pixilators, and fax machines nearly guarantees that such a tyrant will be—the indictment is likely to be returned in television soundbites captured by the ubiquitous minicams.

CEAUŞESCU-ISMS: FIVE SUREFIRE WAYS TO GET SHOT ON CHRISTMAS

1. *Hoard:* No one will forget the sight of liberating soldiers crying as they discovered refrigerators jammed with salamis in Ceauşescu's bunker at a time of widespread famine throughout the country.

2. *Lie:* When the citizens of the free world finally saw the flimsy clothing on the backs of the Romanian people, they

knew why Ceauşescu issued an official decree that news broadcasters could never report that the temperature was below zero.

3. *Nepotize:* Spouse, siblings, offspring—all shared in an egregious case of all-in-the-family power gorging.

4. *Stonewall:* Instead of yielding to the sea change of peaceful protest seen in Leipzig, Ceauşescu's troops gunned down children on the streets of Timisoara.

5. *Condescend:* Minutes before being executed, a man totally devoid of perspective declared he was not answerable to his captors.

There are executive Ceauşescus too:

1. The hoarders who help themselves to a disproportionate share of the stock options, or accept hefty bonuses in the middle of massive layoffs or even bankruptcy.

2. The liars about the state of the business who fail to prepare their people for reality when the bottom falls out.

3. The nepotists who advance only those cut from the same ideological or social cloth.

4. The stonewallers who resist change until it overwhelms their organization and visits widespread destruction.

5. The condescenders who deny reality and dismiss the idea that leaders must have the consent of the led.

COMMON COURTESY

While we can learn from the mistakes of a Ceauşescu, most leaders fortunately deal mostly with more modest behavioral problems, such as courtesy. Courtesy may seem like a tame topic on which to end a briefing for leaders, but it is a foundation for goodwill and can even be considered a fundamental methodology for leadership.

Those of us in the business of public relations generally try very hard to be polite to people. Occasionally, we slip up. Once a PR firm did some work for the president of a small African republic, and had some trouble getting paid. The former head of its European and African operations proceeded to impound the president's personal DC-8 until the bill was settled. This rash move lost them that country's business for over a decade. When I became the communications company's CEO, to get the business back, I had to fly to the capital and wait in one minister's office after another, until finally I was able to plead with the president himself, who was still mad as blazes. In the end, my personal mission worked, but it was not a pleasant job. So I am very sensitive to anything that I see as a lapse of courtesy: First, because it is wrong, and second, because as the leader, I will end up atoning for it.

People say I'm a stickler for courtesy, but there are few skills that will carry you further in the highly visible world of business today.

THE CANON
OF LEADERSHIP
AND ITS GOALS
Conclusion to Part IV

LEADERS CAN BEST UNLEASH THE CREATIVITY OF THEIR ORGANIZATIONS through the creative and provocative use of communications.

Among the most effective techniques are the thoughtful use of silence, perceptive questioning, role reversals, and projective thinking.

Visionary leaders relentlessly pressure the organization to achieve its long-term goals by constantly asking for progress toward those goals.

ACCESS AND PENETRATION

Serious-minded leaders focus on the quality of the organization's results before spending considerable time on gaining access to power bases and opinion leaders.

Discerning leaders learn that the real gatekeepers to power and influence are often diverse and unexpected.

Since political agenda dominate so much of the agenda when leaders gather, a leader should learn as much as possible about the political agenda of other leaders who may be encountered in social situations.

Leaders maximize their travel experience by acting as their own "advance" persons to gain knowledge about regional and local issues and power bases.

Leaders penetrate the minds of other opinion leaders through giving speeches at important forums, radiating the impact of their communications, and using "single-story" strategies to help set the public record.

STEADY, SENSIBLE GROWTH

In guiding the organization toward its financial goals, leaders resist short-term performance pressures by freeze-framing time and steering the organization toward long-term opportunity.

When they carry the organization's message to the financial community, leaders use target marketing to sell the underlying value of their organizations. They also use grass-roots marketing to encourage ownership and commitment to the organization at the local level.

As good stewards, leaders make sure that all of the organization's assets—including intangibles such as brand identities—are kept working hard.

As responsible members of the leadership community, leaders help to change public policy and attitudes on key issues.

GOODWILL

The first step today's leaders take to help their organizations earn and maintain goodwill is to learn the character of the new antiestablishment thinking and to monitor its evolution.

Many organizations maintain giving programs as part of their broader social responsibility. Thoughtful leaders insist that statistical analysis—not personal whims—drive the structure of these programs. They will also see that the organization gets credit for its giving, through identification programs and other appropriate means of recognition.

When raising money, leaders use the influence network to help predispose donors to making gifts—thinking through timing and campaign strategy before making individual solicitations.

Lastly, thoughtful leaders make courtesy an abiding foundation of their efforts to build and maintain goodwill toward the organization.

EPILOGUE

At the end of each of my leadership briefings, I have tried to leave leaders with a sense of empathy for them and their jobs. Leaders have to be empathetic to others in their organizations, but they rarely receive empathy in return, nor should they ask for it. The job has its shortcomings for those dependent on a steady diet of praise or glamour. Realizing a vision may be the goal, but the leader's daily menu is likely to be jammed with telephone calls from beleaguered subordinates needing moral support and inch-thick stacks of faxes demanding action now. Many people say they want to be leaders, but as they advance upward and the grail comes to their lips, they see the rigor and the relentless demands that are involved, and most shirk away.

Even those who sincerely want to lead will always find themselves tested: That is the nature of leadership. Leaders have told me over the years of the various tests they have faced and how they have tried to overcome them. All the challenges they mentioned seemed to fit into one of seven categories below. The odds are high that every leader will need to confront each of these problems at one time or another.

TREATING THE AILMENTS OF LEADERSHIP

1. *Loneliness:* The only cure is to build bonds with other leaders outside of your own organization and to talk with them on a regular basis. No one else in your organization is going to understand how isolated you will at times feel.

2. *Failed inspiration:* No intelligent leader can cheer the troops on all the time. Don't fake it. People will see right through you. Go micro and work with small groups of people in very focused ways. Find those parts of the organization, those ideas and plans, that really excite you—even in the face of your own apathy—and let them be the foundation on which you rebuild your enthusiasm.

3. *Disloyalty:* In any case of subordinate disloyalty, always establish in your own mind whether the disloyalty is directed toward you as a person, toward the mission of the organization, toward other members of the management team, or toward that person's own goals and values. Leaders often overreact and assume that disloyalty must be directed toward them personally. Leaders who radiate confidence about the loyalty of their people and seek to build trust are the ones likely to earn loyalty in return.

4. *Internal dissent:* Internal dissent is usually a blessing in disguise, because it really manifests interest and energy. The foremost challenge for a leader facing internal dissent is to harness it toward the achievement of positive goals.

5. *Getting too far ahead:* More leaders than you can imagine lose their following because they fail to develop their vision for the organization with enough participation from their colleagues. To prevent the problem, constant communication is necessary. In the end, the organization must own the vision every bit as much as the leader. If the leader keeps this continually in mind, the problem will rarely occur.

6. *External threats:* Any leader with a clear, positive agenda is bound to collide at times with the vested interests of others. Quite bluntly, that is why some of the finest and most determined political leaders are assassinated. The threats to your agendas—if not to your person—cannot be minimized or avoided. Before choosing to pursue leadership, you must reconcile yourself to this reality.

7. *Insurmountable odds:* If things don't work on their present scale, on what scale will they work? What exactly must be achieved? Who precisely must you satisfy? In business as in communications, the sharper and clearer the focus, the better. As Bill Cosby once put it, "I don't know the key to success, but the key to failure is to try to please everyone."[1]

History is replete with examples of leaders who succumbed to one or more of these often fatal maladies. On the other hand, leadership can overcome all these trials and produce wonderful things. The key for any leader is to keep learning the lessons of leadership as they emerge. And, new lessons of leadership as they emerge. And, new lessons appear in each day's newspaper and news broadcasts. For leadership is indeed a science and art about which the last chapters have by no means been written.

NOTES

INTRODUCTION

1. Bryan Burrough and John Helyar, *Barbarians at the Gate: The Fall of RJR Nabisco* (New York: Harper & Row, 1990), pp. 282–283.
2. Robert H. Waterman, Jr., *The Renewal Factor* (New York: Bantam, 1988), p. 207.

CHAPTER 1: A CERTAIN TRUMPET

1. "God's Action Man," *Economist*, November 24, 1990, p. 101.
2. Robert J. Flaherty, "Great Businessmen," *Forbes*, September 15, 1977.
3. Thomas Kamm, "French Luxury Firms Are Merging, Turning into Big Multinationals," *Wall Street Journal*, December 28, 1987.
4. Noel Tichy and Ram Charan, "Speed, Simplicity, Self-Confidence: An Interview with Jack Welch," *Harvard Business Review*, September/October 1989, p. 115.
5. Andrall E. Pearson, "Six Basics for General Managers," *Harvard Business Review*, July/August 1989, p. 96.
6. James E. Ellis and Chuck Hawkins, "The Unraveling of an Idea: How

Dick Ferris' Grand Plan for Allegis Collapsed," *Business Week,* June 22, 1987.

CHAPTER 2: SMASHING THE CRYSTAL

1. Janet Bush, "The Man Who Fell to Earth," *Financial Times,* February 24, 1990.
2. Bryan Burrough and John Helyar, *Barbarians At The Gate: The Fall of RJR Nabisco* (New York: Harper & Row, 1990), p. 47.
3. Harris Collingwood, "Where Lying Was Business As Usual," *Business Week,* November 20, 1989.
4. Robert H. Waterman, Jr., *Adhocracy: The Power to Change* (Knoxville: Whittle Direct Books, 1990), p. 77.
5. Arno Penzias, *Ideas and Information* (New York: W. W. Norton and Co., 1989), p. 161.
6. Edward Reingold, "Facing the 'Totally New and Dynamic' " (An Interview with Peter Drucker), *Psychology Today,* January 22, 1990, p. 21.
7. Kathleen Deveny, "Perelman's Much Touted Gloss As a Marketer at Revlon Is Not Without a Blemish or Two," *Wall Street Journal Europe,* March 4, 1991.
8. Al Neuharth, *Confessions of an S.O.B.* (New York: Doubleday, 1989), p. 64.
9. Edmund L. Andrews, "The Five Best Managed Companies," *Business Month,* December 1989, p. 33.
10. "Korea," *Business Week,* September 5, 1989, pp. 44–50.
11. Thomas J. Murray, "Rethinking the Factory," *Business Month,* July 1989, p. 35.
12. Reingold, "Facing the 'Totally New and Dynamic'," p. 21.
13. "Costing the Factory of the Future," *Economist,* March 3, 1990, p. 61.
14. "The Rival Japan Respects," *Business Week,* November 13, 1989, pp. 108–111, 114, 118, 121.
15. William Wiggenhorn, "Motorola U: When Training Becomes an Education," *Harvard Business Review,* July/August 1990, p. 71.
16. "Quality Wins," *Inc.,* July 1990,
17. Robert Howard, "Values Make the Company: An Interview with Robert Haas," *Harvard Business Review,* September/October 1990, p. 134.

CHAPTER 3: THE POWER CLOCK

1. Clare Ansberry, "National Intergroup's Chairman to Resign After Firm Sheds All Units but FoxMeyer," *Wall Street Journal Europe,* June 7, 1990.

2. Gregory L. Miles, "National Intergroup: How Pete Love Went Wrong," *Business Week,* March 6, 1989, p. 56.
3. Paul Kennedy, *The Rise and Fall of the Great Powers* (New York: Random House, 1987), p. 194.
4. "Many Feel Bennett Quit Drug Post Too Soon," *New York Times,* reprinted in *Stars and Stripes,* November 11, 1990.
5. Al Neuharth, *Confessions of an S.O.B.* (New York: Doubleday, 1989), p. 352.
6. "Jimmy Carter's Second Coming," *Economist,* December 15, 1990, p. 42.

CHAPTER 4: RALLYING A GREAT FOLLOWING

1. Wallace H. Offutt, Jr., "How Come the Japanese CEO Gets More Sleep?" *Across the Board,* April 1990, p. 60.
2. Hedley Donovan, "Managing Your Intellectuals," *Fortune,* October 23, 1989, p. 177.
3. Peter F. Drucker, "The Emerging Theory of Manufacturing," *Harvard Business Review,* May/June 1990.
4. J. S. Ninomiya, "Wagon Masters and Lesser Managers," *Harvard Business Review,* March/April 1988, p. 86.

CHAPTER 5: THE BIG I AM

1. "Martyrs to Their Share Price," *Economist,* March 24, 1990, p. 76.
2. Alix M. Freedman and Frank Allen, "Family Misfortune: John Dorrance's Death Leaves Campbell Soup with a Cloudy Future," *Wall Street Journal,* April 19, 1989.
3. "Martyrs to Their Share Price," p. 76.
4. Peter F. Drucker, "Leadership: More Doing Than Dash," *Wall Street Journal,* January 6, 1988.
5. David A. Nadler and Michael L. Tushman, "Beyond the Charismatic Leader: Leadership and Organizational Change," *California Management Review,* Winter 1990, p. 84.
6. Michael Schroeder, "The Quiet Coup at Alcoa," *Business Week,* June 27, 1988.
7. Otto Friedrich, "There are 00 Trees in Russia: The Function of Facts in News Magazines," *Harper's,* October 1964, pp. 59–65. As cited in Susan P. Shapiro, *Caution! This Paper Has Not Been Fact Checked! A Study of Fact Checking in American Magazines,* Gannett Center for Media Studies, Columbia University, New York.

8. Rick Atkinson, "The Chief Who Said Too Much," *Washington Post*, September 23, 1990.

CHAPTER 6: BUSTING UP THE GENERAL CONTEXT

1. "Last Days of Maggie: The Agonised Calculations, and the Men in Grey Suits," *Daily Mail*, November 23, 1990.
2. "Cabinet Revolt Ends Thatcher's 11-Year Reign," *Daily Telegraph*, November 23, 1990.
3. Colin Brown, "Cabinet 'Rats' Blamed for Leader's Demise," *Independent*, November 23, 1990.
4. "The Long Good-bye," *Economist*, November 24, 1990, p. 36.
5. "Playin' It (Dolphin) Safe," *Food and Beverage Marketing*, June 1990.
6. "Newly Labeled Perrier to Be Made Available," *New York Times*, February 27, 1990.
7. K. Patrick Conner, "The Conversion of Star-Kist," *The San Francisco Chronicle*, June 17, 1990.
8. Lori Silver, "Perrier Crowd Not Taking the Waters; Sales After Recall Off Sharply in Area," *Washington Post*, July 4, 1990.
9. Matthew Grimm, "McDonald's Flip-Flops Again and Ditches Its Clamshell," *Adweek's Marketing Week*, November 5, 1990, p. 4.
10. Karen Woolfson, "Heinz Dolphin-Friendly Tuna Policy Backfires," *The European*, December 21–23, 1990.
11. Julie Liesse and Judann Dagnoli, "Kellogg, Nabisco Fight for Shreds," *Advertising Age*, August 20, 1990.
12. Ron Hawkins, "An Open Door For Marketing," *Channels Field Guide 1991*, p. 46.
13. Kenneth R. Clark, "Network Audience Share at Record Low," *Chicago Tribune*, November 30, 1990.

CHAPTER 7: MOVING THE NEEDLE

1. Don Wycliff, "With Money and Talent, Emory Raises Its Status," *New York Times*, August 23, 1990, p. A18.
2. Joe Quinn, "Delay over Bomb Warning Photo 'Unfortunate'," *Press Association Newsfile*, November 27, 1990.
3. "Playing the Thrift Blame Game," *Economist*, July 21, 1990.
4. David Hoffman, "The Frictionless Presidency," *Gannett Center Journal*, Spring 1990, p. 90.

CHAPTER 8: FIRST ON THE SLATE

1. Monica Roman, "The Changes at Revlon Are More Than Just Cosmetic," *Business Week*, November 20, 1989, p. 74.

CHAPTER 9: NATIONS AND NICHES

1. "Sneakers + Walkmen = Capitalism," *Economist*, July 7, 1990, p. 69.
2. Subrata N. Chakravarty, "How Pepsi Broke into India," *Forbes*, November 27, 1989, p. 43.
3. George V. Grune, "Global Marketing," speech delivered May 20, 1989, at the Roy E. Crummer Graduate School of Business, Rollins College, Winter Park, Florida.
4. Wolfgang J. Koschnick, " 'I Can Think of More Important Things Than Being Loved by Everybody': An Interview with Rupert Murdoch," *Forbes*, November 27, 1989, p. 102.
5. "Field Trip: The *Economist*'s Editor on His Brand of Business Journalism," *TJFR*, February 1989.
6. Kenichi Ohmae, *The Borderless World* (New York: HarperBusiness, 1990), p. 17.
7. Thomas A. Stewart, "New Ways to Exercise Power," *Fortune*, November 6, 1989.
8. "Globesmanship," *Across the Board*, January/February 1990.
9. John Naisbitt and Patricia Aburdene, *Megatrends 2000* (New York: Morrow, 1990), p. 149.
10. "Towards Two Nations," *Maclean's*, February 11, 1991.
11. Peter F. Drucker, *The New Realities* (New York: Harper & Row, 1989), p. 115.
12. Kamran Kashani, "Beware the Pitfalls of Global Marketing," *Harvard Business Review*, September/October 1989.
13. Preston Townley, "Global Business in the Next Decade," *Across the Board*, January/February 1990, p. 17.
14. Subrata N. Chakravarty, "Acceptably Sexy," *Forbes*, November 13, 1989.
15. Melinda Grenier Guiles, "Ford's 1991 Escort Symbolizes Future; Car is Engineered by Japan's Mazda," *Wall Street Journal*, February 27, 1990.
16. Nan Stone, "The Globalization of Europe: An Interview with Wisse Dekker," *Harvard Business Review*, May/June 1989, p. 92.

PART III: THE COMMUNICATOR'S TEMPLATE

1. James P. McCollom, *The Continental Affair: The Rise & Fall of the Continental Illinois Bank* (New York: Dodd, Mead & Co., 1987), p. 69.
2. Jeff Bailey, John Helyar, and Tim Carrington, "Anatomy of a Failure: Continental Illinois: How Bad Judgments and Big Egos Did It In," *Wall Street Journal,* July 30, 1984.
3. Ibid.

CHAPTER 10: SEEING AROUND CORNERS

1. Technimetrics, Inc., *1990 International Target Cities Report.*
2. "Do Today's Kids Follow Current Events?" *Children's Express Quarterly,* Spring 1990, p. 4.
3. Dick Thompson, "Big Problems for Big Science," *Time Bureau Chiefs' Report,* p. 4.
4. "Porsche's Mind Set," *The Delaney Report,* September 17, 1990, p. 2.
5. "Macho Out, Gentleness In for '90s Man," *The Stars and Stripes,* December 27, 1990, p. 12.
6. Mark Stuart Gill, "You've Come a Long Way, Buddy," *Working Woman,* March 1991, p. 77.
7. Anne B. Fisher, "What Consumers Want in the 1990s," *Fortune,* January 29, 1990, pp. 108–111.
8. "Nuclear Energy Group Has a Cow over 'Simpsons,'" *The Stars and Stripes,* December 7, 1990.
9. Malcolm Gladwell, "Risk, Regulation and Biotechnology," *American Spectator,* January 1989.
10. "West to the White House," *Economist,* March 3, 1990, p. 18.
11. Marc Beauchamp, "Made in Los Angeles," *Forbes,* November 13, 1989, p. 68.
12. Joel Kotkin and Yoriko Kishimoto, "America's Asian Destiny," *Washington Post,* July 3, 1988.

CHAPTER 11: THE UNIVERSE OF 25,000

1. Paul Keegan, "The Case of the Missing Minute," *Pursuits,* Fall 1989, p. 10.
2. "Competitive Intelligence," *Conference Board Research Report* no. 913, 1988, p. 9.

3. "The Greening of Shopping," *Economist*, March 31, 1990.
4. "Marketing Greenery: Friendly to Whom?" *Economist*, April 7, 1990, p. 87.
5. Beth Enslow, "Degradable Liaisons," *Across the Board*, January/February 1990, p. 44.
6. Victor Orlov, "When Spies Fool Themselves," *World Monitor*, March 1989, p. 42.

CHAPTER 12: GUIDANCE CONTROL

1. "Talking European, But Going Dutch," *Economist*, July 9, 1983, p. 73.
2. "The Next Age for Japan's cars," *Economist*, July 21, 1990, p. 63.

CHAPTER 13: THE EARNEST EAR

1. Hedley Donovan, "Managing Your Intellectuals," *Fortune*, October 23, 1989.

CHAPTER 14: THE KING'S SEAL

1. Robert A. Caro, *The Years of Lyndon Johnson: Means of Ascent* (New York: Knopf, 1990).
2. Alison L. Sprout, "America's Most Admired Corporations," *Fortune*, February 11, 1991.
3. "Leaders of the Most Admired," *Fortune*, January 29, 1990.

CHAPTER 15: BEYOND THE GATEKEEPERS

1. Randall Rothenberg, "P. R. Firms Head for Capitol Hill," *New York Times*, January 4, 1991.

CHAPTER 16: FREEZE-FRAMING CHANGE

1. Stewart Alter, "A Crisis of Confidence," *Adweek*, March 12, 1990.
2. Bruce Buursma, "Annual Reports Take on Look of More Frugal Times," *Chicago Tribune*, January 20, 1991.

CHAPTER 17: GOODNESS AND GOODWILL

1. Christine Gorman, "Listen Here, Mr. Big!" *Time,* July 3, 1989, pp. 40–41.

EPILOGUE

1. Jefferson Graham, "The Cosby Wisdom," *USA Today,* June 16, 1989, p. 1D.

INDEX